World Trade and Development Report 2003

Cancun and Beyond

World Trade and Development Report 2003

Cancun and Beyond

RIS

Research and Information System for the Non-Aligned and Other Developing Countries
NEW DELHI

Published by :

Academic Foundation
NEW DELHI

The World Trade and Development Report 2003 has been prepared by an RIS research team led by Dr Nagesh Kumar, Director-General, RIS. The core team comprised Dr Rajesh Mehta, Senior Fellow, RIS, and Dr Sachin Chaturvedi, Dr Ram Upendra Das and S.K. Mohanty, Fellows of RIS.

Key inputs have been provided by Dr. J. George, Senior Consultant and Rajesh Sehgal, Consultant. The Report Team benefited a great deal from perceptive comments and advice of Saikat Sinha-Roy.

The team has benefited from interactions with a number of scholars, experts and negotiators at different stages including Yilmaz Akyuz, T.K. Bhaumik, K.M. Chandrasekhar, Ha-Joon Chang, Carlos Correa, B.L Das, Muchkund Dubey, Enrique Lendo Fuentes, Torbjörn Fredriksson, Murray Gibbs, R. Gopalan, Branislav Gosovich, Ashok Gulati, Anwarul Hoda, Raj Kanoria, Saman Kelegama, Martin Khor, Ivan Mbirimi, S.N. Menon, Rajiva Misra, Amit Mitra, S. Narayanan, Hardeep Puri, Lakshmi Puri, Shishir Priyadarshi, S.L. Rao, Pedro Roffe, Karl Sauvant, Prabir Sengupta, S.P. Shukla, Rajiv Sikri, V. S. Seshadri, M. Sornarajah, Ronald Steenblik, J.P Verbiest, Richard Kojul-Wright and Shashank. However, the views presented are those of the members of the core team.

Production of the Report was managed by Tish Kumar Malhotra with DTP assistance by Pradeep Kumar.

Research and Information System for the
Non-Aligned and Other Developing Countries (RIS)
Zone IV B, 4th Floor, India Habitat Centre
Lodhi Road, New Delhi 110 003, India.
Tel. : 91-11-24682177-80
Fax : 91-11-24682173-74
Website: www.ris.org.in
Email: dgoffice@ris.org.in

Published in India in association with RIS by:

Academic Foundation
4772/23 Bharat Ram Road
(23 Ansari Road), Darya Ganj
New Delhi 110 002.
Tel. : +91-11-23245001-04
Fax : +91-11-23245005
e-mail : academic@vsnl.com
www.academicfoundation.com

Contents

List of Boxes, Tables and Figures

Boxes

Tables

Figures

कृष्ण चन्द्र पन्त
K. C. PANT

उपाध्यक्ष
योजना आयोग
भारत
DEPUTY CHAIRMAN
PLANNING COMMISSION
INDIA
& Chairman, RIS

August 28, 2003.

FOREWORD

The various multilateral trade agreements under WTO have, over the years, come to exercise a great deal of influence on a number of policy issues that have conventionally been in the domain of decision-making at the national level. Therefore, the up-coming negotiations have the potential to affect even further the patterns of international development, specially in developing countries. While expansion of market access for goods and services produced by developing countries could expand the economic opportunities available to them, the negotiations could also threaten the livelihood of millions of smaller and vulnerable farmers and of small-scale industries, hence adversely affecting employment, income distribution, and poverty reduction.

Therefore, the challenge before the developing country negotiators is to try to maximise their gains from market access, while minimising the potential adverse consequences. The challenge becomes particularly formidable in view of the fact that the WTO negotiations essentially represent power plays between unequal protagonists. A handful of developed countries generally exercise disproportionate influence on the outcomes of these negotiations, while the developing countries, which form the majority of the membership, have little effective say in the process.

To some extent, the lack of good research and analytical back-up from the developmental perspective on different aspects of the negotiations is also responsible for the inability of the developing countries to make their case forcefully. In this context, I believe that it is incumbent on countries and institutions, in the developing world which possess such research and analysis capability to assess the developmental consequences of different issues on the negotiating agenda and to make them available to a wider constituency.

I am glad that the RIS has taken the initiative to launch a series of World Trade and Development Reports on the WTO agenda. With its analysis, and policy implications, on the broader patterns of trade and development as well as select specific sectoral issues, this Report brought out on the eve of the Cancun Ministerial, I believe, will be found useful by the negotiators, policymakers, and civil society in developing countries.

[K.C. PANT]

योजना भवन, संसद मार्ग, नई दिल्ली–११० ००१ दूरभाष (कार्यालय) : २३०९६६७७, २३०९६६८८ फैक्स : २३०९६६९९
Yojana Bhawan, Parliament Street, New Delhi - 110 001 Phones (Office) : 23096677, 23096688 Fax : 23096699
दूरभाष (निवास) : २३०९२६१८, २३०९४४३१ फैक्स : २३०९२५५३ Phones (Resi.) : 23092618, 23094431 Fax : 23092553

Preface

This Report is the first in a series of new Reports launched by RIS to provide a developmental perspective on the agenda of multilateral trade negotiations. We propose to bring out the World Trade and Development Reports every two years to synchronize with the WTO Ministerial Conferences.

The launch of World Trade and Development Reports is a sequel to the growing activities of RIS on the WTO issues. As part of its work programme on WTO issues, RIS organized several conferences and seminars on the agenda for Cancun Ministerial over the past year. The first such Seminar was organized in July 2002 itself on the World Trading System and South Asia: Post-Doha Challenges. Subsequently, major Conferences and Seminars have been organized in November 2002, December 2002, March 2003, May 2003 and August 2003. RIS has also brought out several research monographs, discussion papers and policy briefs on the specific issues on the agenda of the multilateral trade negotiations, and have set up a special webpage on the Cancun Agenda at RIS website.

This Report represents the collective work and wisdom accumulated at RIS from the different conferences and seminars organized and reports and papers prepared. It examines the trends and asymmetries in the emerging multilateral trading system from a development perspective and outlines an agenda for developing countries for the Cancun Ministerial and beyond to restore the development focus in the multilateral trading system. We argue that trade liberalization should be seen as a means and not the end by itself.

In the preparation of this Report, we have benefited from the overall guidance of Chairman of the Governing Council of RIS, Hon'ble Shri K.C. Pant, Deputy Chairman, Planning Commission. Ambassador S.T. Devare, Vice-Chairman has been a source of inspiration and advice at different phases of its preparation.

This Report is the outcome of an excellent team work of the members of the RIS faculty. I would like to put on record my appreciation to all the members of the Report Team as listed elsewhere.

New Delhi
27 August 2003

Nagesh Kumar
Director-General, RIS

1

World Trading System and Developing Countries: Agenda for Cancun and Beyond

An Executive Summary

1. Introduction

The completion of the Uruguay Round with the setting up of WTO in 1995 marked an important turning point for the world economy. What started as a process of trade liberalization under GATT has come to embrace broader parameters of policy hitherto subject to decision making at the national levels. The Ministerial Conferences of WTO generate a lot of interest among the policy makers and the civil society, given the importance of decisions taken for the development prospects of the member countries.

The express purpose and objective of the multilateral trade negotiations (MTNs) is to liberalize trade so that efficiency gains become available to the world economy at large. However, it has been recognized that there are unequal players in the game and developing countries are limited in their financial and physical capacities to undertake equal commitments. They need flexibilities to pursue their development policy objectives that have been available to developed countries in the early stages of their development. Hence, the concept of special and differential treatment (S&DT) to developing countries on a non-reciprocal basis was built into the process.

In the Uruguay Round (UR), developing countries undertook substantially higher commitments for trade liberalization compared to developed countries. Developed countries continued to impose peak and high tariffs, specific duties and NTBs on imports from developing countries. A startling example is the fact that tariffs collected by the US on $2 billion worth of imports from Bangladesh are higher than those imposed on imports worth $30 billon from France.

Developing countries were lured into accepting these substantially higher commitments with the promises of additional market access in agriculture, textiles and clothing and movement of natural persons under services. The experience of the past seven-eight years suggests that this promised market access has been a mirage. Precious little has been delivered under any of these areas in real terms. The S&DT provisions were also diluted in the UR.

As a part of the strategic trade policy, developed countries are increasingly subsidizing industrial and innovative activity and are imposing policies akin to outlawed local content requirements. Resort to regionalism and contingent protection has also grown. These trends have adversely affected the place of developing countries in the world trade and their terms of trade. With the liberalization of trade and investment regime, growth rates of developing countries have declined in the 1990s compared to the previous decade and inequalities have increased. These trends do not bode well for the long-term sustainability of the world trading system.

The Doha Ministerial Conference attempted to restore the emphasis on development in the WTO. The Doha Declaration called for positive efforts to ensure developing countries benefiting from enhanced market access and balanced rules. In substantive terms the highlights of the Doha Agenda included a commitment in the area of agriculture to substantially improve market access, progress towards phasing-out of all forms of export subsidies and substantial reduction of trade distorting domestic support. It also accepted the primacy of public health concerns and offered to provide flexibility to poorer countries from the provisions of TRIPs Agreement to import cheaper generic medicines. In the area of market access for industrial products, commitments were made to eliminate or reduce peak tariffs, high tariffs, tariff escalation and NTBs, in particular, on products of export interest to developing countries. Commitments were also made to review the S&DT provisions for developing countries to make them more precise, effective and operational.

However, the progress since the Doha Ministerial has been far from satisfactory. Almost all the deadlines proposed, that were important from the point of view of developing countries, have been missed. On the other hand, pressure is mounting on developing countries to agree to giving the negotiating mandate on the Singapore Issues at the Cancun Ministerial. The draft modalities for market access in agricultural as well non-agricultural goods that are being proposed by developed countries suggest that the principle of less-than-full-reciprocity as enshrined in the Doha Mandate is being undermined.

It is clear that the multilateral trade negotiations have failed to liberalize the trade and industrial policy regimes in the world's richest and most developed countries that could have enabled equitable sharing of the fruits of globalization, as articulated in the preamble of the Marrakesh and Doha Declarations. The Cancun Conference provides an opportunity to the WTO membership to seek a redressal of the emerging asymmetries before they take on any new commitments.

Against this background, the *World Trade and Development Report 2003* examines the trends and asymmetries in the emerging multilateral trading system from a development perspective. It also outlines an agenda for developing countries for the Cancun Ministerial and beyond to restore the development focus and, more importantly, popular confidence in the multilateral trading system. In this respect, trade liberalization should be seen as a 'means' and not the 'end by itself'. The 'end' beyond any doubt should be sustainable development in all parts of the world, with principles of efficiency and equity providing the basis.

The substantive contents of the Report are organized in eight chapters. Chapter 2 examines the broad trends in the protectionism in the developed world and their implications for development. The subsequent chapters deal with the select important sectoral issues from a development perspective: Chapter 3 deals with the Singapore Issues. Chapter 4 deals with the issues concerning the Agreement on Agriculture. Chapter 5 covers Market Access in Non-Agriculture goods. Chapter 6 deals with TRIPs. Chapter 7 deals with the SPS Agreement and the implementation issues concerning it. Chapter 8 covers the issues and concerns raised by the Dispute Settlement Understanding Rules for developing countries. Chapter 9 summarizes the evolution of the S&DT provisions and highlights the concerns with the provisions.

The rest of this chapter summarizes the highlights of the individual chapters and puts together the key policy recommendations made in these chapters for the governments and negotiators of developing countries for consideration at the Cancun Ministerial and beyond to evolve a multilateral trading system more responsive to their developmental needs.

2. WTO, Rising Protectionism and Development: An Analysis of Trends and Their Implications

The emerging WTO regime has important implications for national development and evolution of trade, investment and technology policies of the developing countries. The UR also placed substantial obligations on developing countries with respect to the liberalization of trade and their policy regimes with respect to intellectual property rights, investments, and trade in services. Developing countries undertook commitments to expand tariff bindings to cover 61 per cent of their imports compared to 13 per cent earlier and have offered $ 15 billion worth of concessions by way of reducing their trade-weighted average bound tariff on imports from industrialized countries by 28 per cent.

Developing countries were tempted to accept these substantial commitments by the promise of additional market access to them by developed countries through liberalization of agricultural trade, textiles and clothing and movement of natural persons. The gains from the UR proposals of liberalization in these areas were estimated to the tune of US$ 213 to US$ 510 billion-a-year rise in world income with developing countries benefiting to the tune of $86 to $122 billion. Contrary to these claims, it has now been empirically shown that much deeper commitments have been undertaken by developing countries in the UR and the mercantilist balance resulting from trade liberalization has been in favour of developed countries. The UR Agreements, such as TRIPs and TRIMs, are leading to significant income transfers from developing countries besides reducing the policy space for development. The S&DT provisions have been considerably diluted and reduced to just longer transitions for implementation.

The developed countries while preaching the virtues of free trade to developing countries have been resistant to bringing down peak tariffs, high specific duties, and tariff escalation that affect imports from developing countries. The market access commitments in textiles and clothing have been backloaded and only about 20 per cent of imports under specific quota restrictions have been liberalized in the seven years of implementation till 2002. The agriculture trade liberalization in developed countries has been undermined by dirty tariffication. The average applied tariff rates applicable to agricultural products compared to those on industrial goods have been higher by 641 per cent in Japan, by 353 per cent in the EU, and by 100 per cent in the US.

Despite the promise of improved market access in the services of interest to developing countries, very few commitments have been made by developed countries in Mode 4. Furthermore, almost all these commitments are subject to limitations, such as economic needs test that usually render them ineffective. New barriers to movement of natural persons are being evolved in different parts of the world, such as legislations outlawing business process outsourcing. Studies have found staggering welfare losses for the world economy from the protected markets for labour. Even a limited liberalization of labour markets covering just 3 per cent of work force has the potential to generate welfare gains of US$ 156 billion per year, according to recent studies.

There has been continued resort to quotas and other NTBs. As many as 30 per cent tariff lines in basic metal industries in the US (and 34 per cent in Japan), for instance, are subject to core NTBs. There has been a proliferation of NTBs in the form of environmental and food safety standards much higher than the internationally agreed norms. There has been increased resort to contingent protection against developing countries. There is a proliferation of regional and bilateral free trade arrangements in the developed world that are diverting trade and investments away from developing countries.

There seems to be a protectionist backlash in the developed countries inspired from the strategic trade policy aiming to strengthen the competitiveness of their national champions at the cost of sustainable and equitable growth of world trade. While heavy subsidization of developed country agriculture has become well known from the ongoing debates in the context of WTO's Agreement on Agriculture, the continued and rising subsidization of industrial sector remains virtually unnoticed. Not only have developed countries exploited the grey areas available in the multilateral rules, they have included exceptions for the kind of policies and practices that they wish to make use of such as R&D subsidies and huge financial incentives for investment that are as distorting as other actionable subsidies. The US has been giving US$ 4 billion in subsidies to the exporting enterprises under the Foreign Sales Corporations (FSC). These subsidies have been deemed illegal by the WTO's Panel on a complaint brought by the EU. These are now being replaced by even bigger tax cuts worth US$ 120 billion over the ten years for companies having manufacturing bases in the US.

The agricultural subsidies too are growing despite the promises of reduction made in the Uruguay Round and the Doha Declaration. The US has announced the most generous farm subsidy package in history in its Farm Bill 2002. Arguments like multifunctionality are made to justify ever increasing agricultural subsidies. Even export subsidies (called export credits in the US) are not reduced. While trade related performance requirements such as local content regulations have been phased out under TRIMs Agreement, developed countries extensively resort to policies like screw driver regulations, rules of origin, buy local regulations that are akin to local content regulations.

The process is not leading to growth of world trade either. Quantitative studies do not find the process of GATT/WTO to be leading to either trade liberalization or growth of trade. The developing countries, with the exception of China, have not been able to increase their share in world trade. The terms of trade of developing countries have deteriorated. As a result of these trends, the growth rates in a large number of countries in 1990s has been lower than in the 1980s and inequalities have risen in a large number of developing and transition economies.

This situation is in sharp contrast to the avowed goals of the WTO as set out in the preamble to the Marrakesh Agreement recognizing the 'need for positive efforts designed to ensure that developing countries... secure a share in the growth in international trade commensurate with the needs of their economic development... mutually advantageous arrangement directed to the substantial reduction of tariffs and other barriers to trade and to the discriminating treatment in international trade'.

3. Singapore Issues

The effort of developed countries in WTO has been towards expansion of negotiating agenda since its inception. At the first ever Ministerial Conference of WTO, held in Singapore in 1996, itself they demanded the negotiating mandate of WTO be broadened to include trade and investment, trade and competition policy, government procurement, trade facilitation, labour standards and environmental standards. Having undertaken heavy commitments in the just concluded Uruguay Round, developing countries resisted these demands. As a part of the compromise arrived, Working Groups were set up at the WTO on investment, competition policy, and transparency in government procurement to conduct study processes without any negotiating mandate. The Council for Trade in Goods was also directed by the Ministerial Conference to 'undertake exploratory and analytical work .... on the simplification of trade procedures in order to assess the scope for WTO rules in this area'. Developing countries managed to put labour standards and environment off the WTO agenda for the time being.

These so-called Singapore issues, viz. investment, competition policy, government procurement, and trade facilitation, were the most contentious ones at the Doha Ministerial. Even though the Working Groups set up on these issues by WTO at the Singapore Ministerial have not completed their work, the developed countries wanted to launch negotiations right away. Developing countries resisted a negotiating mandate and wanted the Working Groups to complete their assigned work prior to negotiations. After much deliberations, developing countries succeeded in postponing the decision on the launch of negotiations on these issues subject to an 'explicit consensus' on the modalities of negotiations.

Although the four issues are unrelated and raise different types of concerns, they are being bundled together. However, there are similarities in the sense that the North-South divide is quite apparent in each case. Secondly, in most cases there is a wide divergence of views even among the developed countries themselves. Debates at the Working Groups on the subject over the past six-seven years have failed to produce a consensus and establish conclusively the need for binding rules.

Studies find a critical role of host governments' interventions such as selective policies and performance requirements in determining the developmental impact of FDI. Evidence on extensive use of such policies by developed countries in different stages of development has also been documented. Given the high opportunity cost of the policy flexibility for the process of development and no reciprocity or gains even in the form of higher inflows of FDI, the most prudent option for developing countries would be to resist a negotiating mandate on investment at Cancun. A compromise solution could be to negotiate a multilateral treaty on investment outside the WTO such as in the framework of UN.

Given the little experience that developing countries have in dealing with competition policy even at the national level, it is premature to consider a multilateral framework. There is also divergence of views even among developed countries on the subject especially with some countries seeking only a non-binding voluntary framework for cooperation among competition authorities. Developing countries also have genuine development concerns in implementing competition policies.

Transparency in government procurement seems to be an intermediate step in evolving a framework providing national treatment. Binding rules on the subject may thus take away valuable development policy space from governments. Similarly, there is hardly any rationale for binding rules in the case of trade facilitation either. Technical assistance and autonomous policy decisions should be preferred over binding rules which will put heavy burden of compliance on developing countries.

4. Agreement on Agriculture

The Doha Ministerial focused on the development dimension of agriculture by bringing on board the issues of food security and rural development. It also emphasized the need to take up the non-trade concerns in the negotiations as provided for in the WTO Agreement on Agriculture (AoA). The emphasis was also on phasing out of domestic support to agriculture and export subsidies in the developed countries. The Doha Declaration expressed concerns about the possible negative effects of reforms on the LDCs and net food importing developing countries. S&DT was considered to be an integral part of all elements of agricultural negotiations.

In the post-Uruguay Round phase, developing countries have provided most of market access in agriculture. On the other hand, expanded access to markets of industrialized countries promised to developing countries under the AoA has been very slow in materializing. There have been tendencies to either under-implement these commitments or to implement in a manner that makes the fruits of liberalization unavailable to the developing countries. Developed countries continue to provide significant domestic support to agricultural production along with substantial of export subsidies. The agricultural subsidies by OECD countries have increased from $ 266 billion during 1997-99 to US $ 311 billion which added up to as much as 31 per cent of the gross value of agricultural output in these countries. In addition, the industrialized countries have increasingly used provisions of anti-dumping and other restrictive measures to deny the benefits of trade liberalization in agriculture to their trade partners, especially in the developing world.

The proposed changes in the AoA need to be attempted in a manner that ensures equitable distribution of gains. The US-EU proposal of August 13, 2003, however, does not go far in this direction. Prior to this, the Harbinson's proposals in the form of an 'Overview Paper' were presented on December 18, 2002 (HT1) for possible negotiation. However, based on the feedback and responses from the member countries two more drafts, viz. Harbinson-2 (HT2) and Harbinson-3 (HT3) were presented in February and March 2003. All these deliberations intend to lay down the modalities in agricultural negotiations. The finalization of the modalities is an important step towards agricultural negotiations themselves as issues left out for consideration during finalization of modalities cannot be retrieved in the later stage of agricultural negotiations.

5. Non-Agricultural Market Access

A major concern of developing countries with the process of trade liberalization for non-agricultural products in the Uruguay Round has been the persistence of high and peak tariffs, specific duties, tariff escalation and non-tariff barriers in developed countries on goods their export interest. It has also been shown that process of trade liberalization has been asymmetric with developing countries taking deeper commitments compared to developed countries. The Doha Ministerial Conference sought to address this asymmetry by proposing negotiations on the market access for non-agricultural goods on the basis of the modalities to be agreed by May 2003 to eliminate barriers to market access in particular on products of export interest to developing countries. Subsequently, a Negotiating Group on Market Access (NGMA) has been set up at the WTO and different countries have presented proposals on modalities for trade liberalization. Following these proposals, the Chairman of NGMA has proposed draft modalities in May 2003 and on 19 August 2003. Broadly the approach to modalities proposed by developed countries is to undermine the concept of less-than-full-reciprocity and seeking sharp reduction in tariff rates in developing countries using non-linear formulae.

Market Access for the non-agricultural products thus has been one of the principal agenda items in the WTO negotiations in post-Doha phase. The basic mandate in the Doha Declaration under the category 'tariff and trade of industrial products' is both broad and comprehensive. Developing countries should concentrate on reduction in peak tariffs and tariff escalations. They should also demand that all the countries should define their binding rates in the form of ad valorem rates, because it has been noticed that ad valorem equivalence of non-ad valorem duties are very high.

While discussing tariff elimination the implications of revenue losses for developing countries need to be kept in mind, besides the competition to domestic industry. The revenue losses could affect the developmental effort in developing countries that is highly dependent on public investments. As endorsed in the Doha mandate, the principle of "less-than-full-reciprocity" needs to be respected.

6. TRIPs, Public Health, Traditional Knowledge and Geographical Indicators

The international environment with respect to intellectual property has changed considerably with the conclusion of the TRIPs Agreement in the Uruguay Round. The TRIPs Agreement accommodates the demands of the industrialized countries for higher international standards of protection by mandating the extension of patentability to virtually all fields of technology recognized in developed country patent systems, by prolonging the patent protection for a uniform term of twenty years, and by providing legal recognition of the patentee's exclusive rights to import the patented products.

Besides its wide-ranging adverse effects on the technological capability, balance of payments and economic growth of developing countries, the implementation of TRIPs has raised three sets of negotiating concerns in recent times. Firstly, its impact on prices and availability of essential medicines in the context of HIV AIDS drugs controversy in South Africa. It led the Doha Ministerial Conference of WTO to adopt a Declaration on TRIPs and Public Health, recognizing the supremacy of public health concerns over IPRs and allowing the members some flexibility. However, the US under pressure from its pharma industry is dragging feet from signing an Agreement based on the 16 December 2002 draft text.

Secondly, TRIPs Agreement created an anomalous situation where the knowledge created from traditional and communities innovation systems is left free for commercial exploitation without any compensation as against intellectual property resulting from formal innovation systems being protected from unauthorized commercial exploitation. This resulted in private enterprises obtaining patents on the traditional knowledge of particular communities/countries without the prior informed consent of the owners of knowledge. Developing countries which happen to be rich in genetic resources and traditional knowledge, have been seeking a redressal of this asymmetry. In recognition of this concern the Doha Ministerial instructed the Council for TRIPs to examine 'the relationship between the TRIPs Agreement and the convention on Biological Diversity, the protection of traditional knowledge and folklore'. The TRIPs Agreement needs to be amended to provide a framework for prior informed consent of the holders of traditional knowledge or biological resources and a system of benefit sharing.

Finally, the provision in the TRIPs Agreement for additional protection of geographical indications (GI) for wines and spirits under Article 23 has also created an anomalous situation as geographical indications for other products are not protected. The EU, Switzerland and India, among many others, have sought the extension of protection of GI for other products. The Doha Ministerial agreed to address the issue of extension of the protection of GI to products other than wines and spirits in the Council for TRIPs as an outstanding Implementation Issue. This needs to be addressed.

7. Agreement on Sanitary and Phyto-Sanitary Measures

One important concern of the South in recent years has been the stringent food safety standards and other environmental standards imposed by the North. The WTO Agreement on SPS (Sanitary and Phytosanitary Measures) aims to ensure that these standards and regulations are not used for protectionist purposes and do not cause adverse impacts on trade. However, there is considerable discretion available to importing countries to impose their own rules regarding these standards and other regulations, such as inspection of imported products, specific treatment or processing of products, fixing of minimum allowable levels of pesticide residue, labelling and packaging requirements, good manufacturing practices, etc. provided there is a scientific basis. There is evidence that this flexibility has been exploited by using very minute risk assessments sometimes in a non-transparent manner. The standards are constantly changing and vary across countries even between the partners in a regional trading bloc leading to substantial costs of compliance. The promised technical assistance is often not adequate or arrives too late.

The Doha Ministerial Declaration while recognizing the right of countries to take measures for the protection of human, animal or plant life or health, has argued against their application 'in a manner which would constitute a means of arbitrary or unjustifiable discrimination between countries where the same conditions prevail, or a disguised restriction on international trade. In addition, the Ministerial Conference in its Decisions on Implementation-related Issues and Concerns adopted at Doha under Para 12 of the Declaration, included six points concerning SPS Agreement. However, the progress has been very unsatisfactory.

8. Dispute Settlement Understanding

The Dispute Settlement Understanding (DSU) is one of the most important developments in the WTO. Although the conflict resolution provision was provided in the GATT, the DSU introduced number of other effective provisions for the setting up of trade disputes. The DSU provides for panels to examine complaints from Member countries, appellate review of panel decisions, and the ability to render binding decisions. The DSU mechanism has gained credibility among the Members Countries. However, the participation of developing countries and LDCs in the DSU has not improved due to some existing lacunae in the current dispute settlement procedure. For example, the lack of effective sanction in DSU System, owing to which the complaining party is largely left alone in its struggle against violator. Consequently countries that are economically and politically weak stand at a relatively disadvantageous position.

The DSU is a principal tool which could potentially help developing countries protect and promote their interests. Reforms are needed to improve its effectiveness for developing countries.

9. Special and Differential Treatment (S&DT) for Developing Countries

S&DT has been an integral part of the multilateral trading system right from the 1950s in recognition of the inherent inequality between the players. Despite the strong conceptual basis for S&DT stemming from the infant industry argument, the Uruguay Round Agreements have tended to dilute them and reduced them into best endeavour clauses. Developing countries have expressed concern about the non-mandatory nature of some of the important provisions, lack of specificity and also over the rigid nature of some provisions that fail to take into account the specific needs of these countries. They have demanded a framework agreement to make these provisions binding. The developed countries have been resistant to operationalize the S&DT provisions beyond a longer transition period.

Although the Doha Ministerial agreed to review the S&DT provisions to make them meet demand of developing countries, the progress has been unsatisfactory. All the proposed deadlines for reviews have been missed. The case for S&DT, that may foster growth and development in developing countries allowing policy flexibility to pursue development policy objectives, today is stronger than in the 1960s. In the age of global economic interdependence, rapid development of developing countries eventually supports growth in developed world by creating demand for their goods and services. Hence, WTO needs to pay attention to implement the Doha Mandate on S&DT in the letter and spirit.

10. Some Issues for a Developing Countries' Position at Cancun and Beyond

The Report outlines a number of recommendations for developing country position at the Cancun Ministerial and beyond on specific issues. In what follows, some major recommendations are recapitulated.

10.1. Systemic Reforms

a) An Independent Commission to Make a Development Review of the Multilateral Trading System

Given the key importance of the emerging world trading system for the development and sustainability of the world economy, it is important to pause and undertake a thorough review of the type of asymmetries that have crept in; as outlined in the Report. The Cancun Conference provides an opportunity to the WTO membership to seek a redressal of the emerging asymmetries in the world trading system before moving forward to expand its agenda. The developing countries should call for appointment of an Independent Commission to review the developmental consequences of Uruguay and Doha Rounds before moving forward. This Commission should identify asymmetries that have crept into the system and recommend directions of reform of the priorities, procedures and rules to giving a real meaning to development on the trade agenda.

The Director-General of WTO Secretariat has recently appointed a consultative group to advise him on the world trading system. However, a high powered Independent Commission appointed by the Ministerial Conference will have greater credibility, influence and authority for action and suggesting a thorough reform of the system.

b) Reform of Decision-making Process

The decision-making process in WTO clearly needs a reform for its long-term sustainability. The general perception is that the decision-making process in WTO is non-transparent, and not inclusive. The will of a handful of powerful countries, viz. Quad countries, is imposed on the entire membership in the name of 'Consensus'. In an organization whose membership comprises of countries at varying levels of development, their concerns and interests are expected to be different. Obviously these differences limit the possibilities of arriving at a consensus. In order to arrive at the 'consensus' sometimes powerful members push relatively poorer members to accept their position by several means including diplomacy and even arm-twisting.

Members have also complained of the lack of participation in decision-making process where informal consultations between few powerful players have far greater influence on WTO decision-making than the formal processes.

A more democratic system of decision-making based on secret voting and decision based on majority would serve the organization better and make it more participatory. All negotiating texts and drafts should be introduced in open ended meetings and late night meetings and marathon sessions should be avoided. No decisions should be imposed on members without wide consultations and discussions. Chairpersons drafts should be representative of all the interventions. The Ministers may consider changing the statute to bring about this profound change in the decision-making process in the interest of its long-term survival.

c) Broadbased and Representative Secretariat

Given the large stakes of different players in the multilateral trading system, vested interests begin to operate. In this context the role of the Secretariat becomes critical. It has some times been observed that Secretariat is not discharging its role with the kind of objectivity that it should be. As of now the WTO Secretariat is highly dominated by the developed countries. More than 80 per cent of the staff members of the Secretariat came from the OECD countries with over 61 per cent coming from just six developed countries, viz. France, the UK, the US, and Canada, Spain and Switzerland. There is hardly any representation from a large number of developing countries. It is important that the WTO Secretariat has a proportionate representation of developed and developing countries. A more representative Secretariat will be able to discharge its mandate much more objectively.

d) A WTO Watch Dog of Developing Countries

Developing countries, individually, lack the capacity – physical, analytical and financial – to identify and pursue the cases of non-implementation or unilateral policy decisions concerning trade policy on the part of developed countries and seek their redressal under the existing framework. The recent case of the trade distorting export subsidy valued at $4 billion under Foreign Sales Corporations (FSC) by the US government which was successfully brought by the EU to the DSB is a case in point. Needless to mention that no developing country possesses the capability to do the same.

There is a need for setting up a WTO Watchdog by developing countries. In the interest of building a fair and just world trading system, developed countries should create a trust fund for maintaining the WTO Watchdog. This body should be equipped with the necessary professional, analytical, legal and financial expertise to scrutinize the implementation of commitments by developed countries and where appropriate to bring them to DSB on behalf of developing countries.

e) Strengthening the Provision ofTechnical Assistance

Developing country implementation of their commitments often implies major changes in their legal and institutional framework and involves substantial technical and financial resources that may be beyond the capability of many countries. In this regard it is often being felt that the WTO should provide major technical and financial assistance not only to least developed countries but also to the developing countries for implementation of their commitments in an effective manner.

This would require that the WTO's Trust Fund for Technical Assistance needs to be augmented. In this regard the three Geneva based agencies (ITC, UNCTAD and WTO) have endorsed the launching of the new phase of the Joint Integrated Technical Assistance Programme (JITAP). JITAP seeks to build capacity to understand the emerging trade issues and help comply with them, and also to derive benefit from it. However, the proposed support of $ 12.6 million dollar, over a period of four years is rather modest.

The Doha Development Agenda Global Trust Fund was created following the WTO Ministerial Conference in Doha, in November 2001. In December 2002, the General Council has approved a budget for this fund.

The G-8 countries should augment their contributions to these Funds.

f) Mobilising Support for 'Trilateral Cooperation'

It is often being observed that though different developing countries which are at different stages of economic development are better placed to help and cooperate with fellow developing countries than any other countries from developed part of the world. However, owing to lack of resources the potential for South-South cooperation has remained untapped.

In this regard, adopting a different strategy of trilateral cooperation may help to a great extent. In this a multilateral agency or a donor agency from North may step in to support technical assistance among developing countries.

10.2. Substantive Issues

a) Emphasis on Outstanding Implementation Issues rather than expansion of negotiating agenda

Developing countries should firmly seek full implementation of all outstanding implementation issues before a negotiating mandate on any other issue could even be discussed. Any organization that cannot even handle implementation of the decisions already taken is obviously not justified in asking for more responsibilities.

b) Proactive Initiatives by Developing Countries

A Framework Agreement on Movement of Natural Persons: Given the reluctance of developed countries to make meaningful commitments on the movement of natural persons, developing countries could seek a framework agreement to provide for movement of natural persons.

A Framework Agreement on S&DT: In order to provide a legally binding framework to various S&DT provisions, there is need to negotiate a Framework Agreement, as demanded by developing countries at Doha. Such an Agreement would provide for the notifications requirements and inclusion of commitments in country schedules and for dispute settlement. The framework Agreement should clearly lay out an objectively defined economic criteria for S&DT provisions rather than just longer transition periods. For instance, an objectively defined criteria could be evolved to provide a greater flexibility to countries having a greater proportion of population dependent on agriculture in AoA.

A Framework Agreement on Transfer of Technology: At the request of developing countries a Working Group on Transfer of Technology has been established at WTO. They should now seek a Framework Agreement on Transfer of Technology that would provide for policies and interventions to be taken by governments to facilitate transfer of technology. These could include performance requirements on foreign enterprises, among other policies.

Phase-out of R&D Subsidies and Investment Incentives: The extensive financial subsidies provided by developed countries to their enterprises should come under an international discipline as they are no less distorting than those that have been phased out.

c) No Negotiating Mandate on Singapore Issues

There is very little rationale to support a negotiating mandate on any of the Singapore Issues at the Fifth Ministerial Conference. There does not seem to be an emerging consensus even among the developed countries. Several groups of developing countries such as the least developing countries, the African Union, and the African, Caribbean and Pacific (ACP) countries, at the Meetings of their Trade Ministers have expressed opposition to launch of negotiations on these issues. A group of 13 African countries have even suggested draft Ministerial Text on the subject which should be endorsed. However, the study processes could continue. This seems to be the best course of action as of now for developing countries at large.

d) Issues for Negotiations on Agriculture

Some key issues for Negotiations on Agriculture are as follows:

Economically Active Population Dependent on Agriculture (EAPA) as a Criteria: In 50 developing countries more than half of the population is critically dependent on agriculture for livelihood. Countries with such high dependence on agriculture for livelihood should get a special dispensation under S&DT provisions in agriculture.

Food security: As large number of developing countries have an unstable food security system, a food security box is, therefore, of extreme importance. A more pragmatic approach has to be adopted from the point of view of integrating developing and least developed countries in the international trade regime. In this context, the mere flexibility in terms of a time frame alone under the S&DT may not suffice as against the continuously expanding Green Box.

Facilitating developed country market access for developing countries: The experience of the last six years of implementation of AoA suggests that the developed country policies of high domestic support, coupled with high tariffs, tariff peaks, tariff escalation and a plethora of non-tariff barriers, restrict market access of developing country agricultural exports. It is important that an appropriate formula with a cap on tariff binding is evolved to effect reduction in all tariff levels across commodity lines.

Tariff Rationalisation: For tariff reduction, the principle of higher reduction rates for higher tariffs may be applied, which would cover a large number of products of the developed countries. Further, a ceiling on tariff peaks of developed countries is also a necessity. Developing countries should demand for the conversion of specific tariff to ad valorem tariff for transparency and administration of tariff.

Tariff Rate Quotas (TRQs): It is very unlikely that the TRQ will be abolished. The interest of developing countries would be to have increased volume of the TRQs. Such enhanced TRQs should be available to Member countries on the basis of non-preferential terms and also at the MFN rate. The modalities regarding administration of the tariff rate quotas also need to be ascertained and evolved to the satisfaction of all members.

Special Safeguard Measure for the SP products: In the First Draft of Modalities for Future Consideration (HT2), it is distinctly mentioned that developing countries shall have flexibility to apply SSM in case of Special Products. In the HT3, it is mentioned that the issue "... currently subject to technical work ....". It is developing country position that the proposal made in the HT2 should be made as the basis for negotiation. The developing countries may also negotiate for applying direct import control measures in respect of the products from the developed countries maintaining export subsidy and/ or domestic support.

Domestic Support: The Green and Blue Box subsides of developed countries have to be subject to reduction commitments, aim at a complete elimination. Such reduction may be effected uniformly over a period of five years.

Export Subsidies: The AoA text enables those countries with export subsidies in the base year period (1986-90) to continue with this support. On the other hand, it does not allow any country to provide export subsidies afresh which did not have the provision of export subsidy during the base year nor notified about such provisions for the base year in the country schedule. The regime, therefore, is an extremely uneven in the area of export promotion measures. It is important that the developing countries should re-negotiate this provision and emphasize a progressive elimination of export subsidies.

Expansion of the Sectoral Product Coverage: In the AoA, many primary and agricultural products are not included under the broad sector of agriculture. These products are otherwise eligible for being a part of the agricultural sector, but they are now in the manufacturing sector. Since negotiations in the manufacturing sector are different from that of agriculture, many countries are facing difficulties in gaining market access in these products. A large number of countries from Asia, Africa and Latin America are the victims of this arrangement in the trade regime. In this Round, products like shrimp, rubber, etc. should be included in the agricultural sector, so for making the sector comprehensive for negotiation.

Linking up the three pillars: It is important that the three pillars of AoA, viz. market access, domestic support and export subsidy should have a strong linkage. There has to be a correlation between the disciplines to be adopted on domestic support and agenda for other streamlining measures. The market access commitments which AoA seeks to secure would be viable only if domestic support reduction commitments are ambitious. The continuous effort to enlarge the scope of Green and Blue Boxes is a major concern for the developing countries. Moreover, some of the domestic support measures under Green Box are as trade distorting as the tariffs. In this regard, a clear definition of various components of Green Box which are "non-or minimally trade distorting" is needed.

Special and Differential (S&D) Treatment: Under the provision of S&D, developing countries especially those with more than half of population dependent on agriculture (EAPA) should ask for more liberal terms for reduction commitments and also for a more prolonged implementation period. There should be a downward adjustment of the reduction commitment schedule in the HT3 to accommodate the development requirements of developing countries.

e) Non-Agricultural Market Access

Key consideration in evolving the modalities for market access in industrial goods should be as follows.

Addressing the Peak Tariffs, Specific Duties, and Tariff Escalation in Developed Countries: As per the Doha mandate, the focus of trade liberalization should be on elimination of peak tariffs, high specific duties and tariff escalation on products of export interest to developing countries. A reduction based on differential linear cut or a non-linear formula with significantly different coefficient values for developed and developing countries taking into account of the average base rates should be applied. Developing countries should not accept tariff liberalization on the basis of a Swiss formula.

Preserving the Less-than-full-reciprocity in the Modalities for Tariff Reduction: The Doha mandate promises less-than-full-reciprocity to developing countries. This principle should be preserved in any modality that is agreed to by developing countries.

Retaining the Flexibility to Apply Tariffs in Sector-by-sector /zero-for-x approach: In order to protect small and medium enterprises, developing countries should seek flexibility to apply tariffs in zero-for-zero modality by proposing zero-for-x where x could vary across countries depending upon the level of development.

Addressing the NTBs in Developed Countries: Major barriers for market access for many products are the NTBs in developed countries. Hence, negotiations should evolve modalities to bring down the NTBs as well.

Flexibility to keep Tariff Lines Unbound for Sensitive Products: Developing countries may have concerns about tariff bindings in sensitive products due to small scale enterprises or other reasons. Hence, some flexibility to keep 15-20 per cent tariff lines unbound should be available to developing countries.

Moderating the Effects of Revenue Losses: Besides protection, tariffs are also important sources of revenue in developing countries. A drastic reduction in tariffs will have implications for public finances and fiscal situation in developing countries. Provision should be made for financial assistance to developing countries.

f) TRIPS

An International Framework for Protection of Traditional Knowledge under TRIPs Agreement: The member states should establish *sui generis* systems for protection of traditional knowledge and genetic resources. The protection of TK at national levels will not be complete until there is an international framework for use of TK outside the country of origin. The framework should establish a procedure that requires patent or other IPR applications to disclose the source or origin of TK or genetic resource used and enclose a certificate from a competent authority in the source country of prior informed consent and benefit sharing conditions. This would require an amendment in the TRIPs Agreement.

Delivering the Doha Promise on Public Health: The developed countries, particularly the US, should accept the draft Agreement on TRIPs and Public Health of 16 December 2002. This would be of great symbolic value for developing and least developed countries who are feeling let down on the commitment made at Doha Ministerial.

Granting Flexibility to Developing Countries in Implementing the Provisions of TRIPs on the basis of an Objective Criteria: Most of the adverse effects concerning TRIPs on poor countries arise not because of IPR regimes per se but from the attempt to harmonize them across the countries at different levels of development. There is also a discussion going on whether TRIPs should fundamentally belong to WTO. However, the least that could be done in this connection is to allow flexibility to developing countries to implement the provisions of the Agreement as and when their level of development has reached a certain stage. This could be achieved if a consensus among the developed countries is built on the differential need of developing countries for IPR regime.

Apart from this, a possible revision of TRIPs could incorporate a provision that grants developing countries the flexibility to implement the TRIPs obligations until they reach a certain level of development defined in terms of some objective criteria, such as per capita income. One possibility in this respect is to adopt a threshold of US$ 1000 of per capita income as the Agreement on Subsidies and Countervailing Measures (SCM) adopted, as it would be easier to agree to, having been adopted in one of the WTO's Agreements. This would bring in an element of graduation in the treatment of countries as the preferential treatment would cease as they cross the developmental threshold. Another possibility could be to shorten the term of product patents applicable to low income countries. This way the Agreement will have incorporated development dimension.

Extending the Geographical Indications Coverage to Other Products: Steps should be taken to expeditiously implement the extension of scope of protection of GIs beyond wines and spirits, which is an outstanding implementation issue from the Doha Ministerial.

Moratorium on Further Strengthening of IPR Regime: There is tendency in some developed countries to treat provisions of TRIPs as the minimum standards and are constantly attempting to evolve stronger norms through unilateral or bilateral approaches. A consensus needs to be built on the need to put a moratorium on such approaches for the next couple of decades or so.

g) Agreement on SPS

Linking Implementation with Effective Technical Assistance: The SPS Agreement in WTO contains provisions for technical assistance to be provided by the importing countries to assist the exporters in their compliance with the new standards imposed by them. Furthermore, the SPS Agreement provides that 'where substantial investments are required in order for an exporting developing country Member to fulfill the sanitary and phyto-sanitary requirements of an importing Member, the latter shall consider providing such technical assistance as will permit the developing country Members to maintain and expand its market access opportunities for the product involved' (Art. 9.2).

However, available evidence suggests that promised technical assistance is not delivered in an adequate or timely manner. In this light, it may be useful to seek through reviews of the Agreements in the WTO, effective implementation of standards that are different from international norms, only after technical assistance has been provided.

Restricting the Discretion to Follow International Norms: Developing countries may consider seeking reviews of the Agreement on SPS at the WTO Committee on Sanitary and Phyto-sanitary Measures to reduce the discretion and flexibility available under the Agreement that is being misused; to ensure universal application of international standards; and to bring about greater transparency in the imposition of standards, good manufacturing practices and all other regulations. Countries wishing to adopt higher than international standards should undertake to financially compensate potentially affected developing countries.

Substantive S&DT Provisions: Like other WTO Agreements, S&DT in the case of SPS Agreement has also been reduced to a longer transition period for developing countries. However, the longer transition period provided under these Agreements is of hardly any use because the importing enterprises start insisting on the new product standards due to high consumer consciousness for these standards. Therefore, the SDT has to be of a more substantive type. It could be, for instance, in the form of additional financing (along with technical assistance) to cover the costs of compliance by the developing country exports of the new standards.

Enhancing the Scope of 'Standards and Trade Development Facility': In light of the extremely vocal criticism from the developing countries about the health and environment related standards and the difficulties the developing countries are facing in meeting the disease and contaminant related standards for their food exports to richer countries' markets, the WTO and the World Bank have launched a new fund called Standards and Trade Development Facility. The World Bank has proposed an initial US$ 300,000 to establish the new fund, and the WTO will allocate funding from the Doha Development Trust Fund to launch the Facility.

At present the facility only proposes to help developing countries for better implementing the food safety and plant and animal health measures in the area of sanitary and phytosanitary (SPS) regulations. The developing countries have been finding it difficult to implement stringent standards being implemented by the developed countries. However, one of the factors behind this failure of developing countries in meeting these standards was their lack of participation in the existing institutional mechanisms for setting global standards like Codex Commission and other food safety standards-setting organizations, run jointly by the FAO and WHO. The scope of this facility should be enhanced to facilitate the participation of developing countries in the meetings of such organisations as well. Apart from providing the first hand information to the developing countries this will also ensure the long needed rationalisation of standard setting exercise itself.

h) Dispute Settlement Understanding

Some of the issues that may facilitate more effective use of DSU by developing countries are as follows.

Adjustment of time-period: At present the period between the start of a dispute and its final determination may go up to three years. This period is too long for complainant developing countries as their capacity to absorb the adverse effects of measures taken against them is considerably low. This can be improved by making suitable amendments in the time-frame of the relevant provisions of Articles 4, 5, 6 and 12 of the DSU, especially in all the complaints brought by a developing country against a developed country.

Provision of compensation for loss during the pendency of the dispute: Developing countries that are dependant on a limited number of export products/ markets may suffer heavy trade losses during the course of a dispute regarding a measure taken against them by a developed country. The damage is not limited to foregone exports. The market may be lost permanently to competitors and substitute products. Article 22 (Compensation and the Suspension of Concessions) of the DSU can be extended to provide for compensation for the loss suffered by a complainant developing country during the pendency of a complaint against a developed country. The Panel should be mandated to determine the amount of compensation in all cases where measures by developed countries against developing countries are found to be violative the WTO rules. This will help prevent the initiation of trade-related measures on frivolous grounds by developed countries.

Implementation of decisions: Hardly any developing country is in a position to take retaliatory action against a developed country even if it is authorized to do so by the DSB. This seriously limits the implementation of the DSU rulings. In cases brought and won by developing countries against developed countries, DSU provisions can be amended to provide payment of compensation to the developing country, or joint retaliatory action by all WTO members against the offending member; or mandatory removal of the measure violative of WTO rules.

Making S&D Provisions Effective: A review of the existing S&D provisions should also involve a comprehensive analysis of the implementation of all S&D provisions. This thorough analysis should lead to the elaboration of an implementation mechanism wherever such a mechanism is missing in the present provisions. For example, the "special attention" mentioned in Article 4:10 may be interpreted to mean, inter alia, that consultations initiated against a developing country by a developed country are held at a place convenient for the developing country concerned. This would certainly help the developing country because owing to financial constraints they are often unable to bring experts from their capitals during the consultation period. It should identify the reasons as to why certain special and differential treatment provisions, for example, Articles 12.10, 12.11, 21.7, 21.8 (panel procedure and surveillance of implementation), have so far not been used by developing countries. Such an analysis will also enable improvements that would lead to a more extensive use of these provisions by developing countries.

Legal and Financial support to Developing Countries: It is important to ensure that the costs associated with using the dispute settlement process do not act as barriers for gaining access to the process for the developing and especially the least-developed countries. It will require making provision for adequate legal assistance to both the complainant and defendant developing countries by strengthening and expanding the coverage of present Article 27.2 of the DSU. The Advisory Centre for WTO law has recently been set up by WTO. It is, however, yet to be used effectively by developing countries. Besides increasing the number of consultants, setting up an independent legal unit within or outside the Secretariat, appointment of a permanent Defence Counsel, or establishment of special arrangements with private lawyers, adequate financial resources, etc. should be made available.

Strengthening the existing Legal Provisions in the various WTO Agreements: Owing to the asymmetric legal and economic capacities of developed and developing countries, the former may bring a large number of disputes, some even on frivolous grounds, against the latter. There have also been instances where developed countries brought repeated cases, on the same grounds, against developing countries. The proposals to address these issues should include:

(i) The complainant developed country may be asked to pay the cost of the dispute incurred by the defendant developing country, if the case brought by the former is not maintained by the panel/Appellate Body.

(ii) WTO members may be prohibited from bringing cases against a developing country member once a case on similar grounds involving the same developing country has been decided by a panel/ Appellate Body.

(iii) The panels and the Appellate Body should be directed to give, to the extent possible, transparent and clear rulings that are less prone to conflicting legalistic interpretations so that once the case decided, it should not be appealed on the similar grounds again.

10.3 An Agenda for Cooperation among Developing Countries on WTO-related Issues

The emerging WTO regime is important for the national development, trade, investment and technology policies of member countries. The ongoing round of negotiations will have an important bearing on the developmental process of the developing countries. Therefore, the developing countries need to deliberate over the mandate given by the Ministerial Meetings and prepare themselves to take part in the ensuing negotiations effectively to safeguard their interests. Issues of preparedness on their part would also include taking advantage of the emerging multilateral regime rather than passively implementing their commitments. This calls for strategic thinking and concerted action at different levels.

Not only do developing countries lack strong analytical capabilities in fully comprehending the developmental implications of the commitments implicit in the negotiations, the situation is further complicated by the mis-information that is promoted by developed countries to achieve their strategic objectives. Very often the training courses offered by international organizations in the name of technical assistance are also influenced by the view-point of the donors, viz. the developed countries and fail to highlight the concerns of developing countries.

The technical cooperation among developing countries could cover the followings:

Exchange of Experiences in Implementation of Commitments: Developing countries should fully exploit the policy spaces that may be available in the WTO Agreements. An example in this regard is the TRIPs Agreement where several flexibilities are available to be exploited to moderate the potential adverse effect of the Agreement such as provisions for compulsory licensing, research exception, Bolar provisions, grey market imports, anti-trust regulations, breeders exceptions, among others. Exchange of experiences and professional expertise among developing countries may facilitate such possibilities.

Technical Assistance and Cooperation in Implementation or Compliance of Commitments: Compliance with some SPS standards require huge technical and financial costs. Cooperation among developing countries may be in sharing the services of experts, setting up the common testing and verification laboratories, translations of standards, etc.

Effective Coordination of Positions: WTO negotiations are power games. Any coordination between developing countries at the issue level or regional levels would be more effective than individual country positions. Developing countries should establish communications among their respective trade ministries and their missions at WTO to facilitate such coordination.

Vigilance and Active Participation in the Proceedings: Given the high stakes involved, developing countries need to participate in the negotiations effectively and with extreme vigilance. They need to back up their preparations with adequate legal and analytical expertise. Introduction of small phrases which may appear innocuous may eventually lead to some burdensome commitment, as is clear from the example how a reference to counterfeit goods in the Punta del Este Declaration snowballed into the TRIPs Agreement.

Proactive Agenda: Developing countries generally confine themselves to defensive and reactive strategy. They should have their own positive and proactive agenda. They should identify and articulate their concerns with the asymmetries creeping into the multilateral trading system and seek their redressal with effective coalition-building.

*****

To sum up, therefore, these are some of the many issues that may be kept in mind by developing country trade diplomats in negotiations at the Cancun Ministerial and subsequent meetings in the WTO. The lenght of this policy agenda gives an indication of the complexity and enormity of the challenges before them.

2

WTO, Rising Protectionism and Development

"...industrialized countries, while preaching the virtues of free and fair trade, are practising protectionist policies which actively discourage poor countries from developing their own industries... if the barriers were lifted...the minimum net gain would be over $100 billion—more than twice the amount of annual aid flows"

Kofi A Annan, Secretary-General of the United Nations[1]

Introduction

The emerging WTO regime his important implications for national development and evolution of trade, investment and technology policies of the developing countries. The Uruguay Round (UR) also placed substantial obligations on developing countries with respect to the liberalization of trade and their policy regimes with respect to intellectual property rights, investments, and trade in services. Developing countries undertook commitments to expand tariff bindings to cover 61 per cent of their imports compared to 13 per cent earlier and have offered $ 15 billion worth of concessions by way of reducing their trade-weighted average bound tariff on imports from industrialized countries by 28 per cent.

Developing countries were tempted to accept these substantial commitments by the promise of promised additional market access to them by developed countries through liberalization of agricultural trade, textiles and clothing and movement of natural persons. The gains from the UR proposals of liberalization in these areas were estimated to the tune of US$ 213 to US$ 510 billion-a-year rise in world income with developing countries benefiting to the tune of $86 to $122 billion. Contrary to these claims, it has now been empirically shown that much deeper commitments have been undertaken by developing countries in the UR and the mercantilist balance resulting from trade liberalization has been in favour of developed countries. The UR Agreements, such as TRIPs and TRIMs, are leading to significant income transfers from developing countries besides reducing the policy space for development. The S&DT provisions have been considerably diluted and reduced to just longer transitions for implementation.

The developed countries while preaching the virtues of free trade to developing countries have been resistant to bringing down peak tariffs, high specific duties, and tariff escalation that affect imports from developing countries.

There are also clear signs of protectionist backlash in the developed world in different sectors with market access for the developing world becoming ever elusive. While developing countries are constantly being pushed to undertake increasing liberalization commitments, developed countries are finding new ways to protect their industries, agriculture and services. This situation is in sharp contrast to the avowed goals of the WTO as set out in the preamble to the Marrakesh Agreement recognizing the 'need for positive efforts designed to ensure that developing countries... secure a share in the growth in international trade commensurate with the needs of their economic development... mutually advantageous arrangement directed to the substantial reduction of tariffs and other barriers to trade and to the discriminating treatment in international trade'.

In this chapter, we summarize the different forms of protectionism that prevail in the developed world despite the GATT/ WTO process especially on the goods and services of particular interest to developing countries. It then summarizes the features of protectionist industrial and strategic trade policies pursued by developed countries that often contradict the spirit of a number of WTO Agreements if not the letter. In the following section the implications of these trends for development are examined. The chapter ends by drawing some implications of these trends for the forthcoming negotiations.

Market Access in Agriculture, Industry and Services: Chasing a Mirage

Trade Barriers for Goods of Export Interest to Developing Countries

Despite the trade liberalization mandated by different rounds of multilateral trade negotiations, trade barriers and subsidies in industrialized countries continue to limit the growth of developing countries' exports. In general, the average tariff and other trade barriers are low in industrialized countries. However, "their tariffs and trade barriers remain much higher on many products exported by developing countries". The low average tariff rates in the developed countries also tend to mask the very wide ranging variation as between 0 to 350 per cent as in the case of the US.[2] Furthermore, the industrialized countries impose specific

Table 2.1: Post-UR Tariffs in Quad Countries on Select Items of Exports from Developing Countries

Product description	EU	Japan	USA	Canada
Agricultural products				
Milk (>3% fat)	113	220[1]	66[2]	241
Milk in powder, with or without sugar	55-66	160-280[1]	55-85[2]	243-243
Yogurt and Butter	69	300-620[1]	63-80[2]	238-300
Cereals and Preparation	32-84	70-900	0-2	1-77
Groundnuts, shelled	0	470	132[2]	0
Cane sugar, raw and white	71-73	85-100[1]	77-90[2]	7
Grape juice	215	30	14	10
Coffee preparations	8	130	27[2]	0
Tea preparations, essences	0	100	91[2]	0
Smoking tobacco	52	30	310	5
Industrial Products				
Woven fabrics of >80% combed wool	12	8	25	14
Babies garments, knitted or croch synthetic fibres	11	22	16	18
Women's blouses and trousers knitted or croch., man-made fibres	11	9-11	32	18
Men's shirts, woven, of cotton and man made fibres	11	7	20-28	17-18
Waterproof footwear	13	27	38	20
Footwear with leather uppers	6	140	10	18
Ceramic tableware, kitchen-ware, etc., Drinking glasses of glass Glassware for kitchen, toilets, etc.	8-9	0	28-29	0

Notes: Post-Uruguay Round MFN rates above tariff quotas; or applied MFN rates (1998-2000) or general GSP rates, if lower.
[1]Including additional amounts levied by the Government, mark-ups, levies.
[2]Progressive additional safeguard duties are levied if import prices are below the level indicated in the tariff.
Source: RIS based on UNCTAD/WTO, 2000.

tariffs on a significant number of commodities that make protection less transparent. Finally, tariff escalation according to stage of processing characterizes tariff structure in a number of industrialized countries that discourages industrial diversification and value-addition of exports in developing countries.

Tariff Peaks: Nearly 10 per cent of the tariff lines in Quad countries are subject to peak tariffs of more than 12 per cent.[3] A bulk of the commodities facing high tariffs in the industrialized countries covers agricultural and fishery products and leather and textiles and clothing. However, the proportion of industrial products is also substantial, especially for the USA and Canada. Commodities subject to high tariff rates in the industrialized countries consist largely of those products where developing countries have a comparative advantage. Some of the products with high tariffs in Quad countries in which developing countries have a comparative advantage are summarized in Table 2.1. These include major agricultural staple food products, such as meat, sugar, milk, dairy products, and chocolate, where tariff rates often exceed 100 per cent; tobacco and some alcoholic beverages; fruits and vegetables—including 180 per cent for above-quota bananas in the European Union and 550 per cent and 132 per cent for shelled ground nuts in Japan and the US, respectively; food industry products, including fruit juices, canned meat, peanut butter, and sugar confectionery with rates exceeding 30 per cent; and textiles, clothing and footwear, where tariff rates are in the 15 to 30 per cent range for a large number of products.[4]

Box 2.1 highlights the differential tariff system of developed countries with regards to other developed countries vis-a-vis developing countries citing an example of the US. The tariff revenue collected by the US on $2 billion imports from Bangladesh is higher than that collected on $ 30 billion imports from France.

Tariff Escalation: Escalation of tariff rates with the extent of processing of imports in industrialized countries has been a major concern for developing countries as it discourages their value-added manufactured exports. The UR commitments were expected to level the variation by the stage of processing with relatively higher cuts for finished goods. However, as Table 2.2 shows, tariff

Box 2.1:
Poor Pays Higher: Asymmetries in Tariff Policy of the United States

The Bush administration's decision last March to impose tariffs of 8-30 percent on steel has attracted widespread criticism. The steel tariffs, even if one believes they are bad policy, are just temporary aberrations from the norm. But for dozens of other products — sneakers, spoons, bicycles, underwear, suitcases, drinking glasses, T-shirts, plates, and more — tariffs of 8-30 percent are neither aberrant nor temporary. In fact, they are normal and permanent parts of U.S. trade policy.

The US tariff policy, has evolved into something astonishingly tough on the poor. Young single mothers buying cheap clothes and shoes now pay tariff rates five to ten times higher than middle-class or rich families pay in elite stores. Very poor countries such as Cambodia or Bangladesh face tariffs 15 times those applied to wealthy nations and oil exporters.

Malign Neglect

The average trade-weighted tariff for the United States is now under 2 percent. But the low overall average masks something more troubling.

Tariffs on industrial imports are not just low but extremely low. For expensive consumer goods such as cars, appliances, and televisions, rates are also generally low and are further reduced in practice by trade agreements with Mexico and Canada. But for light consumer goods, the story is different. Tariffs on these products (with a few exceptions, such as toys and furniture) remain at levels other industries last saw in the 1960s and 1970s: for instance, 8.7 percent for cutlery and tableware, 13.8 percent for suitcases and handbags, 10 percent for bicycles, and 11.4 percent for shoes and clothes, the largest category of consumer imports for the United States.

In effect, the United States now has two tariff systems. One, for low-tech consumer goods, has an average rate of 10.5 percent. The other, for everything else, has an average rate of 0.8 percent. As a result, most tariff revenue now comes from a very small number of goods. Shoes and clothes in particular, make up less than 7 percent of imports but bring in nearly half of all tariff revenues.

Box 2.1 continued

Box 2.1 continued

Finally, tariffs also vary from one consumer good to the next. Most notably, they are much higher on cheap goods than on luxuries. This disparity occurs because elite firms, selling image and brand name, find small price advantages relatively unimportant. They have not pressed the government to keep tariffs high, and tariffs on luxury goods such as silk lingerie, silver-handled cutlery, leaded-glass beer mugs, and snakeskin handbags are now very low. But makers of nylon lingerie, stainless steel cutlery, cheap water glasses, and plastic purses benefit by adding a few percentage points to their competitor's prices. So on the cheapest goods, tariffs are even higher than overall averages for consumer goods suggest. For instance, tariff on men's knitted shirts made of silk is just 1.9 per cent but is steep at 32.5 per cent if it is made of synthetic fibre. Similarly, tariff on drinking glasses costing 30 cents or less is 30.4 per cent but only 5 per cent for leaded glasses costing $5 or more.

Do high tariffs preserve jobs in America?

No. Employment in high-tariff industries now accounts for only about three percent of U.S. manufacturing jobs. It has fallen by half since 1990, and the plunge is fastest in some of the most protected industries. In 1992, for example, 20,000 Americans worked making women's shoes. No shoe tariffs have been cut since the 1970s, but since 1992 employment in women's shoes has fallen by 90 percent, to only 2,000 workers. Likewise, the number of workers making children's clothes is down from 44,000 to fewer than 7,000. For the manufacture of goods such as watches, bicycles, and drinking glasses, job totals are even lower.

The International Trade Commission's July 2002 study finds that employment in high-tariff industries is already so low that eliminating all U.S. trade barriers would mean a net gain of about 35,000 jobs rather than a loss.

Punishing the Poor

Average tariffs on European exports to the United States — primarily cars, power equipment, computers, and chemicals — now barely exceed one percent. Developing countries such as Malaysia, which specialize in information-technology products, get rates just as low. So do natural-resource exporters such as Saudi Arabia and Nigeria. Middle-income exporters that ship a broader variety of goods, such as China, Thailand, and Brazil, face rates typically between two percent and four percent — above average but still not exorbitant. The least-developed Asian countries, however, take it on the chin.

For Bangladesh, Cambodia, Nepal, Mongolia, and a few others, clothes make up 90 percent of all exports to the United States. So they face average tariff rates of 14.6 percent — nearly 10 times the world average, and 15 times the rate for wealthy Western countries. Translated into real dollars, the disparities can be remarkable.

As Table 1 notes, the U.S. now collects more tariff revenue from Bangladeshi goods than from French goods, even though Bangladesh exports $2 billion in goods a year to the United States and France $30 billion. Cambodia's exports to the United States total $900 million and Singapore's usually reach $15-$20 billion — but the U.S. collects more revenue from the former.

Table 1: The Poor Pay More

Country	Per Capita *GDP*	2001 Exports to U.S. *in billions*	Tariff Paid *in millions*	Rate
Nepal	$240	$0.20	$25	12.3%
Ireland	$22660	$18.60	$29	0.2%
Bangladesh	$370	$2.35	$331	14.1%
France	$24,170	$30.02	$330	1.1%
Cambodia	$260	$0.96	$152	15.8%
Singapore	$30,170	$14.90	$96	0.6

Source: **World Bank, World Development Indicators 2002; ITC dataweb.**

In fairness, such disparities are not universal, and some attempts to ease tariff burdens have been successful. The African Growth and Opportunity Act, set up under the Clinton administration, is the best example. Since it was enacted two years ago, African clothing exports to the United States have nearly doubled, but tariff collection on African goods has dropped by more than half. The results of the Caribbean Basin Initiative are less dramatic, but Haiti, Honduras, and several other beneficiaries also face fairly low rates.

The U.S. system is not uniquely bad. Europe's tariffs on clothes and shoes — not to mention food — are also high, and European Union tariff collection is far less transparent and accessible than America's.

To sum up: ***one point seems quite clear. A system that makes maids pay higher rates than corporate vice presidents, and hits Cambodians 15 times harder than Germans, is an ethical scandal.***

Source: **Excerpted from Edward Gresser 'Toughest on the Poor: America's Flawed Tariff System', *Foreign Affairs* 81(6), November/December 2002: 9-14. Edward Gresser is Director of the Project on Trade and Global Markets at the Progressive Policy Institute.**

Table 2.2: Tariff Escalation in the "Quad" by 2-digit ISIC Industry

		United States 2001	Canada 2002	EU(15) 2002	Japan 2002/03
Food beverages and tobacco	First stage of processing	3.2	7.9	12.4	25.4
	Semi-processed	9.0	6.8	19.1	30.3
	Fully processed	13.1	34.3	18.8	22.6
Textiles and leather	First stage of processing	2.2	1.0	0.9	9.8
	Semi-processed	9.8	7.0	6.7	6.8
	Fully processed	10.3	13.5	9.7	12.0
Non-metallic mineral products	First stage of processing	0.0	0.0	0.0	0.0
	Semi-processed	2.3	0.7	2.9	1.5
	Fully processed	5.4	3.8	4.0	1.1
Basic metal	First stage of processing	0.3	0.0	0.0	0.4
	Semi-processed	2.1	0.9	1.9	1.1
	Fully processed	2.5	3.0	0.0	3.0

Note: For countries with non-*ad valorem* rates AVEs have been used as available. In case of unavailability, the *ad valorem* part is used for compound and alternate rates.

Source: RIS based on WTO Annual Report 2003, Appendix, Table II.1.

escalation has continued in most industrialized countries. In the US, for instance, the average bound rate for finished products is five times that for raw materials. In specific sectors the extent of variation by stage of processing is much higher. For instance, in the case of imports of textiles, leather products, wood products, etc. substantial variation has been observed in the tariff rates applicable to various stages of processing in the EU.[5]

Specific Tariff Rates: Table 2.3 shows that nearly 12.5 per cent of the EU tariff lines and over 14 per cent of the US tariff lines are subject to specific tariffs rather than *ad valorem* rates. These rates make it difficult to comprehend the level of protection applicable. For example, Japan defines the specific rate for 'groundnut not roasted' (HS 120910010) as 70 yen per kilogram + 7 yen for every 1 per cent exceeding 10 per cent by weight of lactose content'![6] It has been noticed that the *ad valorem* equivalent of the specific duties is generally very high.[7]

Table 2.3: Proportion of Tariff Lines Subject to Specific Tariff Rates in Industrialized Countries

Country	% of Tariff Lines Subject to Specific Tariff	
	All	Manufactured Products
EU	12.49	0.75
Japan	5.15	1.28
US	14.28	8.35
India	0.22	0.20

Source: Mehta, 2001 based on TRAINS database.

Elusive Market Access in Textiles and Clothing

The imports of textiles and clothing by most developed countries such as the US and EU are regulated by quotas under the Multifibre Agreement. These quotas are to be phased out under the WTO Agreement on Textiles and Clothing in three successive stages ending 2004. However, the phase out commitments have been backloaded so that even with the implementation of stage 3 (1 January 2002) at the most 51 per cent of the total volume of the respective Members' 1990 imports of products falling under the ATC have been integrated. Furthermore, the integration has been confined to a lower value-added range implying that the value of products integrated during the three phases is lower than in volume. Even with the 51 percent integration requirement, only about 20 per cent of imports under specific-quota restrictions had been liberalized by the EU and the US at the beginning of the third stage.[8] Furthermore, as discussed earlier, textiles and clothing face some of the highest tariffs in developed countries and are subject to substantial proportion of anti-dumping initiations besides other NTBs. It is doubtful if the market access in these labour intensive products would actually be provided to developing countries in the letter and spirit.

Continued Protection of Agricultural Goods

As observed above, the trade in agricultural goods is subject to high tariffs and non-tariff barriers in developed countries. Simple average applied tariff rates on agricultural products compared to those on industrial goods have been higher by 641 per cent in Japan, by 353 per cent in the European Union and by 100 per cent in the case of the US. A very high proportion of the agricultural products are subject to peak tariffs and specific duties in the developed countries. For instance, nearly 98 per cent of tariff peaks in the case of the European Union and as many as 85 per cent in Japan are related to agricultural and fishery products. The agricultural trade liberalization as agreed under the Uruguay Round has been undermined by the developed countries through dirty tariffication. The European Union has, for example, set the tariff bindings for the base period at about 60 per cent above the actual tariff equivalents on average while the US has set it at 45 per cent above the recent rates.

Continued Resistance to Movement of Natural Persons

Developing countries were lured into accepting the liberalization of trade in services by the prospect of increased market access in the developed countries for their skilled professionals under the Mode 4 (viz. the movement of natural persons). However, an overview of the commitments made by developed countries in services suggests that most of the commitments made by industrialized countries simply maintain the existing status quo with regard to binding without providing meaningful market access. Significant commitments have not been made in the mode of greatest importance to developing countries, namely, movement of natural persons, notwithstanding Article IV.1(c), viz. "the liberalization of market access in sectors and modes of supply of export interest to them". Furthermore, 100 per cent of their commitments made in market access and 83 per cent in case of national treatment in Mode 4 are with limitations which tend to nullify the commitments made, if any (Table 2.4). On the other hand, developing countries have made substantial commitments under GATS with respect to many service industries, often binding recently adopted legislation or pre-committing future policies without having had much experience in their implementation, and have undertaken a higher share of full bindings under the cross border and commercial presence modes of supply.[9]

Besides, potential exporters of services from developing countries are prevented

Table 2.4: Summary of Commitments under GATS made by Countries by Modes of Supply (Percentage of commitments on service activities)

Country group	Cross-border			Consumption abroad			Commercial presence			Natural persons		
	No limits	Limits	Un-bound	No limits	Limits	Un-bound	No limits	Limits	Un-bound	No limits	Limits	Un-bound
Market Access												
Total	56	10	34	80	8	13	30	66	4	2	92	6
Developed	65	11	25	87	12	2	39	60	1	0	100	0
Developing	44	10	46	70	2	28	20	75	5	5	81	14
Transition	52	11	37	79	11	10	37	61	12	0	99	1
National Treatment												
Total	63	4	33	83	2	15	11	83	6	30	61	9
Developed	70	5	25	95	3	2	0	97	3	17	83	1
Developing	52	3	45	66	1	33	28	63	9	45	34	21
Transition	70	3	27	93	3	4	0	88	12	51	48	1

Source: RIS based on WTO data.

from competing effectively in foreign markets by anti-competitive situations, market dominance, restrictive business practices, subsidies and other barriers. Major entry barriers continue to deny market access to outside suppliers in a number of services, especially those in which developing countries have some capability to compete. Subsidization, investment incentives and tied aid policies followed by developed countries are highly distorting of trade in services.

Furthermore, there is an attempt to raise other barriers to export of services by developing countries. For instance, besides economic needs tests and quantitative restrictions on visas, some countries like the US are discouraging the service enterprises of developing countries by imposing fees/charges applicable for providing social safety nets even for temporary movement of natural persons. According to a study, the US government is collecting US $ 22.5 billion annually in payroll taxes from Indian professionals holding temporary HI-B visas, even though these workers do not get any social security benefits nor tax refunds upon their return to their native lands.[10] Secondly, the individual States of the United States are bringing legislation prohibiting the business process outsourcing (BPO) that is bound to adversely affect the exporters of the BPO services such as India, the Philippines, and China among other countries.

The restrictions on movement of natural persons across regions impose a cost on developed and developing economies far exceeding that of trade restrictions on goods. Studies conducted in the framework of a CGE model suggest that an increase in developed countries' quotas on both skilled and unskilled temporary workers equivalent to just 3 per cent of their labour force will lead to over US$ 150 billion of welfare gains for developed and developing economies.[11] Considering that the estimation of gains resulting from all the liberalization under Uruguay Round was put between US $212 to US $510 billions, US $150 billion welfare gain resulting from limited liberalization of labour alone movement is substantial.

Continued Resort to Quotas and other Non-tariff Barriers

In the post Uruguay Round phase, only 1.2 per cent of the tariff lines are subject to NTBs in the Quad countries. However, most of the NTBs are applicable to agriculture (e.g. tariff quotas), and textiles and clothing (MFA quotas), where developing countries have a comparative advantage.[12] But NTBs are not limited to textiles or agriculture products alone. As many as 30 per cent of the tariff lines in basic metal industries in the US and 34 per cent in Japan were subject to core NTBs, as were 17 per cent of the EU tariff lines pertaining to food, beverages and tobacco.[13] Industrialized countries are also known to employ a wide array of non-tariff protectionist measures such as orderly marketing arrangements (OMA) and other grey area measures with impunity.[14] These include voluntary export restraints (VERs), quotas, screw driver regulations, rules of origin, and various anti-dumping measures.

Proliferation of Environmental Requirements as Non-Tariff Barriers

There has been a proliferation of environmental and health requirements imposed on trade especially in developed countries. These requirements not only include product standards and regulations, but also voluntary measures, standards set by the private sector, buyers' requirements and supply chain management, which may involve non-product-related production and process methods (PPMs) such as recycling requirements. These regulations have often been applied in such a manner that they act as non-tariff barriers.

The WTO Agreements on SPS (Sanitary and Phytosanitary Measures) and TBT (Technical Barriers to Trade) intend to ensure that these standards and regulations are not arbitrarily used for protectionist purposes and do not have an adverse impact on trade while protecting the interest of the consumer. However, at present there is considerable discretion available to importing countries to impose their own rules regarding these standards and other regulations such as inspection of imported products, specific treatment or processing of products, fixing of minimum allowable levels of pesticide residue, labelling and packaging requirements etc. This flexibility in these Agreements has been exploited to impose environmental norms and standards that are much more stringent compared to international standards thereby acting as a significant barrier for exports. This provision too has been used by various countries to check market access of specific countries.

A case in point is unmanufactured tobacco where Japan insists on a DDT residue level of 0.4 particles per million (PPM) while the international standard is 6 PPM. Indian tobacco has a DDT residue level of 1-2 PPM which is well below the internationally permissible levels. But tobacco imports from India are prevented on phytosanitary grounds. Often very minute risk assessments are used to justify imposition of these higher standards. For instance, adoption of a new aflatoxin standard in the European Union that would reduce health risk by approximately 1.4 deaths per billion a year, is a case in point. While there are not a billion people in the whole of EU, African exports of cereals, dried fruits and nuts to EU are expected to decline by 64 per cent as a result of adoption of these standard with an estimated loss of export earnings of the order of US$ 670 million.[15]

Even though international standards such as Codex are evolved by developed countries, they themselves do not adopt them. Many of these environment related standards are imposed in a less than transparent manner and sometimes are accompanied by other requirements such as Good Manufacturing Practice. There are cases of detention of consignments of Indian spices in Spain, Italy and Germany without any satisfactory explanation forthcoming on the changes made in their regulations on microbial contamination and pesticide residue despite transparency obligation under the Article 7 of the SPS Agreement.[16]

Increasing Resort to Contingent Protection

The resort to trade defence measures such as anti-dumping, countervailing and safeguards has risen significantly since 1995. The number of antidumping investigations initiated have risen steadily from 157 in 1995 to a peak of 355 in 1999 and 347 in 2001.[17] The bulk (60 %) of the investigations have been initiated by developed countries and 72 per cent (overall 68%) of them have targeted developing countries (as summarized in Table 2.5).

A large number of these measures have been eventually deemed illegal by the WTO Dispute Settlement Mechanism, e.g. antidumping on bed linen by EU, or on steel by the US. However, in the meanwhile the damage to exporters in developing countries is made. The worst affected in the process are the smaller and medium exporters in

Table 2.5: Number and Percentage of Antidumping Initiations by Country Groups (1995 – 2001)

Initiated by / Against	Developed countries	Developing countries	Total
Number of antidumping cases			
Developed countries	231	575	806
-USA	82	173	255
-EU	22	224	246
Developing countries[1)]	360	674	1040
Total	597	1249	1846
Percentage of antidumping cases			
Developed countries	28	72	100
Developing countries[1)]	35	65	100
Total	32	68	100

[1] Including transition countries.
Source: WTO database at http://www.wto.org/english/tratop_e/adp_e.htm accessed May 8, 2002.

developing countries who may even cease to exist due to their inability to sustain the losses.

Proliferation of RTAs and Distortion of Trade and Investment Patterns

The past decade or so has seen a major trend of formation of regional trading arrangements (RTAs). Around 240 such arrangements are currently in force and the number is likely to go up to 300 in the next couple of years.[18] The Single European Market (SEM) in the European Union and North American Free Trade Area (NAFTA) are the major RTAs. Developed countries account for the bulk of the functioning RTAs. An immediate effect of these regional integration agreements (RIAs) has been that nearly half of the world trade is conducted on a preferential basis rather than on an MFN basis. Exports of non-member countries are discriminated against. Hence, RTAs act as protectionist barriers against exports of non-member countries. The trade diversionary effect of these RTAs is clear from the fact that the intra-regional trade within these RTAs has been rising twice as fast as the extra-regional trade of the member countries.[19] The RTAs' preferences granted to the participants also erode the GSP preferences given to developing countries.

RTAs among industrialized countries are also expanding themselves to integrate select developing countries. That privileged access to major RTAs affects other developing countries by trade diversion away from them. For instance, EU has accepted Cyprus, Malta and Turkey besides 10 Eastern European countries viz. Bulgaria, Czeck Republic, Estonia, Hungary, Latvia, Lithuania, Poland, Romanis, Slovak Republic, and Slovenia as full candidates for accession. These countries have been extended free trade agreements with the European Union ahead of their full membership. In NAFTA, Mexico enjoys a privileged access to the North American Market as a member. NAFTA is also considering to extend its membership to cover more Latin American countries. These trade preferences have already resulted in a diversion of trade away from other developing countries such as those in South Asia. In the case of textiles and clothing exports, for instance, that is the most important item of exports of South Asian countries, Mexican exports of clothing to the United States have grown at the rate of 27 and 15 per cent in 1998 and 1999, respectively with the growth rate of exports to Canada in these years being 30 percent and 26 percent, respectively. Similarly, exports of clothing from Bulgaria, Hungary, Poland, Romania, Turkey to the European Union in 1998 have grown at 26 percent, 14 percent, 11 percent, 23 percent and 11 percent, respectively. Compared to these rates, growth rates of exports of textiles and clothing of South Asian countries have been far more modest if not negative owing to trade diversion and high tariff and non-tariff barriers.

Besides diverting the patterns of trade in favour of partners in RTAs and discriminating against third countries, RTAs also tend to distort investment patterns. The regional champions are protected by common external tariffs and a variety of non-tariff measures such as voluntary export restraints, screw driver and local content regulations and anti-dumping levies. In the post-WTO world, these regional trading blocs enjoy additional advantages as they can still use the instruments of policy to deepen their industrial structure such as rules of origin under regional trading agreement (RTA) exemptions under the WTO Agreements that are not permissible to other WTO members. Hence, the formation of trade blocs has been followed by tariff jumping FDI inflows and M&As as outside MNEs attempt to secure their access to the markets. Hence, the share of RTAs in global FDI inflows has gone up.[20] For instance, EU member countries accounted for 66 per cent of FDI outflows originating in the EU countries in 1990 compared to just 28 per cent in 1985. Recent quantitative studies have observed the significant influence of memberships in RTAs such as EU and NAFTA as well as privileged access to major markets through preferential trading arrangements on the location of export-orientation of affiliates of US and Japanese corporations.[21]

Protectionist Industrial Policy and Strategic Trade Policy

Growing Subsidization of R&D Activity of Enterprises

While developed countries have sought to phase out of all subsidies under the Agreement on Subsidies and Countervailing Measures (SCM), R&D subsidies up to 75 per cent of the costs of industrial research or 50 per cent of the cost of pre-competitive development activity are 'non-actionable' under Article 8.2 of the Agreement. Growing internationalization of markets of the past years has emphasized the role of technology as a key element of international competitiveness. In order to retain and further sharpen the technological edge of their corporate enterprises, governments of industrialized countries have been supporting the technological activities of national enterprises through a wide variety of government - industry complexes.

The governments of Japan, the US, and major European Union (EU) member states such as Germany, France, the UK, and the Netherlands have already taken steps to strengthen the technological competitiveness of national enterprises through increasing subsidization of research in a manner that could be termed as 'technology race'.

The focus of the extensive subsidies provided by the governments to their enterprises is on core technologies viz., microelectronics and information technology, biotechnology and new materials.[22]

The governments in France, Germany, the U.K. and the US, for instance, accounted for 48.8, 37, 34, and 47 per cent of total gross R&D expenditure in their respective countries with a substantial proportion of the funding directly going to business enterprises.[23] Furthermore, nearly 20, 11, 15, and 28 per cent of R&D performed by business enterprises was directly funded by the governments.

Complementing the national programmes of collaborative research, the European Commission has established a number of Community wide technology development programmes called Framework Programmes for funding research activities of entities public or private, large or small. The EC contributes one half of the costs of the projects, the other half being borne by the participating firms. Currently the Sixth Framework Programme (FP6) (2003-2003) is in operation covering a budget of Euro 17.5 billion representing an increase of 17 per cent from the previous programme and accounting for 3.9 per cent of EU's total budget (2001).[24] FP6 is an important building block in the Union's drive to increase its overall research effort to 3 per cent of GDP by 2010 from the present level of 1.9 per cent by stimulating private investment in R&D and creating a favourable environment. The major focus of these programmes is on strengthening the EC's competitiveness in new and emerging technologies such as microelectronics and information technology, biotechnology, and advanced materials in view of the widespread linkages these core technologies have with other sectors of the economy. Almost all the subsidies go to the private enterprises that undertake R&D projects or participate in the joint projects undertaken with other EU enterprises for eventual commercialisation of the technologies developed.

Government subsidization of R&D activity is widely perceived to be a part of strategic trade policy in the industrialized countries, designed to enhance their national enterprises' competitive edge.

Distortionary Investment Incentives

Yet another asymmetry in the SCM Agreement is its failure to discipline the investment incentives given by host governments to attract FDI inflows. The empirical evidence has shown that these incentives tend to distort the investment patterns much in the same way as export subsidies do to patterns of trade.[25]

Industrialized countries have largely indulged in incentive wars to attract foreign investments to particular locations and have been offering substantial subsidies to MNEs to attract investments (see Table 2.6 for some illustrations). Because developing countries lack the capacity to provide matching financial subsidies, investment incentives do tend to distort the normal pattern of location of investments in favour of industrialized countries.

Table 2.6: An Illustrative List of Investment Incentives Given by Industrialized Country Governments

Site	MNE and Year	Subsidy	Jobs created	Subsidy per job
Kentucky, US	Toyota, 1985	$150 million	3,000	$50,000
S. Carolina, US	BMW, 1992	$150 million	1,900	$79,000
Alabama, US	Mercedes Benz, 1996	$300 million	1,500	$200,000
New Mexico, US	Intel, 1993	$289 million	2,400	$120,000
Setubal, Portugal	Ford, 1991	$484 million	1,900	$254,000
Germany	Dow, 1996	$6.8 billion	2,000	$3,400,000
United Kingdom	Samsung, 1994	$89 million	3,000	$30,000
United Kingdom	Siemens, 1995	$77 million	1,500	$51,000
United Kingdom	Lucky Goldstar, 1996	$320 million	6,100	$48,000

Sources: RIS based on Moran (1998), UNCTAD (1996) and sources cited therein.

Export Subsidies to Manufacturers

Although export subsidies have been phased out under the provisions of the Subsidies and Countervailing Measures Agreement of WTO, some developed countries continue to provide substantial subsidies to their enterprises. The United States, for instance, has been giving subsidies worth US$ 4 billion every year to large American exporters under the Foreign Sales Corporation (FSC) Programme. The European Union had recently brought a complaint against the US to the Dispute Settlement Undertaking of WTO which deemed these subsidies as illegal. The EU has warned that it could retaliate with as much as $4 billion in trade sanctions unless the US makes significant progress towards repealing the FSC scheme by the end of 2003. Under EU pressure the US is now proposing to repeal the FSC. However, the subsidies to US enterprises are likely to increase if the proposed scheme promising to cut taxes for a broader range of US companies by US$ 120 billion over the next ten years comes into effect. The proposed new tax cuts will benefit the companies that manufacture in the US with accelerated depreciation, extended R&D tax credit and a lower tax rate for smaller companies.[26]

Growing Subsidies to Agriculture Producers

Gross subsidization of agriculture in the developed countries has been a well known fact. Despite the promises made in the Uruguay Round regarding the phasing out of export subsidies to agricultural exporters and domestic support to farmers, developed countries continue to protect their agriculture sector with high subsidies and trade barriers. In 2001, the OECD countries subsidized their agriculture sector to the tune of US$ 311 billion. These subsidies added up to as much as 31 per cent of the gross value of agricultural output in OECD countries. In Japan, the subsidies amounted to as high as 59 per cent of the gross value of agricultural output. In the EU the subsidies account for 35 per cent of total agricultural earnings in 2001. Furthermore, for all the Quad countries, the extent of support increased considerably between 1997 and 2001.

The developed countries have been resisting elimination of agricultural subsidies. At the Doha Ministerial Conference, after much resistance, the European Union and other developed countries agreed to only 'a substantial reduction' and 'not elimination' of trade-distorting domestic support. The Doha Agenda included a commitment on progress towards phase-out of all forms of export subsidies and substantial reduction in trade distorting domestic support on the basis of modalities to be agreed upon by 31 March 2003. However, the deadline of 31 March 2003 has been missed as the EU could not agree to the modalities for subsidy reduction.

The United States has announced the most generous farm subsidy package in its history under the Farm Security and Rural

Investment Act of 2002 promising additional federal spending of US$ 82.6 billion over the next 10 years on farming. Developed countries keep arguing about multifunctionality of agriculture and decoupling support from prices to justify high levels of subsidy. The EU and the US have been resistant even to phase out export subsidies (export credits in the US parlance). These subsidies, like those imposed on industrial products are clearly trade distorting and need to be phased out immediately.

Continued Use of Local Content Regulations in the Industrialized Countries

Policies such as local content regulations are supposed to have been phased out under the provisions of the TRIMs Agreement. Developed countries of today have extensively employed performance requirements (PRs) in their process of development especially when they were net importers of capital.[27] Even in the post-World War II period, countries such as Australia, Canada, France, Japan, among others have made extensive use of PRs.[28] A closer look reveals that they continue to impose performance requirements either changing their form or exploiting some grey areas in the WTO Agreements. Among the specific types of PRs, local content requirements (LCRs) have been employed by most of the developed countries and developing countries at one time or other.[29] In particular, governments have employed LCRs in the auto industry to promote backward integration and localization of production of value added until recently. For instance, Italy has imposed 75 per cent local content on Mitsubishi Pajero, the US has imposed 75 per cent rule on Toyota Camry and the UK 90 per cent on Nissan Primera, Australia imposed the 85 per cent local content rule on motor vehicles until 1989.[30]

The form of these PRs employed by developed countries in the 1990s, however, changed in favour of trade policy measures that achieve objectives similar to those of PRs but which are consistent with the provisions of TRIMs. These include rules of origin, screw-driver regulations, voluntary export restraints (VERs) and anti-dumping.[31] The European Union countries have extensively used the screw-driver regulations which are in effect like local content regulations. EU countries have also used anti-dumping measures to regulate imports of cars and other products from Japan and Southeast Asia. The US has aggressively used similar anti-dumping measures in attempting to achieve reciprocity (i.e. 'substantially equivalent competitive opportunities') in trade and investment with Japan and other countries.[32] The provisions of the Buy American Act have also been used as local content requirements in the USA. For instance, in order to qualify as domestic product to claim a 25 per cent price preference under the Buy American Act, a Hungarian manufacturer of buses had to buy US made engines, transmissions, axles and tyres.[33]

Even currently, the industrialized countries, especially the EU and NAFTA member countries, taking advantage of RTA exceptions that are available under Section XXIV of GATT, are effectively using the Rules of Origin to increase domestic value addition. Rules of origin determine the extent of domestic content a product must have to qualify as an internal product in a preferential trading agreement. Hence, considerable evidence is available on the use of rules of origin by EU and NAFTA countries to increase the extent of localization of production by MNEs supplying to them (see Box 2.2 for illustrations).

Therefore, developed countries have managed to circumvent the provisions of trade distorting investment measures to deepen their industrial structure—measures that are denied to developing countries under the provisions of the TRIMs Agreement.

Implications of WTO Process for Development

The above analysis has highlighted that MTNs and the WTO have failed to remove the existing asymmetries in the world trading system. Despite the rhetoric of positive efforts designed to benefit the developing countries, protectionism in

Box 2.2: Rules of Origins Imposed by NAFTA and EU to Increase Local Content: Select Case Studies

NAFTA Rules of Origin

The objective of the US effort in NAFTA through rules of origin has been to prevent "screwdriver" assembly operations from being set up within the region that could utilize low-cost inputs from outside. NAFTA rules of origin require that a substantial portion of inputs originate within the region for automobiles, electronic products (printers, copiers, television tubes), textiles, telecommunications, machine tools, forklift trucks, fabricated metals, household appliances, furniture, and tobacco products. For example:

- **Telecommunications:** NAFTA rules require that 9 of every 10 printed circuit board assemblies, the essential component of office switching equipment, be packaged within the NAFTA countries. In response, AT&T shifted some production from Asia to Mexico, and Fujitsu and Ericsson brought new investments to Mexico as well.
- **Color Televisions:** NAFTA requires that television tubes be produced within the region to qualify for preferential status. Prior to NAFTA, there was no North American manufacturer of television tubes; in the first two years after NAFTA's passage, five factories took shape within the NAFTA region, with investments from Hitachi, Mitsubishi, Zenith, Sony, and Samsung.
- **Computers:** US negotiators proposed a rule that would have required two of the three key components (the motherboard, flat panel display, and hard disc drive) to be North American in origin. With forceful opposition from IBM and other companies that wanted to maintain their more flexible international sourcing patterns, the negotiators settled on a final rule requiring at least the motherboard to be North American.
- **Office Equipment:** NAFTA tightened origin rules for printers, photocopiers, and fax machines, requiring more components to be manufactured locally. For printers and photocopiers, all major subassemblies have to be produced in North America (equivalent to an 80 per cent domestic-content requirement). Apparently this rule was instrumental in motivating Canon to construct a plant costing more than US $100 million in Virginia, rather than somewhere in Asia where the production costs would be lower.
- **Automobiles:** The domestic content rule was raised from 50 percent in the United States-Canada Free Trade Agreement to 62.5 percent in NAFTA. It required Japanese and European firms to replace imports from their home countries.

EU Rules of Origin

The European Union has adopted high domestic-content rules of origin in automobiles and other industries such as photocopiers, as well, and has also entertained proposals for even tighter requirements for printed circuit boards and telecom switching equipment. The European Union also established product-specific rules that require printed circuit board assembly within Europe. It has negotiated association agreements in Central and Eastern Europe that require 60 percent domestic content for products to qualify for entry into the European Union. Select examples are as follows:

- **Semiconductors:** In 1989, the European Union abruptly changed the rule of origin to require that wafer fabrication for semiconductor be done within Europe to avoid 14 percent semiconductor tariff. Whereas US companies performed most of their diffusion operations in the United States prior to the decision, 7 of the largest 10 US producers built fabrication facilities in Europe following the rule change. Citing the need to comply within the new rule of origin, for example, Intel invested $400 million in Ireland for wafer fabrication and semiconductor assembly. Even though wafer fabrication was not cost-competitive in Europe, compared to Asia or the United States, 22 new fabrication facilities were set up in Europe within two years of the change in the rule of origin.
- **Automobiles:** The United Kingdom and France proposed an 80 percent local content rule for the Nissan Bluebird to qualify as an EC product. In the end, they backed down in the face of Italian and German opposition and decided to rely on quantitative restrictions to protect against Japanese imports. The 60 percent domestic content in the automotive sector has forced the General Motors engine plant in Hungary to use high cost German steel as an input, preventing utilization of locally available cheaper steel.
- **Textiles and Apparel:** The near 100 percent domestic-content requirement in textiles and apparel has forced the German partner in the Brinkmann-Prochnik joint venture in Poland to load a truck with cotton fabrics, thread, buttons, and even labels in Germany; transport it to Lodz for stitching into trench coats; and re-import it for sale in the European Union-rather than allow the Polish Partner to source from cheaper supplies locally.

Source: **Kumar 2001 based on Moran, 1998; Belderboss, 1997, and other sources.**

developed countries has continued and has even increased while developing countries have been pushed to liberalize their trade and investment regimes.

WTO, Mercantilist Balance and Growth of Trade

The balance of commitments under trade liberalization under Uruguay Round has been clearly in favour of developed countries. As is evident from Box 2.3, in the Uruguay Round, developing countries undertook much deeper reductions in trade barriers compared to developed economies. Hence, the resulting mercantilist balance has been in favour of developed countries.

A number of other WTO Agreements such as TRIPs and TRIMs are likely to result in significant income losses for developing countries. For instance, implementation of stringent IPRs regime under the TRIPs Agreement will lead to net flows of royalties out of developing world to developed countries. As summarized in Table 2.7, countries like China (US$ 5bn.), India (nearly $ 1bn.), Mexico ($2.5bn), Brazil ($ 530mn), Israel ($3.9bn) will see annual net transfers of billions of dollars in the coming years on account of patent rents while the developed countries will be the net gainers with the US receiving US$ 19 billion a year in net receipts. Similarly, with the phasing out of performance requirements such as local content requirements and foreign exchange neutrality under the provisions of the TRIMs Agreement, enterprises in developing countries will either increase import dependence or lose export earnings that could run into billions of dollars. Obviously these income transfers and increased imports will adversely affect the net benefits accruing to developing countries.

The evidence presented in the previous sections on continuing protectionism in developed countries is also consistent with the evidence reported in the rigorous quantitative studies on the role of GATT/WTO process, as summarized in Box 2.4. The empirical evidence presented in these studies

Box 2.3:
Balance of Commitments: The Uruguay Round Scorecard

The outcome of the Uruguay Round was a good one for the North. Not only did the industrial countries gain from the concessions they received; the economics of the concessions they gave was also positive, through the opening up of their own agriculture and textiles sectors. And for the South? On the gain dimension—market—access—developing countries did not achieve a mercantilist surplus (see Table below). Their tariff reductions covered as large a share of their imports as did those of the industrial countries, and their tariff cuts, measured by how these reductions will affect importers' costs, were deeper than those of the industrial countries. This is true even when we take into account the tariff equivalent of the Multifibre Arrangement (MFA) quotas that the industrial countries have committed themselves to remove.

For developing countries as well as industrial countries, concessions made in the grand bargain make for difficult domestic politics. For developing countries, these concessions will also mean real economic costs. The scorecard on the Uruguay Round grand bargain? The South's concessions in the new areas are, as mercantilism, unrequited—and as real economics, they are costly.

Table: Uruguay Round Tariff Concessions, All Merchandise

	Industrial Economies		Developing Economies	
	Percentage of imports	Depth of cut[a]	Percentage of imports	Depth of cut
Includes tariffication and bound reductions on agricultural products	30	1.0	29	2.3
Includes the above plus the tariff equivalent of elimination of the Multifibre Arrangement	30	1.6	29	2.3

[a]Depth of cut, *dt*/(1+T), is a weighted average across all products, including those on which no reduction was made.
Source: Finger and Winters 2002 Reciprocity in the WTO, in Hoekman, B. et al. (eds.) *Development, Trade, and WTO: A Handbook*, The World Bank.

Table 2.7: Income Transfers Resulting from TRIPS in Select Countries

Country	Net Income Transfers following TRIPs Agreement (millions of 1995 or 2000 dollars)
Major Net Gainers	
United States	19,083
Germany	6,768
Japan	5,673
France	3,326
United Kingdom	2,968
Switzerland	2,000
Australia	1,097
Major Net Losers	
Rep. of Korea	-15,333
China	-5,121
Israel	-3,879
Mexico	-2,550
India	-903
Brazil	-530

Source: RIS based on the World Bank, *Global Economic Prospects and the Developing Countries 2002*, Table 5.1.

suggests that the GATT/WTO process is neither indicative of trade liberalization nor led to growth of world trade. On the other hand the system of trade preferences that developed countries offered to developing countries under GSP have facilitated growth of world trade significantly according to the empirical studies.

While the GATT/WTO process has not been able to liberalize the trade and investment regimes in developed countries, increasing pressure of liberalization commitments on developed countries has had important implications for their development process especially because of the lack of reciprocity.

Box 2.4: WTO, Trade Liberalization and Trade Growth: Lessons from Quantitative Studies

The multilateral trade negotiations under the framework of GATT and its successor WTO have engaged the attention of policy makers and negotiators due to their wide-ranging effects on development policies in developing countries. The explicit objective of these all encompassing rules demanding tremendous effort is to promote trade by liberalizing the trade and policy regimes in the member countries. What is the empirical evidence on the effectiveness of these negotiations in achieving their objectives?

Recent empirical studies conducted by Professor Andrew Rose of the University of California at Berkeley, a seat of higher learning well known for its orthodox views, and brought out by the London based Centre for Economic Policy Research (CEPR) does not find any evidence of effectiveness of WTO in trade promotion.[36]

WTO has No Effect on Trade Liberalization

The research included a rigorous analysis using a large panel data set covering 175 countries with observations over 50 years and 67 measures of trade policy and trade liberalization conducted in the framework of 'gravity' model of international trade. The study does not find membership of GATT/ WTO to be related with any of the measures of trade policy or liberalization.[37]

WTO has No Effect on Trade Growth Either

Then the question Professor Rose asked was whether GATT/ WTO membership has promoted trade? The research is unable to find a positive effect of GATT/WTO membership on trade. "Despite an extensive search", he is unable to find a "compelling evidence showing that the GATT/WTO has actually encouraged trade".[38]

GSP has led to Doubling of Trade

Unlike GATT/WTO membership's effect on trade, the GSP (Generalized System of Trade preferences) that developed countries give to developing countries "does seem to have a strong effect on trade, and is associated with an approximate doubling of trade".[39]

Source: RIS based on Rose (2002a, 2002b, 2003).

Table 2.8: Region-wise Share in Global Exports in Percentage

	1980	1985	1990	1995	2000	2001	2002
Industrial Countries	65.01	67.91	71.37	67.77	63.15	63.19	62.39
Developing Countries	34.99	32.09	28.63	32.23	36.85	36.81	37.61
Africa	4.93	3.47	2.44	1.81	1.98	1.94	1.89
Asia	8.18	10.91	13.06	18.09	19.8	19.3	20.03
South Asia	0.68	0.76	0.8	0.9	0.99	1.03	1.08
East Asia	6.58	8.7	10.45	14.28	14.86	18.28	18.95
China Mainland	0.93	1.45	1.81	2.91	3.95	4.34	5.11
Western Hemisphere	5.46	5.48	4.07	4.37	5.58	5.59	5.37

Source: RIS based on IMF, *International Financial Statistics Yearbook*, various issues.

The Place of Developing Countries in World Trade

As a result of the asymmetries prevailing in the process of liberalization described above, the US and EU were able to increase their share in world trade from 50 to 56 per cent between 1993 to 1999 at the cost of rest of the world.[34] The share of developing countries in overall world exports appears to have increased marginally between 1980 and 2002 from nearly 35 per cent in 1980 to 37.6 per cent in 2002 (Table 2.8). However, a closer look at the shares would bring out that this increase in the share of developing countries is largely on account of rising share of East Asian countries in particular, China. It is evident that China has been able to increase its share in world exports from 0.93 per cent in 1980 to over 4.34 per cent in 2001 on the eve of its entry into WTO and further to 5.11 per cent in 2002. The rest of the sub-regions in developing world have actually lost their shares or barely managed to sustain them. Africa and Latin America have lost their shares of world exports. Therefore, excluding China, the share of developing countries in world exports has steadily declined.

Furthermore, the ability of China to increase its share without membership in either GATT or WTO until 2001 while declining share of other developing countries that are members of WTO also suggests something that is consistent with the empirical finding summarized in Box 2.4.

Declining Terms of Trade: Developing Countries as Losing Trade Partners

Another indicator of the distribution of gains from trade growth is the movement in terms of trade. The movements in the terms of trade for the two broad groups of countries as summarized in Figure 2.1

Figure 2.1: Movement in Terms of Trade of Developed and Developing Countries

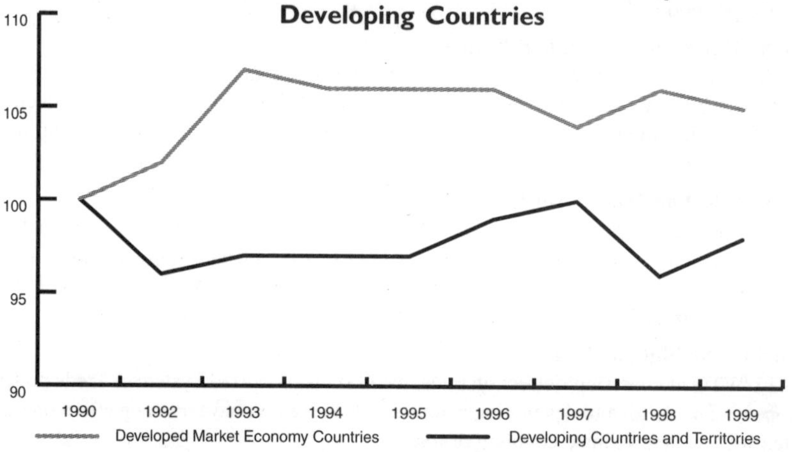

Source: UNCTAD, *Handbook of Statistics*, 2002.

Figure 2.2: Median RCA of Dynamic Products

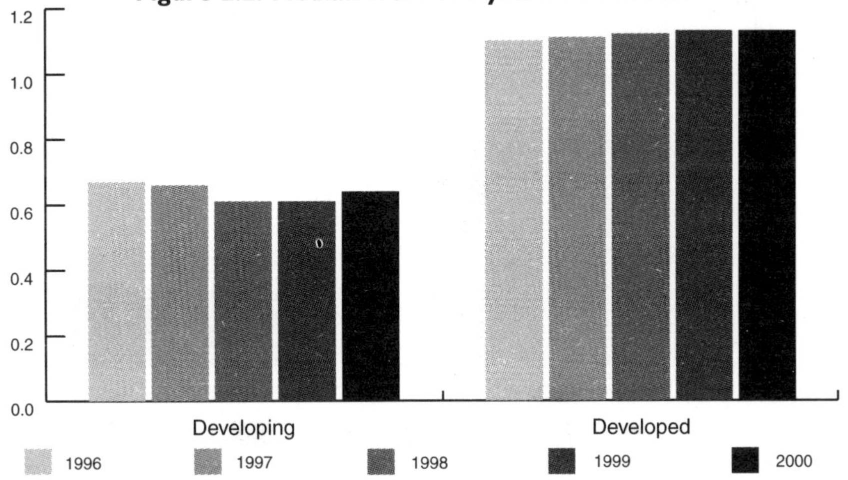

Source: **RIS calculations based on UN/ITC, PC-TAS, 2002, CD-Rom.**

suggests that between 1990 and 1999, the terms of trade of developing countries have deteriorated while those of developed countries have improved. It suggests that unit value realization for the export products of developed countries has increased much more while the unit value realization of developing country exportables has declined in relative terms. It is clear that gains from expansion of trade have been shared unequally between developed and developing countries with latter being on losing side.

Poor Supply Capabilities of Developing Countries in Dynamic Products

An important development effect could be ability of developing countries to upgrade their supply capacities especially in relatively faster growing and higher value adding products or the so called 'dynamic products'. In view of considerable differences in the growth rates of trade in individual products, twenty most dynamic products in world trade have been identified that broadly fall into four categories:[35]

- electronic and electrical goods (SITC 75,76,77)
- textiles and labour-intensive products, particularly clothing (SITC 61, 65, 84)
- finished products from industries that require high R & D expenditures and are characterized by high technological complexity and/or economies of scale (SITC 5,87)
- primary commodities including silk, non-alcoholic beverages and cereals (SITC 261, 111, 048).

It has been found that the major exporters of these most dynamic products are the developed countries and only some of the East-Asian economies among the developing countries have been able to participate in the global trade of these products. It is startling to note that only three of the twenty most dynamic products in world markets are among the twenty fastest growing exports of the first-tier NIEs.

An attempt has been made to examine the relative position of developing countries in the dynamic products with the help of revealed comparative advantage (RCA) indices computed for the period 1996-2000 separately for developing and developed countries. The RCA indices indicate following patterns.

First, as evident from Figure 2.2 the median of RCA of developing countries in dynamic products as a whole are much lower as compared to developed countries. This suggests that developing countries have not been able to build comparative advantage in dynamic products. In other words their export profiles lack dynamism. Third, in most of the products developing countries display relatively more volatile pattern of RCA as compared to developed countries, a fact which is further corroborated by Figure 2.3. It is evident that the standard

Figure 2.3: Standard Deviation of RCA of Dynamic Products

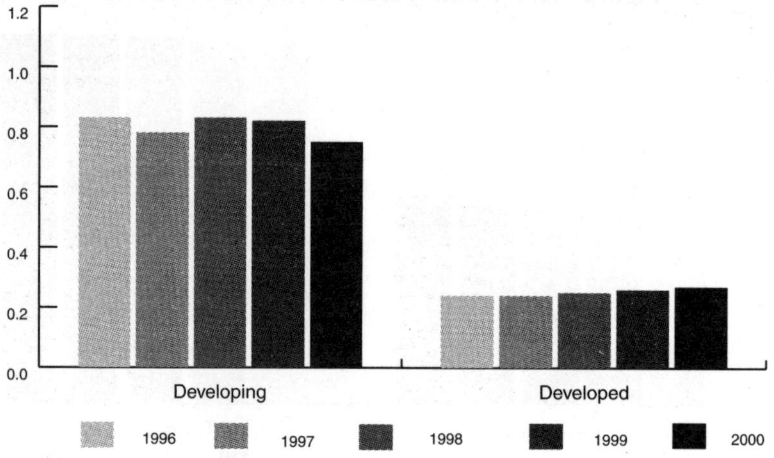

Source: **RIS calculations based on UN/ITC, PC-TAS, 2002, CD-Rom.**

deviation of RCA of dynamic products between 1996 and 2000 is very high suggesting a narrower export base and lack of export specialization compared to the developed countries. Finally, in several dynamic products like cereal preparations, non-alcoholic beverages, silk, pharmaceutical products, leather manufactures, transistors and semiconductors and optical instruments the developing countries' RCA indices have shown some declining trends. The inability of developing countries to develop and strengthen their supply capacities in dynamic products, among other factors, is due to constraints in access to relevant technologies. The provisions of technology transfer in Agreements such as TRIPs have remained ineffective.

Trade, Economic Growth and Equity: Lessons from the Development Experience of the 1990s

It has been argued that trade liberalization leads to growth and hence poverty reduction. While the debate on the issue of the nature of relationship between trade and growth is yet to be settled in the literature (Box 2.5), the evidence on the role of openness to trade in growth of trade is inconclusive. However, as countries develop they liberalize their trade policy regimes. An analysis of the development performance

Box 2.5: Trade and Growth Relationship

The causality issues between trade and growth as well as FDI and growth have been debated for long in the literature. Some of the recent work on this subject is summarized here. On the one hand of spectrum there are analysts who provide empirical evidence in favour of trade and investment liberalization. For instance, Sachs and Warner (1995) have found that developing countries with open economies grew by an average of 4.5 percent per year in the 1970s and 1980s while those with closed economies grew only by 0.7 percent. However, such outcomes of liberalization have been contested by Rodriguez and Rodrik (1999), according to which there is little evidence that 'open trade policies—in the sense of lower tariff and non-tariff barriers to trade—are significantly associated with economic growth.' One of the reasons for getting results in favour of trade liberalization is deemed by them as the usage of poor measures of indicators of openness.

Above facts are further corroborated by Rodrik (2001). According to which, on the basis of cross-national evidence, there is no systematic relationship observed between countries average level of tariff and non-tariff restrictions and its subsequent economic growth. In fact, the evidence for 1990s indicates a positive relationship between tariffs and economic growth. It is argued that the only systematic relationship is that countries reduce trade restrictions as they get richer. It is clear that the problem is one of causality. Whether tariff liberalization results in higher economic growth or countries that have grown richer (under protection) are confident enough to reduce their tariff barriers as they have gained competitiveness over a period of protected trade regime is basically the core of the debate.

Source: **RIS (2003), *Globalization and the Non-Aligned Movement: An Economic Agenda for Action,* New Delhi: RIS.**

Figure 2.4: Change in Average Growth Rate of Real Per Capita Income in Developing Countries between 1980s and 1990s

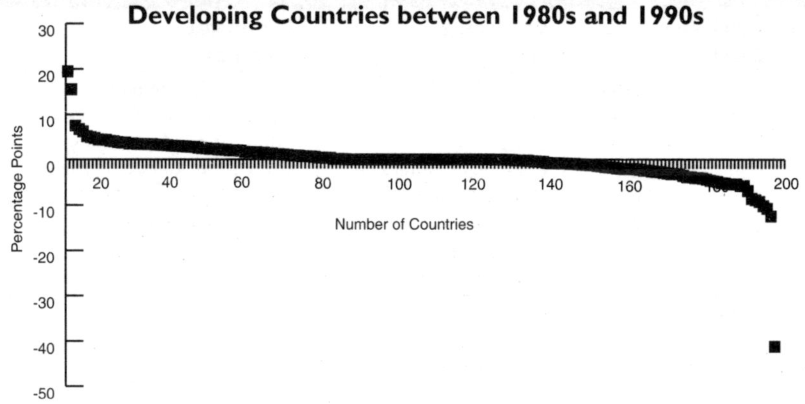

Source: RIS (2003).

of developing countries during the 1990s, the decade of widespread trade liberalization resulting from WTO Agreements vis-à-vis the 1980s may bring out some patterns.

A comparison in the average annual growth of per capita GDP (constant 1995 US $) between the 1980s and 1990s for 180 developing countries shows that only around 65 developing countries have experienced a higher growth rate during the 1990s as compared to 1980s in terms of their real GDP per capita (Figure 2.4). Rest of the countries have either experienced a stagnant progress or their average growth has declined in the 1990s. Figure 2.5 displays some of the prominent countries that have experienced diametrically opposite trends in their economic growth.

It may be pointed out that the success of countries like South Korea and other Southeast Asian economies needs to be understood clearly inasmuch as they followed an export-oriented strategy which must be distinguished from an import liberalization strategy. In the case of South Korea it is argued and demonstrated that it followed an export-oriented strategy along with import substitution. Therefore, it would be naive to relate economic growth of such countries to import liberalization *per se*.

On the whole, the development experience of 1990s suggests that growth process has suffered in the period of global integration in many countries.

What about the equity in the growth process under global integration or

Figure 2.5: Economic Growth in Select Developing Countries between 1980s and 1990s

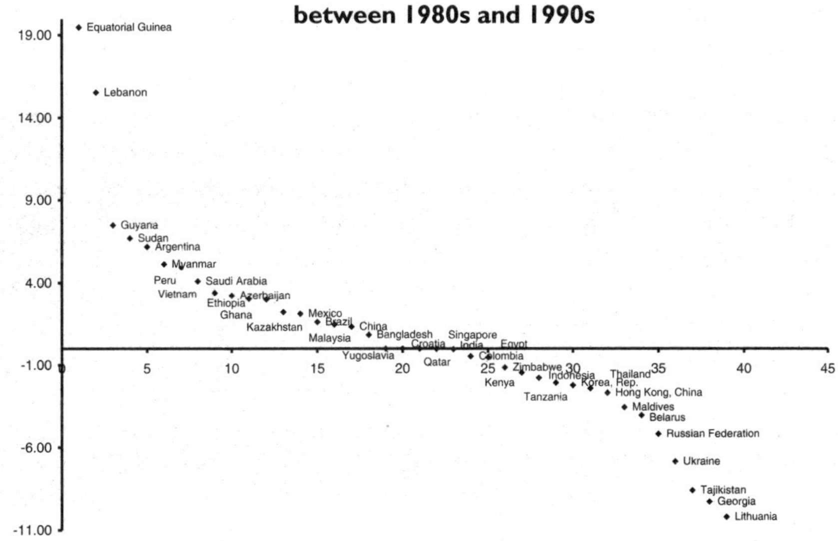

Source: RIS (2003).

Table 2.9: Income Inequality Changes in 73 Countries from 1960s to 1990s

Inequality	Developed Countries	Developing Countries	Transitional Countries	Total
Rising	12:Australia, Canada, Denmark, Finland, Italy, Japan, Netherlands, New Zealand, Spain, Sweden, UK, US	15: Argentina, Chile, China, Columbia, Costa Rica, Guatemala, Hong Kong, Mexico, Pakistan, Panama, South Africa, Sri Lanka, Taiwan, Thailand, Venezuela	21: Armenia, Azerbaijan, Bulgaria, Croatia, Czech Rep Estonia, Georgia, Hungary, Kazakhstan, Kyrgystan, Latvia, Lithuania, Macedonia, Moldova, Poland, Romania, Russia, Slovakia, Slovenia, Ukraine, Yugoslavia	48
Constant	3: Austria, Belgium, Germany	12: Bangladesh, Brazil, Cote d'Ivoire Dominican Rep, El Salvador, India, Indonesia, Puerto Rico, Senegal, Singapore, Tanzania, Turkey 16	1Belarus	16
Declining	2 France, Norway	7: Bahamas, Honduras, Jamaica, South Korea, Malaysia, Phillippines, Tunisia	0	9
All	17	34	22	73

Source: **Cornia and Court (2001) as cited in Rajan (2002).**

liberalization? Again it can be observed from Table 2.9 that between the period 1960s and 1990s number of developing countries falling in the category of declining income-inequality is much smaller than the number of those falling in the category of rising inequality. What is more is the fact that most of the developed countries have also experienced rising income-inequalities during the period under consideration. This suggests that trade liberalization also leads to asymmetric distribution of gains between and within the countries. The richer among the countries and within the countries seem to benefit more from trade liberalization.

Concluding Remarks and Policy Lessons

This chapter has shown that despite several rounds of multilateral trade negotiations attempting the liberalization, strong barriers to trade continue to remain in developed countries. There seems to be a spurt in protectionism in the developed countries inspired by strategic trade policies aiming to strengthen the competitiveness of their national champions at the cost of fair world trade. While heavy subsidization of developed country agriculture has become well known from the ongoing debates in the context of Agreement on Agriculture, the continued and rising subsidization of the industrial sector remains virtually unnoticed. Not only have developed countries exploited the grey areas available in the multilateral rules, they have included exceptions for the kind of policies and practices that they wish to make use of such as R&D subsidies and financial incentives for investment that are as distorting as other subsidies that are actionable under WTO rules. Proliferation of RTAs is again being used by them to undermining the multilateral trading system.

The WTO process has had significant adverse implications for developing countries. It has been shown that given much deeper commitments undertaken by developing countries, the mercantilist balance has been in favour of developed countries. Agreements such as TRIPs and TRIMs are also leading to considerable income transfers to developed countries. The process is not leading to growth of world trade either. The developing countries, with the exception of China, have not been able to increase their share in world trade. The terms of trade of developing countries have deteriorated. As a result of these trends, the growth rates in a large number of countries have declined in 1990s from that in 1980s and inequalities have increased.

Therefore, multilateral trade negotiations have failed to liberalize the trade and industrial policy regimes in the world's richest and most developed countries that could have expedited industrialization and development of the poorer countries by giving them market access and equitable sharing of the fruits of globalization, as articulated in the preamble of the Marrakesh and Doha Declarations.

The Cancun Conference provides an opportunity to the WTO membership to seek a redressal of the emerging asymmetries before they take on any new commitments. Below we list some broader issues that could be taken up by developing countries at WTO negotiations. We also add an agenda for mutual cooperation among developing countries on WTO issues that could be valuable.

Systemic Reforms

a) An Independent Commission to Make a Development Review of the Multilateral Trading System

Given the key importance of the emerging world trading system for the development and sustainability of the world economy, it is important to pause and undertake a thorough review of the type of asymmetries that have crept in. The Cancun Conference provides an opportunity to the WTO membership to seek a redressal of the emerging asymmetries in the world trading system before moving forward to expand its agenda. The developing countries should call for appointment of an Independent Commission to review the developmental consequences of Uruguay and Doha Rounds before moving forward. This Commission should identify asymmetries that have crept into the system and recommend directions of reform of the priorities, procedures and rules to giving a real meaning to development on the trade agenda.

The Director-General of WTO Secretariat has recently appointed a consultative group to advise him on the world trading system. However, a high powered Independent Commission appointed by the Ministerial Conference will have greater credibility, influence and authority for action and suggesting a thorough reform of the system.

b) Reform of Decision-making Process

The decision-making process in WTO clearly needs a reform for its long-term sustainability. The general perception is that the decision-making process in WTO is non-transparent, and not inclusive. The will of a handful of powerful countries, viz. Quad countries, is imposed on the entire membership in the name of 'Consensus'. In an organization whose membership comprises of countries at varying levels of development, their concerns and interests are expected to be different. Obviously these differences limit the possibilities of arriving at a consensus. In order to arrive at the 'consensus' sometimes powerful members push relatively poorer members to accept their position by several means including diplomacy and even arm-twisting.

Members have also complained of the lack of participation in decision-making process where informal consultations between few powerful players have far greater influence on WTO decision-making than the formal processes.

A more democratic system of decision-making based on secret voting and decision based on majority would serve the organization better and make it more participatory. All negotiating texts and drafts should be introduced in open ended meetings and late night meetings and marathon sessions should be avoided. No decisions should be imposed on members without wide consultations and discussions. Chairpersons drafts should be representative of all the interventions. The Ministers may consider changing the statute to bring about this profound change in the decision-making process in the interest of its long-term survival.

c) Broadbased and Representative Secretariat

Given the large stakes of different players in the multilateral trading system, vested interests begin to operate. In this context the role of the Secretariat becomes critical. It has some times been observed that Secretariat is not discharging its role with the kind of objectivity that it should be. As of now the WTO Secretariat is highly dominated by the developed countries. More than 80 per cent of the staff members of the Secretariat came from the OECD countries with over 61 per cent coming from just six developed countries, viz. France, the UK, the US, and Canada, Spain and Switzerland.[40] There is hardly any representation from a large number of developing countries. It is important that the WTO Secretariat has a proportionate representation of developed and developing countries. A more representative Secretariat will be able to discharge its mandate much more objectively.

d) A WTO Watch Dog of Developing Countries

Developing countries, individually, lack the capacity – physical, analytical and financial – to identify and pursue the cases of non-implementation or unilateral policy decisions concerning trade policy on the part of developed countries and seek their redressal under the existing framework. The recent case of the trade distorting export subsidy valued at $4 billion under Foreign Sales Corporations (FSC) by the US government which was successfully brought by the EU to the DSB is a case in point. Needless to mention that no developing country possesses the capability to do the same.

There is a need for setting up a *WTO Watchdog* by developing countries. In the interest of building a fair and just world trading system, developed countries should create a trust fund for maintaining the WTO Watchdog. This body should be equipped with the necessary professional, analytical, legal and financial expertise to scrutinize the implementation of commitments by developed countries and where appropriate to bring them to DSB on behalf of developing countries.

e) Strengthening the Provision ofTechnical Assistance

Developing country implementation of their commitments often implies major changes in their legal and institutional framework and involves substantial technical and financial resources that may be beyond the capability of many countries. In this regard it is often being felt that the WTO should provide major technical and financial assistance not only to least developed countries but also to the developing countries for implementation of their commitments in an effective manner.

This would require that the WTO's Trust Fund for Technical Assistance needs to be augmented. In this regard the three Geneva based agencies (ITC, UNCTAD and WTO) have endorsed the launching of the new phase of the Joint Integrated Technical Assistance Programme (JITAP). JITAP seeks to build capacity to understand the emerging trade issues and help comply with them, and also to derive benefit from it. However, the proposed support of $ 12.6 million dollar, over a period of four years is rather modest.

The Doha Development Agenda Global Trust Fund was created following the WTO Ministerial Conference in Doha, in November 2001. In December 2002, the General Council has approved a budget for this fund.

The G-8 countries should augment their contributions to these Funds.

f) Mobilising Support for 'Trilateral Cooperation'

It is often being observed that though different developing countries which are at different stages of economic development are better placed to help and cooperate with fellow developing countries than any other countries from developed part of the world. However, owing to lack of resources the potential for South-South cooperation has remained untapped.

In this regard, adopting a different strategy of trilateral cooperation may help to a great extent. In this a multilateral agency or a donor agency from North may step in to support technical assistance among developing countries.

An Agenda for Cooperation among Developing Countries on WTO-related Issues

The emerging WTO regime is important for the national development, trade, investment and technology policies of member countries. The ongoing round of negotiations will have an important bearing on the developmental process of the developing countries. Therefore, the developing countries need to deliberate over the mandate given by the Ministerial Meetings and prepare themselves to take part in the ensuing negotiations effectively to safeguard their interests. Issues of preparedness on their part would also include taking advantage of the emerging multilateral regime rather than passively implementing their commitments. This calls for strategic thinking and concerted action at different levels.

Not only do developing countries lack strong analytical capabilities in fully comprehending the developmental implications of the commitments implicit in the negotiations, the situation is further complicated by the mis-information that is promoted by developed countries to achieve their strategic objectives. Very often the training courses offered by international organizations in the name of technical assistance are also influenced by the view-point of the donors, viz. the developed countries and fail to highlight the concerns of developing countries.

The technical cooperation among developing countries could cover the followings:

a) Exchange of Experiences in Implementation of Commitments

Developing countries should fully exploit the policy spaces that may be available in the WTO Agreements. An example in this regard is the TRIPs Agreement where several flexibilities are available to be exploited to moderate the potential adverse effect of the Agreement such as compulsory licensing, research exception, Bolar provisions, grey market imports, anti-trust regulations, breeders exceptions, among others. Exchange of experiences and professional expertise among developing countries may facilitate such possibilities.

b) Technical Assistance and Cooperation in Implementation or Compliance of Commitments

Compliance with some SPS standards require huge technical and financial costs. Cooperation among developing countries may be in sharing the services of experts, setting up the common testing and verification laboratories, translations of standards, etc.

c) Effective Coordination of Positions

WTO negotiations are power games. Any coordination between developing countries at the issue level or regional levels would be more effective than individual country positions. Developing countries should establish communications among their respective trade ministries and their missions at WTO to facilitate such coordination.

d) Vigilance and Active Participation in the Proceedings

Given the high stakes involved, developing countries need to participate in the negotiations effectively and with extreme vigilance. They need to back up their preparations with adequate legal and analytical expertise. Introduction of small phrases which may appear innocuous may lead to some burdensome commitment, as is clear from the example how a reference to counterfeit goods in the Punta del Este Declaration snowballed into the TRIPs Agreement.

e) Proactive Agenda

Developing countries generally confine themselves to defensive and reactive strategy. They should have their own positive and proactive agenda. They should identify and articulate their concerns with the asymmetries creeping into the multilateral trading system and seek their redressal with effective coalition-building.

Endnotes

1 In a Guest Column in the *Economic Times*, 7 March 2001.

2 See WT/TPR/88/15 August 2001.

3 See WT/TPR/88/15 August 2001.

4 World Bank. 2000a. *Global Economic Prospects and the Developing Countries*, Washington, D.C., The World Bank.

5 Mehta, Rajesh. 2001. "WTO, Liberalisation and Industrial Sector: The Case of Market Access", *Occasional Paper No. 63*, New Delhi: Research and Information System for the Non-Aligned and Other Developing Countries.

6. Mehta, Rajesh and S.K. Mohanty. 1999. *WTO and Industrial Tariffs: An Empirical Analysis for India*, New Delhi: Research and Information System for the Non-Aligned and Other Developing Countries.

7 Ibid.

8 See WT/TPR/OV/8 dated 15 November 2002: 16.

9 UNCTAD. 1999d. Assessment of Trade in Services of Developing Countries: Summary of Findings, Background note by the UNCTAD Secretariat, UNCTAD/ITCD/TSB/7, Geneva, UNCTAD.

10 See a study by Mihir Desai *et al.* of Harvard reported in the *Business World*, 9 December 2002:74.

11 Winters, L. Alan, Terrie L. Walmsley, Zhen Kun Wang and Roman Grynberg. 2002. *Negotiating the Liberalization of the Temporary Movement of Natural Persons*, London: Commonwealth Secretariat.

12 World Bank. 2001b. *Global Development Finance 2001: Building Coalitions for Effective Development Finance*, Washington D.C.: The World Bank.

13 WTO. 2001b. *Market Access: Unfinished Business: Post-Uruguay Round Inventory and Issues*, Special Study 6, Geneva: World Trade Organization.

14 ITC/Commonwealth Secretariat. 1996. *A Business Guide to Uruguay Round Agreements*, Geneva: International Trade Centre.

15 Findings of a World Bank Study cited by Jha *et al.*. 2001a. *Impact of Enhancing Environmental Standards on International Trade of South Asian Countries.*

16 RIS. 2002. Impact of Enhancing Environmental Standards on International Trade of South Asian Countries, Report of G-77/PGTF-RIS Project, New Delhi: Research and Information System for the Non-Aligned and Other Developing Countries.

17 WT/TPR/OV/8 dated 15 November 2002.

18 *WTO Annual Report 2003*.

19 World Bank. 2000. *World Development Report 1999/ 2000*, Washington D.C.: The World Bank.

20 Dhar, B. and S. Chaturvedi. 1999. *WTO Agreement and Agricultural Sector: Implications and Options for India*, New Delhi: RIS.

21 Kumar, Nagesh. 1998. "Multinational Enterprises, Regional Economic Integration and Export Platform Production in the Host Countries: An Empirical Analysis for the US and Japanese Corporations", *Weltwirtschaftliches Archiv*, 134(3): 450-483.

22 Roobeek, Annemieke. 1990. *Beyond the Technology Race: An Analysis of Technology Policy in Seven Industrial Countries*, Amsterdam: Elsevier.

23 Kumar, Nagesh, and N.S. Siddharthan. 1997. *Technology, Market Structure and Internationalization: Issues and Policies for Developing Countries*, Routledge and UNU Press, London and New York.

24 See for more details a fact sheet on FP6 at the Http://europa.eu.int/comm/research/fp6/index_en.html.

25 Kumar, Nagesh. 2000. "Explaining the Geography and Depth of International Production: The Case of US and Japanese Multinational Enterprises", *Weltwirtschaftliches Archiv*, 136(3): 442-476.

26 See "Exporters' Subsidy: US to consider big tax break to replace FSC", *Financial Times*, 26 July 2003.

27 Chang, Ha-Joon. 2002. *Kicking Away the Ladder – Development Strategy in Historical Perspective*, London, Anthem Press.

28 Safarian, A.E. 2002. *The Use and Impact of Performance Requirements in the Developed Countries*, Geneva: UNCTAD, memeo.

29 Sercovich, F. 1998. "Best Practices, Policy Convergence and the WTO Trade-related Investment Measures", *Cepal Review*, 64:93-112.

30 WTO/UNCTAD. 2001. UNCTAD Joint Study on Trade Related Investment Measures and Other Performance Requirements, Committee on Trade Related Investment Measures, WTO, G/C/W/307.

31 Belderbos, Rene. 1997. *Japanese Electronics Multinationals and Strategic Trade Policies*, Oxford: Clarendon Press; Moran, Theodore H., (1998), *Foreign Direct Investment and Development*, Washington, DC: Institute for International Economics, and Safarian, A.E. (2002) The Use and Impact of Performance Requirements in the Developed Countries, Geneva: UNCTAD, memeo.

32 Safarian, A.E. 2002. The Use and Impact of Performance Requirements in the Developed Countries, Geneva: UNCTAD, memeo.

33 Krugman, Paul and M. Obstfeld. 2000. *International Economics*, (Fourth Edition), McGraw Hill.

34 *Economist*, 11 November 2000:205.

35 UNCTAD, *Trade and Development Report 2002*.

36 Andrew K. Rose. 2003. "Which International Institutions Promote International Trade?" DP3764 *CEPR*, London, January.

37 Andrew K. Rose. 2002b. "Do WTO Members have More Liberal Trade Policy?" DP3659 CEPR, London, November.

38 Andrew K. Rose. 2002a. "Do We Really Know that the WTO Increases Trade?" DP3538, *CEPR*, London, September 2002.

39 OP.cit.

40 Based on figures reported in *WTO Annual Report 2002*.

3

Singapore Issues: Investment, Competition Policy, Government Procurement and Trade Facilitation

Introduction

The effort of developed countries in WTO has been towards expansion of the negotiating agenda since its inception. At the first Ministerial Conference of WTO held in Singapore in 1996 itself they demanded the negotiating mandate of WTO be broadened to include trade and investment, trade and competition policy, government procurement, trade facilitation, labour standards and environmental standards. Having undertaken heavy commitments in the just concluded Uruguay Round, developing countries resisted these demands. As a part of the compromise arrived, Working Groups were set up at the WTO on investment, competition policy, and transparency in government procurement to conduct study processes without any negotiating mandate. The Council for Trade in Goods was also directed by the Ministerial Conference to 'undertake exploratory and analytical work .... on the simplification of trade procedures in order to assess the scope for WTO rules in this area'. Developing countries managed to put labour standards and environment off the WTO agenda for the time being.

These so-called Singapore issues, viz. investment, competition policy, government procurement, and trade facilitation, were the most contentious ones at the Doha Ministerial. Even though the Working Groups set up on these issues by WTO at the Singapore Ministerial have not completed their work, the developed countries wanted to launch negotiations right away. Developing countries resisted a negotiating mandate and wanted the Working Groups to complete their assigned work prior to negotiations. After much deliberations, developing countries succeeded in postponing the decision on the launch of negotiations on these issues subject to an 'explicit consensus' on the modalities of negotiations. However, there is some ambiguity in the Doha mandate as to whether the explicit consensus will be needed to decide whether or not to launch the negotiations or explicit consensus is required only for deciding the modalities of negotiations.

The Doha Declaration only recognizes a 'case' for but not the 'need' for a multilateral framework. Although the language of the Declaration talks of the need for a consensus on the modalities of negotiations, the Chairman's understanding and clarification that enabled the adoption of the Declaration at the Doha Ministerial suggests that the negotiating mandate would itself be subject to an explicit consensus:

> I would like to note that some delegations have requested

clarification concerning paragraphs 20, ... of the draft declaration. Let me say that *with respect to the reference to an 'explicit consensus'* being needed, in these paragraphs, for a decision to be taken at the Fifth Session of the Ministerial Conference, *my understanding is that, at that session, a decision would indeed need to be taken by explicit consensus, before negotiations on trade and investment ... could proceed.* (emphasis added)

H.E. Youssef Hussain Kamal, Qatari Finance, Economy and Trade Minister, Chairman of Doha Ministerial Conference at the closing plenary session, 14 November 2001.

Going by the Chairman's understanding the negotiating mandate on Singapore Issues is yet to be obtained at the Fifth Ministerial scheduled to be held in Cancun in September 2003. However, the developed countries are seeking negotiating mandate on these subjects at the Cancun Ministerial. Developing countries should not allow the negotiating mandate without an understanding of the pros and cons of the negotiations for their development.

Although the four issues are unrelated between themselves, the demandeurs especially the EU have been bundling them together and are seeking a negotiating mandate for the whole bundle. Given the different types of concerns that relate to different issues, a case is made for unbundling them.

Of the four Singapore issues, investment has emerged as the most contentious and the one which the demandeurs are most anxious to seek. It happens to be most critical from a development perspective. Hence, it is dealt with greater detail in this Chapter. Subsequently, the Chapter discusses the other three Singapore Issues. Finally, the chapter concluded with some remarks as policy options.

Trade and Investment

The attempt of developed countries to seek a multilateral regime on investment through multilateral trade negotiations is a part of their strategy to secure more favourable conditions for overseas operations of their enterprises. The rationale behind this perspective is that these large multinational enterprises, now use FDI as a mode of servicing foreign markets more than trade.

Against that backdrop, this section examines the relevance of a multilateral framework on investment from a developing country perspective in the light of the evidence available on the role of FDI in development. It also suggests the policy options that developing countries may consider at the Cancun Ministerial Conference on the issue of Trade and Investment. It also reflects on the approaches to make different elements of a possible multilateral framework on investment more pro-development and balanced in case a negotiating mandate is unavoidable at the Cancun.[1]

Developmental Impact of FDI:The Role of Policy Space

FDI usually flows as a bundle of resources including, besides capital, production technology, organizational and managerial skills, marketing know-how, and even market access through the marketing networks of multinational enterprises (MNEs) who undertake FDI. These skills tend to spill over to domestic enterprises in the host country. Therefore, FDI can be expected to contribute to growth more than proportionately as compared to domestic investments in the host country. A body of literature that has analyzed the effect of FDI on growth in inter-country framework and another analyzing knowledge spillovers to domestic enterprises from MNEs arrive at mixed findings suggesting that these relationships are not unequivocal. There is also a possibility of MNE entry affecting domestic enterprises adversely given the market power of their proprietary assets.

Therefore, FDI may crowd-out domestic investment and may thus be immiserizing or welfare reducing, as has been revealed by a number of recent studies. The mixed findings on the role of FDI in explaining growth of different countries tend to suggest the role of selective policies and performance requirements that host governments use to influence the quality of FDI inflows. Therefore, policy flexibility is important for developing countries for benefiting from FDI. The studies have also documented the evidence of widespread use of performance requirements and other selective policies by developed countries in different stages of their development.[2]

Relevance of a Multilateral Framework on Investment (MFI)

A basic question before entering into any negotiation on an MFI is to determine to what extent there is need for a new multilateral framework on investment, and what are its costs and benefits for developing country members. Against that backdrop, we now make an assessment of the relevance of MFI from a developing country perspective.

There is no Conceptual Justification of a GATT-Type Framework on Investment

There is a conceptual basis for trade liberalization on the principle of comparative advantage where countries with different comparative advantages benefit from trading mutually. On the other hand, FDI flows emerge because of differences in the levels of development and bundles of created assets of national enterprises. Therefore, MNE entrants enjoy an edge over local enterprises.

Is WTO a Right Forum for Handling Investment?

FDI, like domestic investment, is a development and industrialization issue rather than a trade issue. That WTO lacks competence to deal with investment and development is clear from the fact that the Working Group on Trade and Investment has not been able to complete its work so far. Major differences exist between members on different elements of a possible framework.

One-size-fits-all FDI Policy is not Appropriate for Countries at Different Levels of Development

Countries at different levels of development receive different types of FDI; for instance, an underdeveloped country will attract resource-seeking or labour-seeking inward FDI- and a more developed one-investments in capital and intermediate goods industries. The one-size-fits-all approach to FDI to be evolved through MFI in WTO cannot serve the best interests of countries at different levels of development.

Policy Space is Needed to maximize the contribution of FDI to Development

Evidence suggests that the host government policies have played an important role in extracting the benefits from FDI in developed and developing countries. A multilateral regime will take away the ability of the host governments' to direct FDI in accordance with their development policy objectives and thus will affect the overall 'quality' of FDI inflows.

MFI is Unlikely to Expand the Magnitude of FDI Inflows

In contrast to the argument of its proponents, an MFI is unlikely to increase FDI inflows. Numerous empirical studies have shown that FDI inflows are largely driven by the gravity factors such as market size, income levels, the extent of urbanization, geographical and cultural proximity with the major source countries of FDI, and the quality of infrastructure. Policy factors or investment treaties play a relatively minor role if at all. The US is the most important source of FDI in China and Brazil even though they do not have even a bilateral investment treaty with the US.

International Framework for Investment Protection and Dispute Settlement Exists

A general impression that is created by the protagonists of MFI is the lack of an adequate framework for protection of investment and dispute settlement. However, there exists an elaborate framework for investment protection and dispute settlement at the bilateral as well as multilateral levels. Besides an extensive network of about 2100 bilateral investment promotion and protection agreements or treaties (BIPAs or BITs), multilateral instruments for protection and guarantee of international investments do exist, viz.

the Multilateral Investment Guarantee Agency (MIGA), the International Convention of Settlement of Investment Disputes (ICSID), the UN Committee on International Trade Law (UNCITRAL), and the International Chamber of Commerce (ICC).

A Multilateral Treaty Would Not Substitute the Need for Bilateral Investment Treaties (BITs)

Contrary to the general impression created, the bilateral investment treaties would be needed even with a multilateral agreement just as the presence of GATT in trade in good has not substituted the need for bilateral trade agreements. BITs provide necessary flexibility to partners and are much easier to be concluded. A contrast is the failed OECD's negotiations for MAI.

Asymmetry between Investors' and Host Country's Interests

Proponents of MFI are seeking to protect only the rights of investors or corporations and nothing is being proposed in terms of their obligations or any other provisions for protection of host country interests. MNEs command enormous resources and power granted by their gigantic and global scales of operation that can be misused to pursue restrictive business practices. While the ability of the host governments to impose performance obligations is sought to be curbed, that of corporations to impose restrictive clauses on their subsidiaries that are often trade distorting, is not regulated. An ideal accord would have to have a symmetry between rights and obligations of host as well as home governments and investors.

Asymmetry between Interests of Capital and Labour Exporters

The proposed framework on investment proposes to liberalize capital movements without providing for the labour mobility and hence would create asymmetry. The economic arguments for free movement of labour are no weaker than those for the free movement of capital.

To sum up, therefore, a GATT-type multilateral framework on investment (MFI) is justified on neither conceptual nor policy grounds. It could lead to considerable loss of welfare in developing countries by reducing policy space. It does not offer any reciprocity in the form of more FDI nor labour mobility. In view of all these, developing countries' resistance to a negotiating mandate on investment at the Doha Ministerial Conference held in November 2001 is well justified.

The Way Forward for the Cancun Ministerial Conference

The Doha Declaration only recognizes a 'case' for but does not establish the 'need' for a multilateral framework. The Chairman's understanding and clarification that enabled the adoption of the Declaration at the Doha Ministerial suggests that the negotiating mandate would itself be subject to an explicit consensus.

In the light of the Doha Mandate, there are three possible options for developing countries as follows.

Most Preferred Option: Resist a Negotiating Mandate at Cancun

Keeping in mind the Chairman's clarification, it is still possible to resist a negotiating mandate on investment. For this to happen the coalition of developing countries would be of critical importance. Developing countries will have to draw attention to the practical problems involved in arriving at a consensus on the subject in the light of the OECD's failed MAI negotiation among 29 rich countries. The wide variation in the levels of development in the WTO membership would further limit the chances of arriving at a consensus. The potential cost in terms of world development and welfare could be substantial while promise of gains is negligible, if at all. This option would be by far the most desirable and also most challenging. Yet, it is feasible depending upon the effective coalition building. Least Developed Countries, the African Union, and ACP Countries have also opposed MFI at meetings of their Trade Ministers (see Box 3.1).

Box 3.1: LDC Trade Ministers on Singapore Issues

Second LDC Trade Ministers' Meeting held in Dhaka, Bangladesh, on 31 May-2 June 2003 adopted a Dhaka Declaration. Given below are excerpts of this Declaration Concerning Singapore Issues.

27. The Doha Ministerial Declaration stipulated that negotiations on Singapore issues will take place after the fifth Session of the Ministerial Conference on the basis of a decision to be taken, by explicit consensus, at that session on modalities of negotiations.

28. In view of the overwhelming workload generated from the Doha work programme, LDCs with limited resources are not being able to follow negotiations and evaluate the implications/impact of negotiations on Singapore issues on their economies. Therefore, LDCs shall be given enhanced technical assistance and support to build capacity in these areas. WTO, in cooperation with other relevant intergovernmental organizations, including UNCTAD, ITC, shall provide strengthened and adequately resourced assistance to LDCs.

Trade and Investment

29. In paragraph 22, the Ministers instructed for further work in the Working Group on the relationship between trade and investment on the clarification of certain issues. Progress in the work of the Working Group on Trade and Investment clearly indicates that there would be no agreement between now and Cancun on any of the elements outlined in the Doha Declaration. Therefore, it is still premature to consider the real substantive issues. The views of the LDCs on trade and investment are as follows:

a. Most of the LDCs have not been able to attract Foreign Direct Investment through liberalizing investment regimes owing *inter alia* to very small size, remoteness and extreme vulnerability. Improvements of regulations or policies are unlikely to attract orthodox FDI into LDCs, without a supportive, targeted intervention from the governments of the sending countries. In particular, ODA should assist in creating the infrastructure required for attracting FDI.

b. The Working Group should continue work on the issues referred to in paragraph 22 of the Doha Ministerial Declaration, including studies on whether and how any multilateral investment agreement would facilitate flows of FDI or improve its quality in LDCs.

Trade and Competition Policy

30. The Doha Declaration in paragraph 25 mandated the Working Group on Trade and Competition policies to focus on the clarification of certain issues. Discussions on the Working Group reveal that there are differences even among the *demandeurs* of a multilateral framework on competition policy. The views of the LDCs in this area are as follows:

a. Most LDCs lack competition laws and regulations, and agencies that are able to implement the laws. This lack of exposure to, and experience in, competition laws have hampered the participation of LDCs in the current negotiations. Therefore, efforts aimed at assisting LDCs in formulating national competition laws and in establishing requisite institutions in LDCs shall be undertaken.

b. The Working Group should continue work on the elements referred to in paragraph 25 of the Doha Ministerial Declaration. Studies would also need to be continued/undertaken to reflect on ways in which possible international agreements on competition policy might apply to developing countries, including through preferential or differential treatment.

Transparency in Government Procurement

31. Paragraph 26 of the Doha Declaration states that negotiations on a multilateral agreement on transparency in government procurement shall be limited to the transparency aspect and therefore will not restrict the scope for countries to give preferences to domestic supplies and suppliers.

32. LDCs are yet to assess how an agreement on transparency in government procurement in WTO, would affect social and economic development in LDCs.

33. The Working Group should continue work on issues referred to in paragraph 26 of the Doha Declaration. Studies need to be undertaken to understand the depth and breadth of any possible agreement in this area, and how it would affect LDCs.

Trade Facilitation

34. Paragraph 27 of the Doha Declaration instructed the Council for Trade in Goods to review and as appropriate clarify and improve relevant aspects of Article V, VIII and X of the GATT 1994 and identify the trade facilitation needs and priorities of members, in particular developing and LDCs.

35. Current approach towards trade facilitation pre-supposes the establishment of common procedures, rules and regulations for the movement of goods. Implementation of such laws and procedures will be very costly for the LDCs, which they are unable to afford at this stage. LDCs' institutions should be strengthened to facilitate trade.

36. Work on trade facilitation in other institutions should be taken into account in the current work programme of WTO. Outside of the WTO framework, current efforts to assist the LDCs in this area should continue.

A Compromise Solution: A Multilateral Treaty on Investment Negotiated Outside WTO

In case developed countries persist with their demand for MFI, a compromise solution could be a multilateral treaty on investment negotiated outside the Single Undertaking of WTO. The objective of proponents of MFI is 'to secure transparent, stable and predictable conditions' for cross-border investments particularly FDI, that can be well served by a freely standing independent multilateral treaty on investment negotiated within the United Nations framework like many other international treaties such as a the Law of the Sea.

The Last Resort: Negotiating a Development-friendly Multilateral Framework in WTO

In case a negotiating mandate on investment is unavoidable at the Cancun Ministerial, then developing countries have to ensure that the Framework covers adequate development provisions so that their process of development is not disrupted. For the purpose, sufficient policy flexibility to pursue developmental objectives has to be retained. This will be a big challenge and has to be responded to by proactive home-work by the developing country negotiators.

Incorporating a 'Development Dimension' in a Possible MFI

Some considerations for designing a development-friendly framework negotiated within or outside the single undertaking are as follows:

(a) Scope and Definition

Adoption of a broad assets-based definition and all encompassing sectoral coverage would limit the governments' ability to regulate financial flows and manage the financial crises. The focus of the Doha Declaration is on 'long-term cross-border investment, particularly foreign direct investment, that will contribute to the expansion of trade'. In view of this the scope of MFI could be restricted to FDI especially the export platform FDI that only contribute to expansion of trade. Furthermore, developing countries may wish to limit the scope of MFI to only greenfield investments and not acquisitions in view of the greater potential of the former to contribute to the expansion of trade.

(b) Transparency: A Symmetric Framework

While transparency with respect to FDI policy framework might be unexceptional, some of the procedures for processing and evaluation of proposals might not be made transparent in public interest. Furthermore, governments of developing and least developed countries often experience an information asymmetry in dealing with MNEs with respect to their track record regarding corporate social responsibility, their involvement in bribery and corruption and questionable business practices. Recent evidence on Enron, Anderson, Xerox are cases in point. MFI should provide for transparency on the track record of investors by building obligations on the part of home governments.

(c) National Treatment in Post-establishment Phase: Retaining the Policy Flexibility

MNEs are already much ahead of the domestic enterprises in potential developing host country because of their monopolistic ownership of unique assets, e.g. globally known brand names. Therefore the playing field is already tilted in favour of MNEs. Governments in developing countries often adopt policies supporting 'infant enterprises' or SMEs through some measures favouring them. In view of scarcity of funds, developing countries governments may need to limit such incentives to national firms. However, discriminatory support measures favouring the domestic enterprises in strategic industries are quite common even in the developed world, e.g. SEMATECH in the US. To protect the flexibility, granting of national treatment in the post-establishment phase may be structured on the basis of a GATS-type positive list approach which is subject to limitations, as considered necessary.

(d) National Treatment in Pre-establishment Phase: Exclude any Commitments

In view of great variation in the quality of FDI and its possible adverse impact on domestic enterprises, host governments may wish to protect domestic 'infant enterprises' or SMEs through selective policies towards FDI. Host governments may also impose, subject to the TRIMs Agreement, performance requirements on foreign entrants to regulate their operations in tune with their development policy objectives. The Doha Declaration does provide for such flexibility and suggests due regard to development policies and preserves developing countries' rights to regulate FDI in the public interest. Therefore, developing countries should resist the national treatment obligation for pre-establishment stage to retain the policy flexibility.

The proponents of MFI argue that a GATS-type approach to pre-establishment national treatment commitment allow adequate policy space to developing countries. The experience of GATS suggests that developed countries bring pressure on developing countries to make commitments in the sectors that are of particular interest to them.

(e) Most-Favoured-Nation (MFN): Providing Exceptions for Ethnic Investors

The extension of the MFN treatment to investment may affect the special treatment conferred by many developing countries to "ethnic overseas investors". Exceptions for a differential treatment for ethnic overseas investors may be retained in a possible MFI.

(f) Development Provisions

Developing countries seek FDI as a resource for their industrialization and development. The S&D treatment available to developing countries should include flexibility to impose performance requirements which may require abrogation of TRIMs and provide for balance of payment safeguards, among other provisions.

(g) Balancing the Host Country and Home Country Interests

The Doha Declaration indicates the need for balancing the host and home country interests. However, no indications have been made on the way to balance the interests of developed and developing countries. A balancing of interest between all the stakeholders could be ensured with their rights and obligations and by ensuring a symmetry between capital and labour mobility. Binding obligations should be undertaken by investors regarding transfer of technology, restrictive business practices, consumer protection, environmental protection, disclosure, among other commitments.[3] Home governments should accept an obligation to provide information regarding the involvement of MNEs in any questionable dealings, and cooperate with the host governments in control of RBPs, transfer-pricing manipulation, and in recovery of the liabilities of MNEs resulting from their misconduct in host countries. India, China, Cuba, Kenya, Pakistan and Zimbabwe have made a detailed submission to the Working Group on the subject.[4]

Developing countries could also seek an International Discipline on Incentives that at present distort the pattern of global FDI flows in favour of developed countries.

(h) Investor Protection and Dispute Settlement

Investor to State disputes should not be acceptable in an MFI negotiated in the WTO framework. Furthermore, there is need to adopt a cautious and restrictive definition of expropriation or 'takings' in the light of evidence on litigations brought by affiliates of US corporations against the Canadian Government under NAFTA seeking compensation for the government regulations. Regulatory actions of host governments for pursuing their development policy goals, environmental and social objectives in broad public interest should be specifically excluded from the scope of expropriation or regulatory takings.

Trade and Competition Policy

The Working Group on Trade and Competition Policy over the past six years has been engaged in what is called as 'educative process' with no negotiating mandate assigned to it. There is little debate on the implications of the competition policy coming under the purview of WTO for developing countries. Internationally too, no consensus has emerged as yet on the issue of inclusion of competition policy in the proposed round. While the European Union would like to have a binding multilateral framework on competition policy, the United States does not favour such an approach.

The issue of competition policy coming up in WTO is highly complex. The competition policy at the national level comprises of the competition or anti-trust laws and their enforcement mechanisms. These laws are meant to remedy different types of anti-competitive practices including price fixing and other cartel agreements, abuses of a dominant position or monopolization, mergers that stifle competition and agreements between suppliers and distributors that foreclose markets to new competitors. The national competition policy could play a crucial role especially in a liberalized market setting by preventing enterprises from misusing their market power. Although more than 40 developing and transition countries have adopted competition laws over the past two decades, most of them are at a rather early stage of their implementation or have very weak provisions.

At the international level, various initiatives especially in the framework of UNCTAD have produced a Set of Multilaterally Agreed Equitable Principles and Rules for Control of Restrictive Business Practices adopted in 1980. These Rules are not legally enforceable and are voluntary in nature.

The recent trends of globalization and liberalization have altered the industrial landscape. For instance, the restructuring of the global industry through mergers and acquisitions (M&As) between large multinational enterprises (MNEs) has led to consolidation of their market position. The recently strengthened and harmonized international regime of intellectual property protection also fortifies the monopolistic hold of technologies by large MNEs. Therefore, there is need of effective anti-trust regulations to deal with possible abuse of these trends. Besides the consolidation of market power of affected companies, M&As among MNEs could have more direct adverse effects on the market structures in their host countries. For instance, with the consolidation of Glaxo, Wellcome, Smith Kline and Beecham into a single company after rounds of M&As leading to their affiliates in different host countries coming under common control without any consultation with domestic competition authorities. While EU and the US are equipped with effective anti-trust regulations to deal with possible abuse of monopoly power of patent holders and anti-competitive effects of international mergers, most developing countries either lack anti-trust legislation designed to deal with such situations.

There is also a development dimension of competition policy. The competition policy in a developing country especially in a liberalized regime for trade and investment has to provide a level playing field for domestic enterprises *vis-a-vis* subsidiaries of MNEs which enjoy access to their parent's brand and trade names besides a number of other intangible assets. To use their advantages most effectively, MNE affiliates tend to adopt non-price modes of rivalry dominated by a heavy reliance on advertising and product differentiation. These strategies raise barriers for the entry of new firms and are referred to as 'contrived entry barriers' in the industrial organization literature.[5] In order to promote a healthy competition between local firms and MNE affiliates, competition policy could take the form of either offsetting the monopoly power of MNE affiliation and foreign brands through fiscal measures or assisting national firms to build their own brands and technological capability.

The discussions at the Working Group over the past six years have not produced any convergence of views among the members on different elements of a possible framework even among the demandeurs. For instance, on banning the hard cartels the US, Canada and Japan prefer voluntary cooperation between the competition authorities, the EU seeks a binding framework. Developing countries have sought flexibility and differentiation in treatment of domestic firms as opposed to big MNEs, while developed countries want a national treatment. Therefore, there does not seem to be any consensus emerging on the modalities.

To sum up the discussion on the issue of bringing competition policy on WTO agenda, one does not find the developing world prepared to deal with it. An important first step for developing countries would be to adopt effective competition policy at the national level. Only after grappling with the issue at the national level they could venture to consider an international framework on competition. Otherwise it could jeopardize their development prospects. This is because competition policy negotiations could be used as yet another means of justifying further liberalization of trade and investment regimes of developing countries and facilitation of access to their markets by industrialized country enterprises. A more prudent response on their part would be to defer a negotiating mandate on the issue and use the time bought in the process to establish a competition policy at the national level.

Transparency in Government Procurement

The Doha Declaration recognises the "case for a multilateral agreement on transparency in government procurement and the need for enhanced technical assistance and capacity building" (Para 26), taking into account the development priorities of participants, especially least-developed countries. The Declaration also clarifies that the negotiations "shall be limited to the transparency aspects and therefore will not restrict the scope for countries to give preferences to domestic supplies and suppliers." In addition, Members committed themselves to "ensuring adequate technical assistance and support for capacity building both during the negotiations and after their conclusion."

In the Working Group, major differences among developed and developing countries have been apparent. India has underlined the importance of using government procurement as one of the few policy tools available for achieving socioeconomic objectives. Apprehensive over the 'intrusiveness' of new rules, many developing countries support India's attempt to limit the scope of the discussions in this area. The US, the EU and Switzerland on the other hand are seeking as broad a range as possible.

Australia has outlined a widely supported non-prescriptive approach to procurement methods, leaving it up to the discretion of each government to decide what method to use.[6] Brazil has noted that its procurement laws and regulations are already available on the Internet. But like India, it is opposed to any obligation to notify Members of all tenders or to translate them into the official languages of the WTO, as well as to WTO reviews or examination of domestic laws and regulations.

Canada has stated that while Members require flexibility to choose criteria for awarding contracts, as well as for separate qualification or registration process, decisions should be transparent. Information on the criteria as well as decisions taken should be made available to suppliers, but governments should not be obliged to disclose confidential information. The US has proposed four categories around which to organise the elements of an agreement: general parameters of a potential agreement; transparency of procurement systems; transparency of specific procurements; and operational provisions to fulfil the objectives of a potential agreement.[7] While countries such as Japan want a legally-binding and effective transparency agreement, most developing countries feel this area should not be open to dispute settlement proceedings.

Developing countries see the Agreement on transparency as an intermediate step to a full market access and national treatment in government procurement that developed countries are actually aiming to achieve. In view of the Uruguay Round experience, where a statement concerning regulation of counterfeit goods evolved into TRIPs Agreement, the fears of developing countries are not unfounded. The best option, therefore, would be to exercise caution and hence resist a negotiating mandate until there is a fuller appreciation of the objective of proponents.

Trade Facilitation

Para. 27 of the Doha Declaration provides that until the fifth WTO Ministerial Conference, the Council for Trade in Goods "shall review and as appropriate clarify and improve relevant aspects of Articles V (Freedom of Transit), VIII (Fees and Formalities Connected with Importation and Exportation) and X (Publication and Administration of Trade Regulations) of the GATT 1994 and identify the trade facilitation needs and priorities of members, in particular developing and least-developed countries."

The post-Doha work programme has been organised around the following three 'core' agenda items: (i) GATT Articles V, VIII and X each to be addressed in consecutive meetings (ii) trade facilitation needs and priorities of Members, particularly developing and least-developed countries and (iii) technical assistance and capacity building. Of these points (ii) and (iii) were to be addressed as standing items.

So far, proposals have mainly been submitted by developed countries. The EU along with Japan, Canada and Korea have called for widening the scope of information to be published, a consultation mechanism for affected parties prior to the finalisation of customs regulations, the legal right of appeal against customs decisions, a single inquiry point for trade-related information and expanded technical assistance to developing countries.

Most developed countries, including the EU and Japan, have also called for streamlining the processing of imports under Article VIII (Fees and Formalities Connected with Importation and Exportation). The EU considers this article to be at the heart of trade facilitation and wants 'operational' rather than 'aspirational' rules. An agreement on trade facilitation would ensure a 'locking-in' of reforms that would make WTO rules on customs procedures 'irreversible'.

Broader potential for agreement exists on issues related to transit, especially for land-locked countries. The EU and some other WTO Members have noted that new problems and difficulties have arisen since GATT Article V (Freedom of Transit) was originally drafted in the 1940s. As an example of unjustified restrictions, the EU has pointed to more onerous customs procedures for goods intended for transit than for those destined for immediate import. Consequently, it has called for improving and clarifying Article V especially through the application of non-discrimination with regard to modes of transport, individual carriers and types of consignment among others EU.

In the spirit of para. 27 of the Doha Declaration, a group of developing countries including Uruguay, Pakistan, Malaysia, India, Indonesia and Cuba have reminded Members that the exercise consists merely of a review and not negotiations.

Developing countries such as India and Brazil question the need for new binding obligations on Article VIII, with Brazil expressing particular concern over the potential benefits of 'excessive disciplines' in comparison with the costs. Brazil has suggested that refraining from the abusive and protectionist use of trade instruments, as well as completing the WTO harmonisation work programme on rules of origin (i.e. harmonising the diverging methodologies in use for calculating the origin of a good), could also be included in trade facilitation, adding that the best way to facilitate trade for developing countries would be to eliminate trade barriers to their products. Responding specifically to an EU paper, Brazil noted that a sufficient case had not been made of GATT Article X's (Publication and Administration of Trade Regulations) inadequacy to warrant amending the provision.

Many developing countries prefer trade facilitation measures to be taken autonomously. The need to address the implications of binding rules on human and financial resources, as well as differences in levels of development, has been stressed by some delegations. In response, the EU has outlined elements of special and differential treatment with regard to implementation of future WTO commitments in trade facilitation to help reduce some of these burdens. These include differentiation in commitments particularly for least-developed countries, transition periods to enable progressive implementation and technical assistance.

Although the trade facilitation may appear innocuous, establishment of binding rules may create problems for developing countries. Developed countries are seeking universal application of the rules and procedures evolved by them; this would give them a headstart and an edge. Developing countries have limited financial, and administrative resources to implement the kind of rules and procedure that are being sought to be evolved. Hence, they will impose major burden of compliance on them. While technical assistance may be promised, the experience with SPS/TBT Agreements suggests that it is not easily available. Hence, developing countries should argue for upgradation of trade facilitation procedures through technical assistance rather than binding rules.

Concluding Remarks

This chapter has dealt with some of the most contentions issues for the Cancun Ministerial, viz. the Singapore Issues. Although the four issues are unrelated and to raise different types of concerns, they are often being bundled together. However, there are similarities in the sense that the North- South divide is quite apparent in each case. Secondly, in most cases there is a wide divergence of views even among the developed countries themselves. Debates at the Working Groups on the subject over the past six-seven years have failed to produce a consensus and establish conclusively the need for binding rules.

Given the high opportunity cost of the policy flexibility for the process of development and no reciprocity or gains even in the form of higher inflows of FDI, the most prudent option for developing countries would be to resist a negotiating mandate on investment at Cancun.

A compromise solution could be to negotiate a multilateral treaty on investment on the lines of bilateral treaties outside the WTO. In case a negotiating mandate at the Fifth Meeting is unavoidable, then efforts should be made to ensure that developing countries concerns are built into each element of the proposed framework as outlined.

Given the little experience that developing countries have in dealing with competition policy even at the national level, it is premature to consider a multilateral framework. There is also divergence of views even among developed countries on the subject especially with some countries seeking only a non-binding voluntary framework for cooperation among competition authorities. Developing countries also have genuine development concerns in implementing competition policies.

Transparency in government procurement seems to be an intermediate step in evolving a framework providing national treatment. Binding rules on the subject may thus take away valuable development policy space from governments. Similarly, there is hardly rationale for binding rules in the case of trade facilitation either. Technical assistance and autonomous policy decisions should be preferred over binding rules which will put heavy burden of compliance on developing countries.

To sum up, therefore, there is very little rationale to support the negotiating mandate on any of the Singapore Issues at the Fifth Ministerial Conference. There does not seem to be an emerging consensus even among the developed countries. Several groups of developing countries such as the least developing countries (see Box 8.1), the African Union and the African, Caribbean and Pacific (ACP) countries, at the Meetings of their Trade Ministers have expressed opposition to launch of negotiations on these issues. They would like the study processes to continue, however. This seems to be the best course of action as of now for developing countries at large.

Endnotes

1 This section is draws upon *RIS Discussion Paper #56 (2003)*, "Investment on the WTO Agenda: A Developing Countries Perspective and the Way Forward, for the Cancun Ministerial Conference" by Nagesh Kumar (RIS, New Delhi). For a detailed treatment also see Carlos M Correa and Nagesh Kumar (2003), *Protecting Foreign Investment: Implications of a WTO Regime and Policy Options*, Zed Books (London & New York) and RIS (New Delhi).

2 See *RIS Discussion Paper #52*. 2003. "Performance Requirements as Tools of Development Policy: Lessons from Experiences of Developed and Developing Countries for the WTO Agenda on Trade and Investment" by Nagesh Kumar (RIS, New Delhi).

3 See WT/WGTI/W/152, 19 November 2002.

4 See WT/WGTI/W/152, 19 November 2002.

5 See Kumar, Nagesh. 1990. "Mobility Barriers and Profitability of Multinational and Local Enterprises in Indian Manufacturing", *The Journal of Industrial Economics*, 38:449-61 and Kumar, Nagesh (1991) "Mode of Rivalry and Comparative Behaviour of Multinational and Local Enterprises: The Case of Indian Manufacturing", *Journal of Development Economics*, 35:381-92.

6 (WT/WGTGP/W/31).

7 (WT/WGTGP/W/ 35).

4

Agreement on Agriculture and Developing Countries

Introduction

The Doha Development Agenda (DDA) focused on the development dimension of agriculture by bringing on board the issue of food security and rural development without prejudging the outcome of the negotiations. It also emphasized the need to take up the non-trade concerns in the negotiations as provided for in the WTO Agreement on Agriculture (AoA). Emphasis was also on phasing out of domestic support to agriculture and elimination of export subsidies from the developed countries. The DDA expressed concerns about the possible negative effects of reforms on the least developed and net food importing developing countries. In this regard, it was proposed to give special consideration to the needs of these countries especially in the context of food aid, technical and financial assistance for improving agricultural productivity, infrastructure, and financing normal level of commercial imports of basic food stuff and also review of the follow up. The DDA identified S&DT as an integral part of all elements of agricultural negotiations in a bid to bring development to the centre stage of the WTO process.

In the post-Uruguay Round phase it is the developing countries who have mostly provided market access agriculture.[1] The anticipated increase in developing country exports during the period in the post Uruguay Round phase has not materialized and the share of these countries continues to remain at around 30 per cent of world trade in agriculture.[2] The expanded access to the markets of industrialized countries promised to developing countries under the AoA has been very slow in materializing. There have been tendencies to either under-implement these commitments or to implement in a manner that makes the fruits of liberalization unavailable to the developing countries. Developed countries continue to provide significant domestic support to agricultural production along with substantial export subsidies. The extent of subsidies given by industrialized countries has in fact increased over the past few years. The agricultural subsidies by OECD countries have increased from $ 235 billion a year on average during 1986-88 to $ 266 billion during 1997-99, i.e. roughly equivalent to 60 per cent of total world trade in agriculture and twice the value of agricultural exports from developing countries.[3] In 2001, subsidies to the agricultural sector in the OECD countries amounted to US $ 311 billion, adding up to as much as 31 per cent of the agricultural output in these countries, as observed in Chapter 2. In addition, the industrialized countries have increasingly used provisions of anti-dumping and other restrictive measures to deny the benefits of trade liberalization in agriculture to their trade partners, especially in the developing world. Some examples of these actions are available from the cases brought to the WTO's Dispute Settlement Board (see Annex 1). As a result of these asymmetries, the gains of the Uruguay Round liberalization have been largely cornered by the industrialized countries and development agenda at the DDA is proving out to be rhetoric.

The proposed changes in AoA aim to reduce agricultural subsidies provided by industrialized country governments to the farmers and also intend to dismantle QRs on agricultural commodities and introduce tariff rate quotas. These proposed changes in the AoA need to be attempted in a way that ensures equitable distribution of gains. The US-EU proposal of August 13, 2003, however, does not go far in this direction. Prior to this, the Harbinson's proposals in form of an 'Overview Paper' were presented on December 18, 2002 (HT1) for possible negotiation. However, based on the feedback and responses from the member countries two more drafts[4], viz. Harbinson-2 (HT2) and Harbinson-3 (HT3) were presented in February and March 2003. All these deliberations intend to laying down the modalities in agricultural negotiations. The finalization of the modalities is an important step towards agricultural negotiations themselves as issues left out for consideration during finalization of modalities cannot be retrieved in the later stage of agricultural negotiations.

In what follows is a detailed discussion on the three pillars of AoA, along with country submissions on these issues in light of constraints being faced by developing countries.

The Three Pillars of AoA

The negotiations on agriculture are part of the built-in-agenda under Article 20 of the AoA. There are three major components of AoA, viz. market access, domestic support and export subsidies, which have attracted attention of the developing and the least developed countries.

Market Access

The existence of high average tariffs, tariff peaks, and tariff escalation continue to distort world trade in agriculture. The tariff peaks are the duty rates which exceed the limit of 15 per cent.[5] The Uruguay Round of Multilateral Trade Negotiations led to increased tariff dispersion with tariffication of non-tariff barriers on agricultural products.[6] Some agricultural commodities attract extremely high tariff rates especially in QUAD countries. For instance, it is 340 per cent on butter in Canada, 250 per cent on edible bovine in the EU, 170 per cent on sugar in Japan and groundnuts attract a tariff rate of 120 per cent in the US. Quantitative studies suggest that a 50 per cent reduction in tariffs in agriculture would increase world welfare by US $20 billion.[7] Another recent study by IFPRI finds developing countries losing about US $ 24 billion annually in income lost due to agricultural protectionism in developed countries. The study finds that trade-distorting measures in developed countries displace more than US $ 40 billion of net agricultural exports per year from developing countries.[8]

Apart from this, the tariff structure of developed countries is subject to significant tariff escalation so that market access for processed products remains restricted.[9] In Canada, the tariff on fully processed food products is twelve times higher than the average MFN tariff. Similarly, in cases of the EU and Japan the tariffs are much higher in processed items than for the first stage processed products.

The major areas involved in the negotiations on agriculture market access cover the modalities to be employed for reducing tariffs and other means to improve market access such as exploiting market access opportunities through tariff quota access commitments; rule related issues such as tariff quota administration and special safeguards, non trade concerns and S&DT related issues. Some of the Uruguay Round market access provisions in agriculture are summarized in Box 4.1.

The AoA particularly mentioned that the practice of unbound tariff and persistent use of non-tariff barriers violated Article

Box: 4.1
Some of the Agricultural Market Access Provisions in the Uruguay Round Negotiations

Tariffication, Tariff Bindings, and Reductions

- Non-tariff barriers to be converted to tariff equivalents (tariffication) equal to the difference between internal and external prices existing in the base period.
- All tariffs to be bound (i.e., cannot be increased without notification and compensation).
- Reduce existing and new tariffs by 36 per cent, on a simple average (unweighted) basis, in equal installments over six years.
- Reduce tariffs for each item by a minimum of 15 per cent.

Minimum and Current Access

- Minimum access import opportunities to be provided for products subject to tariffication with imports below 5 per cent of domestic consumption in the base period.
- Countries must agree to maintain current access opportunities equivalent to those existing in the base period. Current access import opportunities (for example under quotas or voluntary export restraints) to be provided for products subject to tariffication with imports exceeding 5 per cent of domestic consumption in the base period.
- To ensure that these access opportunities can be met, countries will establish tariff-rate quotas, with the access amounts subject to a low duty and imports above that amount subject to the tariff established through tariffication.
- Increase minimum access quotas from 3 per cent of domestic consumption to 5 per cent over implementation period.

Safeguards, Exceptions, and Special and Differential Treatment

- Special temporary agricultural safeguard mechanism put in place for products subject to tariffication. Imposed if increase in volume of imports or drop in price of imports exceeds certain trigger levels.
- Special treatment allows countries, under certain conditions, to postpone tariffication up to the end of the implementation period as long as minimum access opportunities are provided.
- Developing countries allowed the flexibility of ceiling bindings, longer implementation period (10 years) and lower reduction commitments in tariffs (24 per cent average reductions with 10 per cent minimum). Least developed countries subject to tariffication and binding but exempt from reduction commitments.

Implementation Period

- Implementation: six years, beginning in 1995 (10 years for developing countries).

Source: **RIS based on International Agriculture and Trade Reports No. 4, 1998**

XI of the GATT. As part of the tariff reduction formula several members have emphasized on the need to tackle tariff peaks and tariff escalation. Within this, members are supporting 36 per cent average reductions targeted with the minimum cut of 15 per cent for developed countries – basically a formula used for calculations during the Uruguay Round. A Swiss type formula suggests harmonization of tariffs with the maximum tariff being 25 per cent *ad valorem* at the end of the implementation period. However, the Chairman of the Committee on Agriculture has proposed a graduated simple average reduction formula to bridge this wide gap. The spirit is that - higher the tariff the greater would be the need to increase the average reduction rate. According to the Chairman's formula, where the tariff on a processed product is higher than the tariff for the product in its primary form, the rate of tariff reduction for the processed product shall be equivalent to that for the product in its primary form multiplied, at a minimum, by a certain factor. In the deliberations of the Committee, the developing countries have largely agreed that tariff reduction formula should also be applicable with appropriate adaptations in terms of reduction targeted rates and implementation periods.

Special Products and Special Safeguards

There are various proposals submitted to the Committee on Agriculture. The idea of *special products* (SP), which would be eligible for significantly lower reduction rates, has also come up for discussion in these deliberations. In the First Draft of Modalities for Future Consideration (HT2), there is a special category of products, which are exclusively for the developing countries. Under this proposal, developing countries can prepare a list of Special Products (SP), which are meant for ensuring food security, rural development and livelihood concerns. Special Products are permitted to be defined either at 6-digit or at 4-digit HS level. According to the Harbinson's Text, there are three concessions proposed for the special products. Firstly, tariff reduction commitments would be smaller than those of the non-SP products. It is proposed that the average rate of reduction of SP products would be 10 per cent where as minimum reduction rate would be 5 per cent. Secondly, it may not be required to increase the volume of Tariff Rate Quota for the SP products, but similar privilege is not granted for non-SP products. However, most developing countries find it difficult to use Special Safeguard Measures (SSM) provisions and very few of them actually use these provisions. There is a provision for SSM for the special products of developing countries, but such measure can be invoked provided there is normal reduction in these products as stipulated in the Text. For many such products, the bound rates are so low that it would be difficult for developing countries to negotiate on these products in the current Round. There is thus a requirement for providing an effective mechanism to provide quantitative restrictions, which could be used by developing countries irrespective of tariffication for all products that they consider sensitive. In this regard, there are some suggestions to amend suitably the Article 5 of the AoA to enable developing countries for using the SSM provisions. One of the suggestions is to amalgamate SP and SSM categories of goods, so that trade protectionism does not come in the way while protecting interests of developing and least developed countries. On the same count developing country members must be allowed to maintain existing level of tariff bindings keeping in mind their developmental needs (There is also the provision of SSM embedded in Article 5 of AoA (see Box 4.2)). This is based on the rationale that enables levying an additional duty on imports when they are priced below a certain reference level or in case of a surge of imports above a specified level. Implementing the SSM requires reliable and timely trade statistics on the volume of imports and prices.

Even though it is proposed in the HT2 that developing countries shall have flexibility in applying SSM for the SP products, this proposal is somewhat diluted in the HT3.

Box: 4.2
Who is Using Special Safeguards?

According to Article 5 of the Agreement on Agriculture Special Safeguards on imports may be taken temporally to deal with special circumstances. As part of this higher safeguard duties can be triggered automatically when import volumes rise above a certain level or if prices fall below a certain level. In either case it is not necessary to demonstrate that serious injury is being caused to the domestic industry. At present 39 WTO Members currently use 6,156 Special Safeguards on agricultural products. Below we provide a number of products which are safeguarded under this Article by member countries.

Canada	150	Barbados	37
United States	189	Bulgaria	21
European Union	539	Colombia	56
Japan	121	Indonesia	13
Korea	111	India	0
Switzerland	961	Malaysia	72
Australia	10	Philippines	118
New Zealand	4	Thailand	52
Mexico	293	South Africa	166
Venezuela	76	China	84

Source: **WTO Secretariat background paper *"Special Agricultural Safeguard" G/AG/NG/S/9/Rev.1***

Domestic Support

The domestic support provided to developed country agriculture provided often creates imbalances in the world trade of agricultural commodities. OECD countries paid $360 billion while US alone paid $15 billion worth of emergency farm aid which depressed the global commodity prices. In case OECD countries do away with their subsidies, according to a University of Adelaide study by Kym Anderson, the international food prices would rise by 5 per cent over the next decade. One of the major emphasis of the AoA is on the reduction of trade distorting domestic support provision.

There are two main categories of domestic support often provided by developed countries, viz. the non trade distorting subsidies placed under the Green Box and those trade-distorting subsidies placed under the Amber Box. The Amber Box has two main measures. First, the "*de minimis*" support which is supposed to have minimal effect on trade. The AoA sets the limit for developed countries at 5 per cent of the value of production of individual agricultural products, while the corresponding limit for developing countries is 10 per cent. Second, certain direct payments under production limiting programmes are classified under the Blue Box. While some of these domestic support measures are allowed under AoA, those included in the Amber Box are subject to progressive reduction commitments.

Green Box

The DDA called for substantial reduction of production and trade distorting domestic support, which by definition would exclude several of the Green Box payments. The various components of Green Box are part of a list suggested in the Agreement. Some of these components are enlisted in the Box 4.3. In the US, $ 6 billion were paid to the farmers in 1998 and $ 9 billion were paid in 1999 under the Green Box. In addition, the Agricultural Risk Protection Act, 2000 provided an assistance to US agriculture worth $5.5 billion in 2000, and $1.6 billion in 2001.[10] Through this Act the Federal Government has also subsidized the premiums paid by farmers to insure against

Box: 4.3
Constituents of Green Box Support

General Services	Includes various rural capital works projects
Research	Agricultural and economic research, statistics, library services, outlook
Pest and disease control	Animal and plant health and disease control
Training, extension, advisory	Cooperative State extension and cooperative services
Inspection and marketing services	Inspection of grain, imports, and food; market news and grading and standardization
Other general services	Conservation operations and other non-payment environmental activities
Stockholding for food security	Food Security Commodity Reserve
Domestic food aid	Food stamps; women, infants, children nutrition
Decoupled income support	1996 production flexibility contract payments
Income insurance and safety nets	(U.S. revenue insurance included in the AMS)
Relief from natural disasters	Livestock and crop disaster payments (U.S. crop insurance included in the AMS)
Structural adjustment: resource retirement	Conservation Reserve Program
Structural adjustment: investment aids	Farm credit, ownership, operating loans (FmHA)
Environmental payments regional assistance, producer retirement	Soil conservation and water quality programs

***Source:** International Agriculture and Trade Reports* **No. 4, 1998**

crop failure. The subsidy has actually encouraged farmers to grow crops in risky situations that they might have avoided otherwise. In addition, total PFC (Production Flexibility Contracts) payments ($5.046 million), under the Federal Agricultural Improvement and Reform (FAIR) Act were lower than by both total loan deficiency payments ($5.894 million) in 1999 and total 'emergency assistance' payments ($7.804 million). As a result, the ratio of total *ad hoc,* or unplanned, to planned payments increased during these years. [11]

In the on-going deliberations at the Committee on Agriculture, the emphasis is on strict discipline in managing the Green Box. In this context, various measures such as the cap on Green Box payments, and even elimination of certain forms of direct payments to producers were discussed. With regard to such support mostly in terms of decoupled and at most minimally trade-distorting payments, the EU, Japan, Korea, Norway, Switzerland and Mauritius – known as the 'Friends of Multifunctionality – and transition economies have called for more flexibility to pursue non-trade issues such as the environment, rural development, food security and animal welfare. A number of developing countries have also asked for more flexibility to address development concerns including food security and rural development. The Cairns Group and some others, however, remain concerned that many of the proposals advocating greater leeway would add new trade-distorting subsidies to the Green Box. Instead, the Cairns Group and some developing countries such as India have demanded overall caps on Green Box spending (e.g. five percent of annual agricultural production), limits on specific types of programmes, or removing some income support programmes from the Box.

Amber Box

The Doha mandate envisages a 'substantial reduction' in Amber Box support. Following this mandate, the EU proposed to cut the support by 55 per cent. With regard to Amber Box, the Harbinson Text proposed reduction of support by 60 per cent (40 per cent for the developing countries) and to cap product specific Amber Box support not exceeding the respective average levels of such support provided during the period 1999-2001. The *de minimis* level of 5 per cent for developed countries is proposed to be reduced by 0.5 per cent point annually over a period of five years. On the other hand, for developing countries, the *de minimis* level of 10 per cent shall be maintained. The developing countries shall have the flexibility to credit to the non product specific *de minimis* support and amount of any negative product specific support upto the equivalent of the 10 per cent of the total aggregate value of production of the basic agricultural product concerns during the relevant year.

Regarding such trade-distorting domestic support, the Cairns Group, the US, China, India and some others advocate its eventual elimination for developed countries that exceed their *de minimis* levels of support of five per cent of agricultural production. Proposals have ranged from elimination of domestic support by developed countries in three years (China) to five years (Cairns Groups and Turkey). The US has advocated a reduction to five per cent of production in five years plus negotiations on a date for its elimination. The Cairns Group (except Canada) has also proposed that developed countries make an initial reduction of their existing domestic support by half. In contrast, advocates of multifunctionality maintain that the Doha Mandate is not binding. Thus, there is lack of consensus on the extent of cut in Amber Box support.

Members also disagree on whether the present system of reduction commitments based on 'total aggregate measurement of support' (AMS) should be maintained – as suggested by multifunctionality Members – or whether new cuts should be made on a disaggregated, production specific basis as proposed by the Cairns Group (except Canada). The protagonists of multifunctionality are countries that are close to their AMS limit (see Table 4.1),[12] and if significant reductions are agreed during the current WTO negotiations, they would be required to reduce their domestic support to agriculture. It is therefore hardly

Table 4.1: Distribution of Domestic Support (Figures in percentage)

	EU[1]		US[2]		Japan[1]	
	1995	1998	1995	1998	1995	1998
Amber Box	62	55	10	7	68	29
De Minimis	NA	1	NA	2	0	0
Blue Box	23	26	0	4	0	0
Green Box	28	21	52	84	25	32

Note: [1]Beierle, 2002.
[2]USDA, 1998.
Source: RIS, based on Beierle, 2002, USDA, 1998 and WTO Documents

surprising that these countries are looking for reasons to have other issues warranting the status of 'exceptional' and therefore deserving subsidies.

According to the Harbinson proposal, Blue Box payments shall be capped at the most recent notified level and bound at that level in member's schedules. These payments are proposed to be reduced by 50 per cent spread over a period of 5 years. Another option in the text is that these payments shall be included in a member's calculation of the current total Aggregate Measure of Support (AMS). Under the S&DT for developing countries the rate of reduction would be 33 per cent instead of 50 per cent and the payments shall be included in a member's calculations of the total AMS as of the 5th year.

Furthermore, developing countries enjoy some privileges under Article 6.2 of AoA in the form of exclusion of varieties of assistance and subsidy measures from the calculation AMS. The Harbinson Text (HT3) has proposed to expand the list of measures which can be exempted under AMS for developing countries. They are investment subsidies for agriculture, input subsidy for low income and resource poor farmers, subsidy for concessional loans, transport subsidies for remote areas, programmes for capacity building measures, government assistance for operation of cooperatives, etc.

The Changing Colour

The developed countries have been trying to adjust their subsidies in those Boxes where reduction commitments least affect the sustenance of protectionist agriculture policies. Thus, the subsidy at best has been changing colours without contributing much towards the intended gains from agricultural trade liberalization. Since Blue and Green Box subsidies are allowed without restriction, both the US and the EU have shifted their subsidies from the Amber to the other two Boxes. The US is ahead in this. In the period 1995-1998 there is a gradual increase in the Green Box measure of domestic support in case of the United States and Japan. The Blue Box support has gone up in case of the EU (see Table 4.1). In 1999, Green Box subsidies by the US were at $50 billion, Amber Box at $16.9 billion and Blue Box at $831 million. The EU had $47.3 billion in Blue and $19.7 billion in Green Boxes. With CAP reform, the EU will also be able to shift more and more of its support to the Green Box in a few years time.[13] The US, the Cairns Group and other developing countries want to move partly decoupled payments from the Blue Box into the Amber Box, which is subject to reduction commitments. They contend that such measures are still trade-distorting, and that the Blue Box exempting them from WTO disciplines has outlived its usefulness. The EU, Japan and Switzerland see the Blue Box as a staging post in the move away from trade-distorting subsidies and argue that it is necessary to allow reform to take place in their countries.

Taking all these into consideration, it is alternatively proposed that, in addition to reduction commitments for Amber Box, the Green and Blue Box subsidies of developed countries have to be subject to steep reduction commitments aiming at a complete reduction over of period of five years.[14]

Export Subsidies

The basic thrust of the export subsidies issue under AoA is to remove the distortions in trade of agricultural products owing to the huge export subsidies given by countries to their farmers and their exports. The various components of export subsidy include direct export payments by government to farms, industries, or producers of agricultural products contingent on export performance; sales or gifts of government stocks at prices lower than the acquisition prices; export payments financed through government action, including payments financed by levies on producers; subsidies to reduce export marketing costs, including handling and export-specific transportation; and subsidies on goods incorporated into export products.

The AoA aimed to reduce the volume of subsidized exports by 21 per cent over six years from a base period (1986 – 90) level and 14 per cent over a 10 year period for developing countries. The Agreement was also to reduce the value of export subsidies by 36 per cent over six years from a base period (1986 – 90) level while for developing countries it was 24 per cent over the time period of 10 years. Developing countries will have to reduce their subsidies by two-thirds of the levels stipulated for developed countries. As in the case of domestic support, least developed countries will not have to undertake any commitment to reduce export subsidies. The measurement of the reductions of the subsidies is to be carried out on a commodity-by-commodity basis, with each member country notifying to the WTO through the schedules. But there is one important provision that member countries not using any subsidies in the base period are prohibited from using export subsidies under the new dispensation.

There are some 25 WTO members who are committed to reduce their export subsidies. The EU, out of the 25 WTO-member countries, by far has the highest user of export subsidies. They cover products like cheese, milk products, bovine meat, olive oil, poultry and fresh fruits and vegetables. Two general approaches have emerged to discipline the use of export credits: first, a 'rule-based' approach proposed by the US and the Cairns Group countries to determine which types of credit are on commercial terms, and which are to be outlawed. The EU, Norway and Switzerland, on the other hand, prefer a dual approach by establishing rules to determine whether credits are on unrestricted commercial terms. Other credits would be subject to the same reduction commitments as export subsidies. The commitments to reforms by South Africa and Canada are noteworthy: both these countries initiated termination of their export subsidy programmes. However, Canada and, to some extent, the EU institute export marketing policies that allow them to circumvent their export subsidy commitments.[15] Further, the case of the EU becomes more interesting to watch particularly after the European enlargement programme.

In the ongoing negotiations, the Cairns Group – with the support of many non-Cairns developing countries - wants to phase out export subsidies within a three-year term (six years for developing countries), with an initial 'down payment' reduction of 50 per cent. The US proposes a five-year period, but without the reduction in down payment, while the EU suggests cutting export subsidies by 45 per cent, and eventually eliminating them on certain products "provided that no other form of export subsidization, including export credits and deficiency payments, is given for the products in question by other Members. Such products should include products of particular significance for developing countries." The Like-minded Group has called for exemptions for developing countries based on S&DT provisions in Article 27 and Annex VII of the Agreement on Subsidies and Countervailing Measures. Even though it is often viewed that S&DT for developing countries would worsen distortions and damage South-South trade, such measures may in fact promote trade among developing countries (see Box 4.4).

Different Proposals for AoA

The report by the negotiation's Chairperson to the Trade Negotiations Committee, circulated on 7 July, 2003, briefly summarises the current status of

Box: 4.4
What About South-South Trade?

A question that has been asked many times by some developed countries and also the members of the Cairns Group is this: What about South-South trade? Would it not be anti-development if protecting our borders for food security reasons affects the exports of other developing countries?

The positive list model does not suggest that all trade comes to a halt. Of course countries will continue to trade. However, if one country's exports are affecting another's food security or livelihoods, the recipient country would then have the right to take the necessary actions to address the situation.

Developing countries' exports not solely, but do mostly come from the big farms and plantations. The rights of small farmers should therefore be exercised. The same principles behind the Development Box would apply even for South-South trade. What if the exports that are affected come from small farmers? The affected developing country would also have its own market that it can choose to protect. It would be up to the farmers to find new markets abroad, or, more likely, up to the government to implement the border measures available in the Development Box, so that their farmers can sell the crops that are in demand in their own domestic market.

The possibility of having anti-development consequences is therefore a fallacy if a country, under a positive list approach, is able to provide its own market to its small farmers. Indeed, quite the opposite outcome is likely, since the local market provides opportunities also for the small players, whereas foreign markets provide access mostly only for the big players.

Source: **Kwa, Aileen. 2001. "Agriculture in Developing Countries: Which Way Forward? Small Farmers and the Need for Alternative, Development – Friendly Food Production Systems". Focus on the Global South, Geneva.**

negotiations in AoA. This follows several meetings of the Committee on Agriculture, covering a wide range of issues with revisions and the text for negotiations on modalities.[16] However, the objective of establishing modalities has continued to remain elusive. In the course of these meetings, it became evident that the failure to establish modalities for further commitments had given an added edge in making the progress in essential technical work, with worthwhile further progress being achieved in a number of the rule-related areas. However, the same could not be said with respect to core issues regarding the modalities for further commitments, notwithstanding repeated appeals by the Chairman for all delegations to work on and converge to solutions that might contribute to the development of a basis for compromise. As a last ditch effort at the informal meeting of 25 Trade Ministers at Montreal, US and EU sought to identify common grounds for farm trade liberalization.[17] The proposed US-EU farm proposals fail to provide any practical dimension as many vital details are missing. The statement does not give any specific target dates and does not specify how individual farm products would be treated. This makes it unclear how far market access would be improved, for say, exports of sugar or dairy products which are highly protected in the US and the EU.[18]

Non-trade Concerns and Multifunctionality

Non-trade concerns form the core of the EU proposals in the AoA defined in terms of protection of environment, sustained vitality of rural areas and poverty alleviation. The EU proposes to increase the market access for developing countries while keeping some degree of protection for the EU farmers. The EU proposes that domestic support for food security in developing countries and sustainable vitality in rural areas should be included in the Green Box and not subject to reduction commitments, and that the developing countries be allowed greater flexibility in their domestic support.

Multifunctionality implies some degree of domestic support under the Blue and Green Boxes, with the latter including measures to support multifunctional agriculture. Norway proposes differentiating production support for domestic consumption from that for exports, and prefers the retaining of the latter. Switzerland considers that a general cap on the volume of support included in the Green Box would be a mistake, because production costs vary greatly from one country to another, while South Korea proposes exclusion of reduction in support for strategic products and small farmers from commitments. The "friends of multifunctionality" echo the EU's case of continuing support in case of some key products.

The above mentioned countries propose improving this treatment by using the concept of multifunctionality; allowing for protection of agriculture on pretext of food security, domestic support higher than the 10 per cent of the *de minimis* provision, and use of export support, and facilitating the access to developed countries for products from developing countries. Some transition economies from Central and Eastern Europe have also submitted proposals calling for special treatment. They want to be allowed to support investment and the purchase of inputs, a higher *de minimis* provision for themselves, and exemption from the reduction of domestic support and lower customs barriers.

The multifunctionality approach however has been articulated by some developing countries so as to cover their developmental and food security needs. At the time of launching of the Doha Development Round some of these countries suggested a Development Box (DB) while India and others in their respective submission proposed a Food Security Box (FSB). In some of the studies the FSB has been proposed to be made part of DB for a more comprehensive redressal of structural problems being faced by developing countries.[19] Box 4.5 gives the details about the comparison between various elements of Food Security Box and Development Box. The Food Security Box, apart from taking food security specific problems, take into account the structural problems with AoA. The FSB comprises measures for agricultural development, poverty alleviation and support for small farmers in developing countries. The FSB also takes into account prevailing malnutrition and concerns about nutritional security. There is a growing shortfall in the intake of fat, calcium and iron along with other micronutrients. The level of deficiency of proteins is somewhat less than that of calories required.

Box 4.5: Broad Contours of Food Security Box (FSB) and Development Box (DB)

Elements of FSB	Elements of DB
• All provisions of Annex 2 of AoA except Para 5, 6 and 7	• The need to protect and enhance domestic food production, particularly in staple crops;
• Measures for poverty alleviation rural development, rural employment, diversification of agriculture to be exempted from reduction commitments	• The need to protect the livelihoods of the rural poor;
• Farm input subsidies to be accounted for in the non-product specific AMS calculations	• The need to protect local producers from dumped imports and excessive fluctuation in import volumes and price;
• Product specific support given to low income and resource poor farmers should be excluded from AMS calculations	• The need to improve distribution systems for local production;
• Developing countries to be exempted from any obligation to provide any minimum market access provision	• The need for increased flexibility in existing trade rules to allow developing countries to manage liberalization more carefully.
• Expending the product coverage of AoA to cover commodity like rubber, jute, coir and other primary forest produce	
• Appropriate level of tariff bindings to be allowed, to be maintained by developing countries as a S&DT measure keeping in mind high distortions in international market	

The contours of the DB are, however, covering a much larger horizon as compared to FSB. The measures proposed as part of the Development Box touch on five key areas.[20] The need to protect and enhance domestic food production, particularly in staple crops; the need to protect the livelihoods of the rural poor; the need to protect local producers from dumped imports and excessive fluctuation in import volumes and price; the need to improve distribution systems for local production; and the need for increased flexibility in existing trade rules to allow developing countries to manage liberalization more carefully. The FSB and the DB represent two different set of concerns, largely remaining independent of each other. Thus the idea to merge the two may not be very feasible from the point of view of developing countries.

Challenges before Developing Countries

While the AoA negotiations are underway, at Cancun and beyond, developing country agriculture confronts certain structural constraints. These challenges are in terms of stagnation in agricultural productivity, limited access to new technology, falling commodity prices, and growing concentration in agriculture. These challenges are of similar nature and needs a similar redressal mechanism. The AoA negotiations need to keep this perspective in hindsight.

Economically Active Population in Agriculture (EAPA)

There are several developing countries in which a high proportion of population is critically dependent on agriculture for their livelihood. It can be very well examined by looking at the proportion of economically active population linked to agriculture in the total. The world average of Economically Active Population in Agriculture (EAPA) for the year 2000 is at 44.7 per cent. In 50 countries, more than half of their population is economically dependent on agriculture, as shown in Table 4.2. Among these countries 34 are from Africa and 13 from Asia.

Under the provisions of S&DT, these counties can be given a separate dispensation as the potential of agriculture in affecting the livelihood of majority of population is very high.

Stagnation in Unit Area Yields

Productivity of most food crops in South Asian countries has been stagnant in the 1990s (see Table 4.3) and the positive impact of the Green Revolution to yield improvement seems to have reached a plateau.[21] Productivity of wheat is almost stagnant in Pakistan and India after 1995. The major rice consuming countries like Sri Lanka and Bangladesh are also facing stagnation. Declining productivity growth in agriculture would have a bearing on per capita food availability especially in the context of rapidly growing populations. One of the reasons behind stagnating agriculture productivity is the growing fiscal constraint on budgetary allocations on R&D.[22] This trend is particularly worrying in view of the changed environment for development of new technologies for agriculture world wide. Further, unlike the Green Revolution varieties that were developed primarily in public funded organizations, these new varieties using biotechnology are being spearheaded by

Table 4.2: Economically Active Population in Agriculture (per cent share in total)

(Year:2000)

Region	Number of Countries
Africa	34
Latin America	1
Asia	13
Oceania	2
Total	50

Note: Reported countries are those whose ratio of Economically Active Population (EAP) in Agriculture to EAP is higher than 50 per cent.
Source: RIS based on *FAO Production Yearbook*.

Table 4.3: Productivity of Different Food Crops in Selected Countries (Kg/hectares)

Commodity	Country	1979-81	1989-91	1995	1996	1997	1999
Cereals	Thailand	1917	2149	2527	2293	2268	2459
	China	3029	4192	4664	4093	4844	4882
	Sri Lanka	2464	2924	3053	3015	3802	3156
	United States	4154	4583	4645	5185	5299	5735
	India	1324	2191	2140	2180	2232	2264
Wheat	China	2047	3112	3541	3734	4087	3969
	Pakistan	1566	1844	2081	2018	2053	2162
	United States	2291	2388	2408	2442	2673	2872
	Argentina	1547	1987	1937	2259	2520	2500
	India	1545	2216	2559	2493	2654	2583
Rice Paddy	Thailand	1494	2098	2441	2172	2143	2327
	China	4244	5613	6022	6206	6331	6321
	Pakistan	2466	2309	2752	2868	2827	2875
	Sri Lanka	2555	3026	3159	3123	3954	3247
	United States	5167	6356	6301	6860	6609	6622
	India	1858	2619	2784	2846	2915	2929

Source: FAO Production Year Book, various years.

commercial companies. Therefore, developing countries need to take steps to enhance their agriculture productivity with appropriate policy measures.

Access to Technology

There has been significant development of new technologies for agriculture worldwide. The advancements in biotechnology seem to offer a way out of this productivity impasse by opening an opportunity to attain higher productivity with sustainable development of agriculture. The spread of agricultural biotechnology have, however, remained concentrated in developed countries. The emerging trade regime through stronger IPR further limits the various public policy options made available by new scientific knowledge and technology. There is a continuous growth in what is called the utility patents in the US while the Biotechnology Directive of EU has suggested a similar mechanism for the protection of biotechnological inventions in the Europe. Along with this, there is also a growing trend of patenting the research tools as well. These changes would have severe implications for the developing countries and their access to technology in a crucial sector like agriculture.

Table 4.4: Annual Average Growth of Primary Commodity Prices of Direct Relevance to the LDCs

(Per cent)

	1989-1993	1994-1997	1998	1999
Total	-3.8	6.0	-13.0	-14.2
All Food	-2.8	7.3	-14.3	-18.3
Food	-1.7	4.8	-13.8	-18.1
Tropical beverages	-8.2	23.3	-17.3	-20.9
Coffee	-10.8	31.3	-28.5	-23.2
Tea	1.9	4.9	4.3	-0.7
Agricultural raw materials	-1.3	2.6	-10.8	-10.3
Tobacco	3.1	7.6	-5.5	-7.0
Cotton	-0.6	10.4	-8.3	-22.9
Jute	-1.5	5.8	-14.2	-2.0
Ores and metals	-7.4	5.6	-16.5	-1.8
Copper	-5.6	6.3	-27.3	-4.9
Crude petroleum	4.2	5.0	-31.8	7.6

Source: UNCTAD (2000), The Least Developed Countries Report.
Notes: Average growth rates refer to the mean annual growth rates.

Commodity Prices

The export of primary commodities occupies an important source of foreign exchange earning of most developing and least developing countries. These countries have been facing declining terms of trade during the 1990s, as shown in Table 4.4. The global agricultural commodity prices have remained depressed since the increase in the domestic farm support in the industrialized countries 1998. In particular, of late, the fall in peak prices was about a quarter and the fall in troughs was about 40 per cent. In both Africa and Latin America, most of the countries are heavily dependent on a few commodities exposing themselves to price fluctuations. 36 of the 51 African countries, 7 of the 13 Caribbean countries and 13 of the 20 Latin American countries fall in this category.[23] Total 11 of the sub-Saharan African countries face shocks to their terms of trade which are permanent. Uganda, South Africa, Nigeria, Mauritania, Kenya, Gabon, Cote d'Ivoire, Congo, Cameroon, Botswana and Angola, and Liberia, Sudan, Tanzania, Zambia, and Congo (Dem Rep) face such periods of more than five years. Almost all the African countries depend on primary commodities for more than half of their export earnings (they account for 45 per cent of sub-Saharan exports) and thus with the possible exception of the oil producers, face declining terms of trade, as observed in Chapter 2.[24] The case of cotton, in this context, narrates even shocking story (see Box 4.6).

Box 4.6: The Red Cotton

King cotton has turned killer cotton in southern India. Since mid-December 2002, more than 100 small farmers in the state of Andhra Pradesh have committed suicide. Saddled with excess production and faced by a simultaneous decline in domestic demand, US cotton farmers are all set to capture the Indian market through exports. This has given rise to a situation in which Indian cotton farmers are being forced to compete with their highly subsidized US counterparts, with their very survival at stake. US cotton exports to India registered an increase from 21,221 tonnes in 1999 to 48,805 tonnes in the year 2000. The falling global prices of cotton since 1997 have turned India from being a net exporter of cotton to being the third largest importer. Between 1995 and 2000, cotton prices declined at a rate of about 46 per cent.

Similar is the plight of West and Central African Countries (WCA) where, more than 10 million people depend directly on cotton production with around 30 per cent of total export earnings and over 60 per cent of earnings from agricultural exports coming from cotton. US farmers are able to offer good quality cotton at cheaper rates largely due to two reasons: the huge subsidies enjoyed by American cotton growers, and the low domestic demand for cotton in the US. There is a glut in the world market for cotton at present, with more than 1 million tons of stock remaining from the previous year. In 2001-02, while world production of cotton stood at 21.24 million tons, consumption of cotton was only 19.94 million tons. According to the International Cotton Advisory Committee (ICAC), when measured in real terms, cotton prices during the current marketing season are at their lowest since 1973.

In July 2002, the International Cotton Advisory Committee (ICAC) indicated that 73 per cent of global production of cotton required direct financial support from governments. Support given to the cotton sector by the United States, China and the European Union was estimated at US$ 6 billion in 2001/02. Of this the US provided nearly $ 2.3 billion and the EU almost $ 700 million while China contributed $1.2 billion. These figures clearly show that the WTO objectives of phasing out production and export subsidies have not been achieved in the case of this product. The classification of subsidies in the various WTO boxes is a major problem because the description of each box is often a matter of interpretation. The WCA countries in their proposal have called for the following:

* **Establishment at Cancun** of a mechanism for phasing out support for cotton production with a view to its total elimination (early harvest): at the Ministerial Conference in Cancun. There should be a decision on immediate implementation, providing for substantial and accelerated reductions in each of the boxes of support for cotton production. This decision should set a specific date for the complete phase-out of cotton production support measures.
* **Transitional measures for LDCs** until cotton production support measures have been completely eliminated; cotton producers in LDCs should be offered financial compensation to offset the income they are losing, as an integral part of the rights and obligations resulting from the Doha Round.

Source: **RIS, based on www.kisanwatch.org; Devinder Sharma, Hindu Business Line 6th January, 2003, WTO (TN/AG/GEN/4, 16 May 2003.**

The declining prices of commodities have exerted a significant squeeze on the earnings of these countries. This has been especially severe for the primary commodity exporting and oil importing economies.[25] These adverse external developments have led to a breakdown of the growth process in these countries. The international trade regime should provide extra attention towards these developments and support the affected countries as they lack the resources to cope with falling and unstable prices.

The financial support mechanisms evolved in the late eighties have helped only few commodities and still fewer countries. However, such support mechanisms cannot deal with larger and long term fluctuations affecting large number of countries. There is a need for restrengthening external assistance programme for improving infrastructure and technical assistance to comply with international standards. Apart from that it is also important to ensure access to markets in terms of tariffs, various NTBs and different marketing requirements for new products so that these economies can diversify. For instance, exports environmentally friendly products such as organic goods from developing countries have a significant potential.

Growing Concentration in Agriculture

Globalization across various developing countries has further enhanced the role being played by transnational corporations in agriculture. The agricultural sector is heavily influenced by large corporations, having scale economies and access to market information. Significant world agricultural trade is thus controlled by these corporation. Small farm operators, on the other hand, are disadvantaged on this count. Agri-business in several developing countries is also controlled by small number of large corporation. The following examples would bring out this point clearly.

For flower exports from Kenya, even though The growing concentration in case of coffee markets in well known (see Box 4.7) the country has emerged as a leading flower supplier to the European Union, this has become possible with foreign affiliates producing most of these exports.[26] Since the arrival of biotechnology, the commercial seeds market with a turnover of $20 billion, has seen consolidation with life sciences farms entering in the seed business. The most prominent example is Monsanto which in the space of few years made $8.5 billion worth of acquisitions and joint ventures. Other companies such as Aventis and DuPont have also joined Monsanto in this race. Their grand plans include transforming drug discovery and apply them to agriculture. In many cases the same transnational companies buy, ship and mill grain, then feed it to livestock or turn it into cereal, often crossing several national borders in the process.[27] In the US, for example, 60 per cent of terminal grain handling facilities are owned by Cargill, Cenex, Harvest States, ADM and General. Mills, 82 per cent. of corn exporting is concentrated in Cargill, ADM and Zen Noh, 81 per cent of beef packing is held by ADM, ConAgra, Cargill and Farmland Nation, and 61 per cent of flour milling capacity is owned by ADM, ConAgra, Cargill and General Mills.

Key Points of Interests for Negotiations on Agriculture

Economically Active Population in Agriculture (EAPA) as a Criteria: It is important for the international trade regime on Agriculture to take note of the fact that in several developing and least developed countries a large number of people are dependent on agriculture. AoA in no provision takes note of this. A special consideration in terms of implementation and agricultural liberalization should be given to those countries in which more than one half of their population is dependent on agriculture. This would help in improving the efficacy of the trade regime. This would help in ensuring the livelihood sustenance of rural population dependent on agriculture. At present S&DT provisions also do not take care of this dimension.

Food security: As large numbers of developing countries have an unstable food security system, a Food Security Box is, therefore, of extreme importance. Though

Box 4.7:
Transnational Corporation in Agriculture: Case of Coffee

The concentration in the coffee market has considerably grown over the year. The local exporters and mid-sized traders could not compete with international traders and have either disappeared or allied with international traders. A large number of these traders have also gone bankrupt and were taken over by the majors.[1] In case of roasted and instant coffee the level of concentration is much higher than in any other category of coffee. The figure shows that top two groups viz. Nestle' and Philip Morris account for 49 per cent of world market share for roasted and instant coffee and the top five groups control 69 per cent of the market. Nestle' dominates the soluble market with a share of 56 per cent. The brands owned by Nestle' are Taster's Choice, Nescafe, Hills Brothers, Lite, Sarks and MJB. Some of the other companies like Procter & Gamble which owns the brands like Folgers, Millstone and High Point has a share of 7 per cent in the market. Sara Lee and Tchibo own 6 per cent and 7 per cent respectively in the roasted and instant coffee market.

Figure : Market Share of Coffee Companies

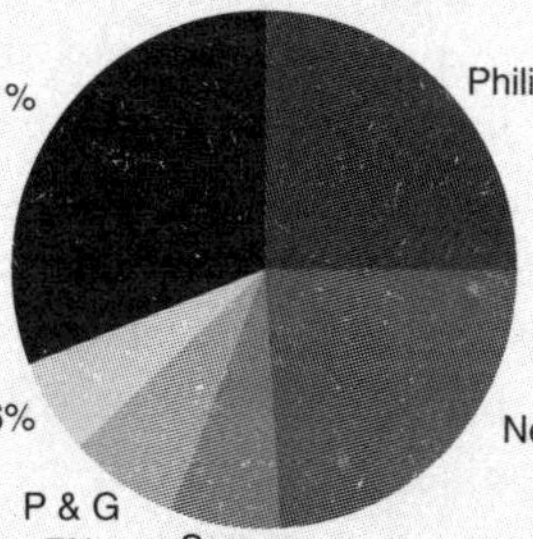

The high concentration in the coffee industry has also affected the distribution of total income generated along the coffee chain. According to Talbot (1997) the share of producers in the income generated through marketing of coffee has consistently declined. In the 1970s share of producers in the total income was 20 per cent while the average proportion retained in consuming countries was 53 per cent. In the period 1980-81 and 1988-89 though producers control similar share, the consuming countries' share increased to 55 per cent. By 1994-95 and the share of producers dropped to 13 per cent while that of consuming countries surged to 78 per cent.

According to an Oxfam International Survey since 1997 the prices of coffee have declined by 70 per cent with costing developing country's loosing about $8 billion of foreign exchange earnings.[2] The survey further points out that for some countries, these losses have outweighed the benefits of aid and debt relief. Poor households have suffered particular hardship. The Oxfam research among coffee farmers in Tanzania, southern Mexico, and Haiti found families reducing their general consumption, taking children out of school, and facing extreme difficulties in meeting health costs. Family and community structures were coming under strain, as women were forced to increase their off-farm labour, and men to migrate in search of work.

Source: **RIS based on [1]Ponte, Stefano. 2001. The 'Latte Revolution'? Winners and Losers in the Restructuring of the Global Coffee Marketing Chain, CDR Working Paper – 01.3, Centre for Development Research, Copenhagen. [2]Oxfam International. 2002. "Rigged Rules and Double Standards: Trade, Globalization and the Fight against Poverty", Oxfam International, UK.**

the concept of food security has been defined differently by different authors, a more pragmatic approach has to be adopted from the point of view of integrating developing and least developed countries in the international trade regime so as to stimulate their economic development.[28] In this context, mere flexibility in terms of a time frame alone under the Special and Differential Treatment may not suffice to counter the continuously expanding Green Box. Here it is also relevant to mention that the Development Box and Food Security Box are to be kept as separate entities.

Facilitating developed country market access for developing countries: The experience of the last six years of implementation of AoA suggests that the developed country policies of high domestic support policies coupled with high tariffs, tariff peaks, tariff escalation and a plethora of non-tariff barriers restrict market access of developing country agricultural exports. It is important that an appropriate formula with a cap on tariff binding is evolved to effect reduction in all tariff levels across commodity lines.

Tariff Rationalisation: For tariff reduction, the principle of higher reduction rates for higher tariffs may be applied, which would cover a large number of products of the developed countries. Further, ceiling on tariff peaks of developed countries is also a necessity. Developing countries should demand for the conversion of *specific tariff* to *ad valorem tariff* for transparency and administration of tariff.

Dealing with Sanitary and Phytosanitary Measures: Another contentious issue is the emergence of Sanitary and Phytosanitary Measures as non-tariff barriers. The developing countries in particular are directly affected by these measures. They not only lack information about them but also often do not possess the necessary technologies and finances to cope with them. Hence, there has to be a provision for technical assistance and information dissemination on the emerging standards. The involvement of developing countries in the international standard setting bodies is equally important in this respect. The SPS/TBT committees should be instructed, as per the DDA, to urgently work towards the harmonization of international food and other standards.

Tariff Rate Quotas: It is very unlikely that the TRQ is abolished. The interest of developing countries would be to have increased volume of the TRQ. Such enhanced TRQ should be available to Member countries on the basis of non-preferential terms and also at the MFN rate. The modalities regarding administration of the tariff rate quotas also need to be ascertained and evolved to the satisfaction of all members.

Special Safeguard Measure for the SP products – In the First Draft of Modalities for Future Consideration (HT2), it is distinctly mentioned that developing countries shall have flexibility to apply SSM in case of Special Products. In the HT3, it is mentioned that the issue "... currently subject to technical work ....". It is developing country position that the proposal made in the HT2 should made as the basis for negotiation. The developing countries may also negotiate for applying direct import control measures in respect of the products from the developed countries maintaining export subsidy and/ or domestic support.

Domestic Support: The Green and Blue Box subsides of developed countries has to be subject to reduction commitments, aiming at complete elimination. Such reduction may be effected uniformly over a period of five years.

Expansion of the Sectoral Product Coverage: In the URAA, many primary and agricultural products are not included under the broad sector of agriculture. These products are otherwise eligible for being a part of the agricultural sector, but they are now in the manufacturing sector. Since negotiations in the manufacturing sector is different from that of agriculture, many countries are facing difficulties in gaining market access in these products. A large number of countries from Asia, Africa and Latin America are the victims of this arrangement in the trade regime. In this Round, products like shrimp, rubber, etc. should be included in the agricultural sector, so as to make the sector comprehensive for negotiation.

Export Subsidies: The AoA text enables those countries with export subsidies in the base year period (1986-90) to continue with this support. On the other hand, it does not allow any country to provide export subsidies afresh which did not have the provision of export subsidy during the base year nor notify about such provisions for the base year in the country schedule. The regime, therefore, leaves member countries at an extremely uneven field in the area of using export promotion measures. It is important that the developing countries should renegotiate this provision and emphasize a progressive elimination of export subsidies.

Peace Clause: The "Peace Clause", Article 13 of the AoA prohibits Member countries to initiate action against other member's subsidies so long as those subsidies remain within the committed level. The "peace clause" is to expire in 2003 unless it is renewed for some more time. The developing countries should press for the termination of the "due restraint" provision, and should not allow for further extension of the provision.

Special and Differential (S&D) Treatment: Under the provision of S&D, developing countries should ask for more liberal terms for reduction commitments and also for a more prolonged implementation period. There should be a downward adjustment of the reduction commitment schedule in the HT3 to accommodate the development requirements of developing countries.

Linking up the three pillars: It is important that the three pillars of AoA, namely, market access, domestic support and export subsidy should have a strong linkage. There has to be a correlation between the disciplines to be adopted on domestic support and agenda for other streamlining measures. The market access commitments which AoA seeks to secure would be viable only if domestic support reduction commitments are ambitious. The continuous effort to enlarge the scope of Green and Blue Boxes is a major concern for the developing countries. Moreover, some of the domestic support measures under the Green Box are as trade distorting as the tariffs. In this regard, a clear definition of various components of Green Box which are "non- or minimally trade distorting" is needed. New rules are to be framed to restrain any attempt to transfer subsidies either from the Amber Box to Green Box/Blue Box or from the Blue Box to Green Box.

Endnotes

1 WTO. 2001a. G/AG/NG/S/6/Rev. 1. Agriculture Trade Performance by Developing Countries 1990-1999. January 31.

2 UNCTAD. 1999. The World Commodity Economy: Recent Evaluation, Financial Crises, and Changing Market Structures, Trade and Development Board Commission on Trade in Goods and Services, and Commodities, TD/B/COM. 1/27, 16 July

3 Olarreaga, Marcelo and Francis Ng. 2002. "Tariff Peaks and Preferences in Development Trade and the WTO" in Bernard Hoekman *et al.* (eds.), *Development, Trade and the WTO – A Handbook*, The World Bank. Washington D.C.

4 The First Draft of Modalities for Future Consideration *was released on 12 February, 2003 (HT2) and* The Second Draft of Modalities for Future Consideration *was released on 18 March, 2003 (HT3).*

5 For details see UNCTAD, 2003, Back to Basics: Market Access Issues in the Doha Agenda, UNCTAD/DITC/TAB/Misc. 9, pp. 22.

6 Olarreaga, Marcelo and Francis Ng. 2002. "Tariff Peaks and Preferences in Development Trade and the WTO" in Bernard Hoekman et. al. (eds.), *Development, Trade and the WTO – A Handbook*, The World Bank. Washington D.C.

7 See UNCTAD. 2003. *Book to Basics: Market Access in the Doha Agenda*. Geneva: UNCTAD. Also see Beierle, C. Thomas 2002. From Uruguay to Doha: Agricultural Trade Negotiations at the World Trade Organization, Resource for the Future, Discussion Paper 02-13, March, Washington, D.C. and Mohanty, S. K., Sanjib Pohit and Saikat Sinha Roy. 2002. 'Implication of Agricultural Trade Liberalisation in Selected Industrialised Countries on Trade Prospects of South Asian Countries: A CGE Modelling Analysis', Paper presented in International Conference on 'Globalisation and Agriculture: Challenges for South Asia', organised by IPS, Sri Lanka, IFPRI, USA and RIS, India, held on 4-5 December, 2002 at New Delhi.

8 See the study conducted by Engenio Diaz-Bonilla of IFPRI, findings reported in *Business Standard*, 27 August 2003.

9 Hoekman, Bernard; Mattoo, Aaditya and English, Philip. 2002. "Development, Trade, and the WTO: A Handbook", The World Bank. Washington, D.C.

10 Glauber, J. 2000. 'The Agricultural Policy Outlook', USDA Agricultural Issues Center, October 26, 2000.

11 European Parliament. 2001. 'The WTO Negotiations in the Field of Agriculture and Food Strategic Positions of the US and China.' Working Paper Agriculture, Forestry and Rural Development Series No. 135 – EN.

12 Wynen, Els. 2002. Multifunctionality and Agriculture – Why the Fuss? Information and Research Services, *Current Issues Brief*, No. 13 2001-02, June.

13 Khor, Martin (2003), Comment on the EC-US Joint Paper on Agriculture in WTO, Third World Network, Geneva.

14 Das, B.L. 2003. Agriculture in the WTO: After the Chairman's Text. 20 February.

15 USDA. 1998. "Agriculture in the WTO: Situation and Outlook Series'. International Agriculture and Trade Reports No.4. December.

16 TN/AG/6, 18 December, 2002.

17 *Financial Times*. 2003. "US and EU Seek Common Ground on Farm Trade", July 31.

18 *Financial Times*, August 15, 2003.

19 Braun. Joachim Von; Wobst, Peter and Grote, Ulrike. 2003. "Development Box" and Special and Differential Treatment for Food Security of Developing Countries: Potentials, Limitations and Implementation Issues. *ZEF – Discussion Papers on Development Policy*, No. 47, Bonn and Green, Duncan and Shishir Priyadarshi. 2001. Proposal for a "Development Box" in the WTO Agreement on Agriculture, Catholic Agency for Overseas Development and South Centre, Geneva.

[20] ACF. 2003. "Agriculture Trade Negotiations in the World Trade Organization" Report of a Meeting of NGOs in Geneva, February. Agriculture and Theology Project: Networking for Biblically Transformed Agriculture.

[21] RIS. 2002. *South Asia Development and Cooperation Report- 2001/2002*. RIS, New Delhi.

[22] Tabor, R Steven, Willem Janssen and Hilarion Bruneau. 1998. *Financing Agricultural Research: A Source Book*, ISNAR, The Hague, April.

[23] European Parliament. 2001a. 'Impact of World Commodity Prices on Developing Countries Directorate-General for Research.' *Working Paper Development Series No. 103 - EN.*

[24] *ibid.*

[25] UNCTAD. 2000. *The Least Developed Countries Report. United Nations*, Geneva UNCTAD.

[26] Africa Online. 2002. Kenya: Flower power boosts economy Nairobi, 1 July.

[27] UNDP. 2003. *Making Global Trade Work for People*. Earthscan Publication Ltd. London.

[28] Gulati, Ashok. 2002. "Trade Liberalization and Food Security" in Hoda, Anwarul, WTO Agreement and Indian Agriculture, Social Science Press, Delhi and Mohanty, S.K. 2002. Food Security and Structural Adjustment. *Productivity*, Vol. 43, No. 1. April-June.

Annex I

Illustrative List of Complaints by Developing Countries Pertaining to Agricultural Commodities			
S.No.	**Problem Areas for Developing Countries**	**Brought by**	**Against Developed country**
1.	Approval and marketing of biotech products	Argentina	European Community (EC)
2.	Export subsidies on sugar	Thailand	EC
3.	Measures affecting the importation of fresh pineapple	Philippines	Australia
4.	Subsidies on upland Cotton	Brazil	United States
5.	Export subsidies on Sugar	Brazil	EC
6.	Measures affecting imports of wine	Argentina	EC
7.	Tax imposed on processed orange and grapefruit products	Brazil	United States
8.	Conditions for the granting of tariff preferences to developing countries	India	EC
9.	Generalized System of Tariff Preferences	Thailand	EC
10.	Measures affecting soluble coffee	Brazil	EC
11.	Measures affecting differential and favourable treatment of coffee	Brazil	EC
12.	Measures affecting import duties on rice	India	EC
13.	Tariff rate quota for imports of groundnuts	Argentina	United States
14.	Regime for the importation, sale and distribution of bananas	Panama	EC
15.	Countervailing Duty Investigation of Imports of Salmon	Chile	United States
16.	Safeguard measure against imports of broom and corn brooms	Colombia	United States
17.	Measures Affecting Importation of Certain Poultry Products	Brazil	EC
18.	Import Prohibition of Certain Shrimp and Shrimp Products	Philippines	United States
19.	Anti-dumping investigation on fresh and chilled tomatoes	Mexico	United States
20.	Implementation of the Uruguay Round Commitments Concerning Rice	Uruguay	EC
21.	Import duties on rice	Thailand	EC

Source: RIS based at WTO Report.

5

Market Access for Non-Agriculture Sector

Introduction

A major concern of developing countries with the process of trade liberalization for non-agricultural products in the Uruguay Round has been the persistence of high and peak tariffs, tariff escalation and non-tariff barriers in developed countries on goods of export interest, as observed in Chapter 2. It has also been shown that process of trade liberalization has been asymmetric with developing countries taking deeper commitments compared to developed countries. The Doha Ministerial conference sought to address this asymmetry by proposing negotiations on the market access for non-agricultural goods to be agreed by May 2003 to eliminate barriers to market access in particular on products of export interest to developing countries' (Para 16). Subsequently, a Negotiating Group on Market Access (NGMA) has been set up at the WTO and different countries have presented proposals on modalities for liberalization.

Against that background this chapter reviews the Doha Mandate on non-agricultural market access (NAMA). It then discusses the priorities for developing countries in NAMA. The different proposals on modalities are summarized. The implications of the Draft Paper on Modalities of Negotiations prepared by Chairman of NGMA in May 2003 on the basis of various proposals is then commented upon from a developing country perspective. Subsequently, a Revised Draft Paper on Modalities was issued by the Chairman of NGMA on 19 August 2003 where a number of provisions of the May Draft were changed. The implications of the changes are also commented upon. Some concluding remarks are made at the end.

The Doha Mandate: A Comment

The Doha Ministerial Meeting had agreed to reduce industrial tariffs under the agenda item "Market Access for Non-Agriculture Products" as per Para 16 of the Ministerial Declaration:

> "16. **Market access for non-agricultural products:** We agree to negotiations which shall aim, by modalities to be agreed, to reduce or as appropriate eliminate tariffs, including the reduction or elimination of tariff peaks, high tariffs, and tariff escalation, as well as non-tariff barriers, in particular on products of export interest to developing countries. Product coverage shall be comprehensive and without *a priori* exclusions. The negotiations shall take fully into

> account the special needs and interests of developing and least-developed country participants, including through less than full reciprocity in reduction commitments, in accordance with the relevant provisions of Article *XXVIII* bis of GATT 1994 and the provisions cited in paragraph 50 below. To this end, the modalities to be agreed will include appropriate studies and capacity-building measures to assist least-developed countries to participate effectively in the negotiations" cf, (WTO, *Ministerial Declaration*, WT/MIN (01)/DEC/W/1, Nov. 14, 2001, Doha, 9-14, November 2001).

There are several implications of the Doha Declaration. The following paragraphs summarise some concerns.

The Declaration thus, lays emphasis on both reduction as well elimination of tariffs, tariff peaks, high tariffs, tariff escalation and non-tariff barriers.

It is sometimes argued that elimination of tariffs by developed countries belonging to Regional Trading Arrangements (RTAs) may give a higher market access to developing countries. Elimination of tariffs, it may be pointed out, will take away the preferential margins to member countries of RTAs for intra-regional trade. Hence, non-member countries can get market access to member countries of mega-trading blocs.

Even though the Ministerial Declaration proposes about reduction in and elimination of high and peak tariffs, there is some ambiguity. The definition of high and peak tariffs has not been made very clear in modalities before negotiations start. Peak tariff in the literature is defined at a specified level, i.e., 10 per cent, 12 per cent or 15 per cent.[1] The level of the peak tariffs cannot be assumed as being the same for developed countries, developing countries and LDCs. In fact, these should be related to average tariff rates.[2]

The Declaration also mentions reduction or elimination of tariff escalation as well as of non-tariff barriers. In the Uruguay Round negotiations actually tariff escalation increased developed countries, particularly for the products in which developing countries have an export interest[3].

The Declaration talks about reduction or elimination of non-tariff barriers, in particular on products of export interest to developing countries. However, it does not talk about different types of non-tariff barriers whether – hardcore or soft. Different issues relating to NTBs, namely identification, examination, linkage with other areas of Doha Declaration, modalities, etc., remained untouched.

The Declaration does not specify the base rate (the tariff rate for starting negotiations) or the modalities of negotiations that have critical bearing on the outcome.

The Doha Declaration also says that a member country cannot *a priori* exclude an item/product for negotiations. In other words, developing countries cannot keep any item in the unbound list on a unilateral basis. It also does not mention of "credit for autonomous liberalization".

The Declaration does not make any reference to an increase in transparency and predictability through a significant expansion of the scope of tariff bindings and through simplifying members' tariffs. A large number of developed countries are defining tariffs in the form of specific and compound duties, which have been found to be relatively high. It is very difficult to put them in the negotiations without knowing *ad valorem* equivalence and the other implications of such duties.

Priorities for Developing Countries

In the pre-Doha era, many developing countries were opposed to comprehensive WTO negotiations on market access for industrial sector. They had taken this stand probably from the consideration that the level of developed countries' average tariff was low, and a further reduction (or even complete elimination) in industrial tariffs of developed countries would not lead to a substantial increase in market access for developing countries. On the contrary, there

Table 5.1: Tariff Reduction on Industrial Products by Select Developing Countries

Country	Trade-weighted tariff averages (%)**			Simple Average (%)
	Pre-Uruguay*	Post-Uruguay* (based on UR commitments)	Applied, 1999	Applied, 2000
Argentina	38.2	30.9	15.4	13.36
Brazil	40.6	27.0	16.2	14.78[2]
Chile	34.9	24.9	10.0	8.96
Colombia	44.3	35.1	11.6	10.99
India	71.4	32.4	27.09[4]	30.82[4]
Indonesia	20.4	36.9	10.5	9.68[2]
Korea Rep.	18.0	8.3	7.6	7.62[1]
Malaysia	10.2	9.1	9.0[3]	
Philippines	23.9	22.2	8.8	8.87[1]
Thailand	37.3	28.0		14.61[1]
Venezuela	50.0	30.9	11.9	

Notes: *Pre-and post-Uruguay Round tariff averages are computed as the trade weighted average of tariff rates on bound lines and applied tariff rates on unbound rates. Due to the significance of ceiling bindings in the post-Uruguay Round tariff averages, no reductions are reported. It excludes the Petroleum sector.

** HS Chapters: 25-97.

[1]For the year 1999, [2] For the year 1998, [3] For the year 1997 and [4] For the year 2001-02.

Source: Mehta (2003), *Indian Industrial Tariffs: Towards WTO Development Round Negotiations*, RIS

was a lurking fear that developing countries would have to give in return substantial market access by significantly cutting down their present level of tariff rates and spread of tariff bindings.

A large number of developing countries, as a part of trade policy reforms, have been unilaterally reducing their custom tariffs on industrial products. Table 5.1 shows that applied tariffs of a large number of developing countries' are significantly lower than the UR commitment level. Nonetheless, the negotiation process is expected to put pressure on developing countries to reduce/eliminate their tariffs. In the light of a number of studies[4] developing countries should give emphasis on the following aspects:

Elimination of Tariffs: A Symmetric Framework of Elimination of all tariffs completely would not be in developing countries' interest as it will lead to very high reductions by developing countries as compared to those of developed countries. It will not be consistent with the development dimension and with the principle of 'less than full reciprocity'. Elimination of low/nuisance tariff in developed countries also should not be considered as equivalent to high or deeper reduction by developing countries.

Focus of Tariff Reduction: Developing countries should not concentrate on reduction in the average tariff but their concerns should be on other aspects like peak tariffs, tariff escalation, 'credit for autonomous liberalization', and non-*ad valorem* duties, etc.

Bringing Greater Transparency in Tariff Rates: A large number of developed countries are used to the practice of imposing specific and complex duties rather than *ad valorem* duties. The total number of commodities for which custom duties are given in the form of specific duties, is very large for developed countries' for instance EU (1780 tariff lines), US (1455 tariff lines). In most cases, non-*ad valorem* duties[5] consist of one single specific tariff. However, many are mixed and complex, consisting of several specific and *ad valorem* tariffs associated with a condition of relationships between them. There are many variants of specific duties in the schedules of different countries. Some of these variants are very complex[6].

It has been noticed that the developed countries have imposed specific duties on a larger number of commodities as compared to developing countries. Although most of the countries believe that the specific duties should be replaced by *ad valorem* rates, no decision was made in the UR. In fact, a significant number of UR bound rates had been committed in the form of specific duties. It has been noticed that these specific duties conceal the fact that the countries are indirectly imposing high tariffs[7] without explicitly mentioning them in different forums[8].

The specific duties are not suitable for analytical and comparative purposes, and require more common *ad valorem* tariffs. Hence these specific duties should be converted to *ad valorem* equivalence[9] (AVEs). A study by UNCTAD (1999-2000) has computed *ad valorem* equivalence of specific duties for 18,000 commodities (of different countries) for the year 1996. It shows that the *ad valorem* equivalence of a large number of products with specific duties are much higher than the average *ad valorem* rates.

The Custom Tariff Database of the US for August 1999[10] also corroborates the above observation. In this database, the US defines specific duties for around 600 industrial commodities (national lines) and provides the corresponding *ad valorem* equivalent rates of most of the specific duties. It shows that the average tariff rate of commodities with non-*ad valorem* duties is almost three times higher than the average tariff rate of the commodities whose custom duties is defined in form of *ad valorem* rates. In this context, it is worth highlighting that *ad valorem* equivalence of bound rates is still not available in the literature.

Dealing with the Tariff Peaks: Even if the tariffs are reduced by developed countries, tariff peaks seem to be the major hurdle in the market access for certain sectors where the developing countries have good export potential.

In the literature[11], a cut-off point has generally been specified for the identification of commodities with peak tariffs. The level of cut-off point is generally taken as 12 per cent (and sometimes 10 per cent or 15 per cent). All those commodities, whose tariff rate is more than 12 per cent *ad valorem* rate, are called commodities with peak tariffs. In the existing literature the selection of a cut-off point is arbitrary and has no relationship with average tariff. Further it does not make any distinction between different groups of countries.

Besides, a number of attempts have been made to identify the commodities with peak tariffs. Notably the study by UNCTAD[12] concludes that, "both frequency and levels of tariff peak rates remain a matter of concern. Over 10 per cent of tariff universe of the Quad countries, corresponding to an aggregate 4,000-tariff line, will continue to exceed 12 per cent *ad valorem*. All four countries maintain high variance in tariff rates. One fifth of the peak tariffs of the US, one quarter of those in EU and Japan, and about one tenth of those of Canada exceed 30 per cent. In the four selected developing countries, tariff peaks are more frequent but reach less extreme rates than in the major developed countries" (emphasis added).[13]

Disciplining the Tariff Escalation: Tariff structures of many countries have traditionally displayed significant escalation favouring domestic processors for a large number of commodities. It was expected that tariff commitments in the UR would provide for gradual reduction of escalation by applying relatively higher cuts to finished goods. However, rapidly rising tariffs have been noticed from low rates for raw material to higher rates for intermediate goods and sometime peak tariffs for finished products. A number of studies[14] have confirmed that tariff escalation has continued after the UR for a large number of sectors, particularly, fish & fish products, textile & textile products, leather & rubber products, footwear and to some extent wood & wood products. Basically, the results conform that tariff escalation is still a major constraint for export industries of India and developing countries.

Addressing the Non-Tariff Barriers: The developed countries employ an impressive array of new measures of protection and government interventions. These have been imposed through different instruments, including non-tariff barriers (NTBs). The agreements of the UR have changed the intensity of different types of NTBs. As a result, while some measures of NTBs have lost their significance, importance in of some other measures of NTBs has increased.

The non-tariff barriers continue to affect the growth of world trade and the UR could not tackle these issues successfully. On the one hand the importing countries generally term them as NTBs, the imposing countries insist that 'these instruments are policy objectives'. Developing countries should look for a coherent approach for dealing with such issues and participate actively in setting up new (and clear) rules and provisions.

In short, the priorities of developing countries should be focussed on *Peak Tariffs, Tariff Escalation* and *NTBs* to get market access, and to see that it is consistent with development dimension and "less than full reciprocatory".

The Present Status of Negotiation on Modalities

To initiate negotiations on market access for non-agriculture products, the Negotiation Group on Market Access (NGMA) has been formed, such negotiations could be concluded by 1 January 2005. The Fifth Ministerial Conference in Cancun will take stock of these negotiations and recommend appropriately.

As part of negotiations a number of meetings of NGMA have been held and many proposals,[15] particularly relating to Modalities, have been submitted by member countries.

These proposals include those submitted by China, EU, India, Japan, Korea and the US. The different modalities can be categorised into the following five broad categories.

1. Request and offer
2. Formulae
3. Sector by sector
4. Zero for Zero
5. Mixed

Proposals submitted by these members to NGMA are summerised below:

Proposals

(a) China[16]

The Chinese formula is specified as:

$$t_1 = \frac{(t_a + (B \times P)) \times t_0}{(t_a + P^2) + t_0}$$

where,

t_a is the simple average of the base rates (*A* in TN/MA/20).

P is a peak factor defined as the ratio of the tariff rate over the average rate (t_0/t_a)

B is an adjusting coefficient for the year of implementation. *B*=1 for 2015 or *B*=3 for 2010.

The formula is very similar to the Swiss formula but instead of a fixed coefficient, a variable factor based on the simple average of the base rates t_a, a peak factor and an additional parameter for the year of implementation have been used. The properties of the Chinese formula are similar to what is known about the properties of the Swiss formula discussed in paragraph 16, such as higher cuts for higher rates. Furthermore it can be shown that for *B*=1 the formula reduces any initial tariff rate below a maximum level which is the current average of the base rates. This is equivalent to the effect of the standard Swiss formula using the tariff average as coefficient.

The percentage cuts for any given tariff rate will depend on the tariff average of the Member concerned. For the same tariff rate, Members with lower tariff averages will experience relatively higher reduction rates than Members with higher tariff averages. Therefore, the overall result of applying this formula will depend on the statistical properties of different Members' tariff profiles.

(b) European Communities[17]

European Communities' proposal is within the class of linear tariff dependent formulae, however, with an adjustment, which gives it the properties of a step-wise linear function. The formula is applied across a set of tariff intervals and the tariff rate cuts depend upon the upper and lower bound of the applicable interval.

The formula is specified as:

$$t_1 = B_1^L + (t_0 - B_0^L) \times \left[\frac{B_1^U - B_1^L}{B_0^U - B_0^L} \right]$$

where B^i_j are the upper and lower bounds of the respective tariff intervals. The superscripted letters U and L are, respectively, the upper and lower bounds of the interval. The intervals are defined as follows:

	Base		Final	
	B^L_0	B^U_0	B^L_1	B^U_1
Interval 1	0	to less than 2	0	to 0
Interval 2	2	to 15	1.6	to 7.5
Interval 3	15	to 50	7.5	to 15
Interval 4	50	to more than 50	15	to 15

(c). India[18]

India proposes a simple linear cut on the individual bound tariff lines of each Member, with a higher percentage cut for developed countries than for developing countries. In addition to the linear cut, any tariff in excess of three times the national average tariff shall be reduced to no more than three times the national average which results after applying the initial linear cut. The formula is specified as:

Step (1) $t_I = c \times t_0$

where $c = (1- (A \times Y/100))$ and

Step (2) $t_I \leq 3 \times t_{al}$

where

A is defined as 'less than full reciprocity' parameter with
$A = 1$ for developed countries and
$A = 0.67$ for developing countries,

Y is the reduction percentage (to be negotiated)

t_{al} is the simple average tariff after applying the linear cut.

The following supplementary modalities are proposed for developing country Members: (a) The actual reductions of at least 15 percent of currently bound rates can differ from the rates calculated under Step (1) under condition that the overall percentage reduction still meets the reduction percentage resulting from Step (1). (b) The flexibility in the application of the formula shall also apply for Step (2).

(d) Japan[19]

Japan proposes that each Member sets a target level of a trade-weighted tariff average according to a formula and that each Member reduce its trade-weighted tariff average to that target level. Each Member will retain flexibility on ways to realize the target tariff level. The formula is specified as:

$$t^w_{1a} = \frac{A \times t^w_{0a}}{A + t^w_{0a}} + \alpha$$

where, t^w_{0a} is the weighted tariff average prior to the application of the formula and t^w_{0a} is the weighted average after the application of the formula. A is a constant whose values varies as follows:

t^w_{0a} £ 10%, $A = 10$

$10\% < t^w_{0a} \leq 20\%$, $A = 20$

$20\% < t^w_{0a} \leq 30\%$, $A = 30$

$30\% < t^w_{0a}$, $A = 40$

The term α in this specification has been proposed as a constant equal to 0.3.

The formula applies to the reduction of the trade-weighted tariff average as opposed to a reduction of the tariff rates on a line-by-line basis. This means that the formula is used to determine the end result, or the objective of the tariff negotiations. A lower coefficient will yield a higher cut and a higher coefficient a lower cut.

(e) Republic of Korea[20]

The objective of this proposal is to lower the weighted tariff average of Members by 40 percent. This is achieved by applying a reduction formula that results in a higher reduction of tariff peaks. The starting point is a 20 percent minimum reduction by tariff line, which is followed by a further reduction aimed at harmonising the tariff profile. Two criteria are used to distinguish which tariff rates should be addressed and the applicable methodology. These are twice the national average and 25 percent.

For the case where tariff rates are above twice the national average but less than 25 percent, the following formula is applicable which includes the initial 20 per cent reduction:

$$t_1 = (t_0 \times 0.8) - (0.7 \times (t_0 - 2 \times t_a))$$

If the tariff rate is less than twice the national average, but still above 25 percent the following formula is applicable which includes the initial 20 per cent reduction:

$$t_1=(t_0 \times 0.8) - (0.7 \times (t_0 - 25))$$

In cases where the tariff rate is above two times the simple national average and at the same time above 25 percent, the final tariff rate shall be whichever is lower after the reduction.

The formula reduces higher tariff rates in a way that takes into account individual tariff profiles since the cut is dependent on the tariff average. This means tariff profiles that have duties predominantly below 25 percent but above twice the national average will still be subject to further tariff reductions. Alternatively, profiles with duties predominantly above 25 percent, but with high overall averages will still be subject to reductions since the 25 percent rule will apply.

The overall result of applying this formula will, therefore, depend on the statistical properties of each Members' tariff profile. It should be noted though that for all tariff profiles with an average of above 12.5 percent the tariff rate reductions in percentage are identical for a given tariff rate because the 25 percent rule applies in all cases where twice the national average is greater than 25 percent.

The Korean proposal is similar to the Japanese proposal in that both seek a reduction of the weighted tariff average. However, the application of the Korean formula for the targeted reduction of weighted tariff averages differs slightly from that of the Japanese proposal as illustrated in figure 8.

(f) United States[21]

The United States has proposed a modality, which includes the elimination of tariff rates at or below 5 percent and the application of a Swiss formula on the tariff profile for all other tariff rates. The proposed coefficient is 8, which converts the general Swiss formula[22] into the following specification:

$$t_1 = \frac{8 \times t_0}{8 + t_0}$$

What is important to note about the US proposal is the value of 8 for the coefficient. This implies a maximum tariff rate of 8 percent after tariff reductions for any tariff profile.

Draft Modalities by Chairman, NGMA: Some Comments

Based on different submissions, as summarized above, Chairman of NGMA has prepared a document 'Draft Elements of Modalities for Negotiations on Non-Agricultural Products', WTO, *TN/MA/W/35*, 16 May 2003. There are four major components of the NGMA Chairman Draft (NGMA-CD).

1. *Formula (Core Modality):* All non-agricultural tariffs shall be reduced on a line-by-line basis using the formula applied to the base rates

$$t_1 = \frac{B \times t_a \times t_0}{B \times t_a + t_0}$$

where,

t_1 is the final rate, to be bound in *ad valorem* terms

t_0 is the base rate

t_a is the average of the base rates

B is a coefficient with a unique value to be determined by the participants

2. *Sector-by-Sector/Zero-by-Zero Approach:* The NGMA-CD has also proposed a sectoral elimination approach, in addition to the application of formula, for seven sectors: Electronics & Electrical goods; Fish & Fish products; Footwear; Leather goods; Motor Vehicle parts & components; Stones, Gems, & Precious Metals; and Textiles & Clothing.

3. Supplementary Modalities: In addition to the above two approaches the NGMA-CD proposes that member countries should adopt other procedures for additional tariff reduction and elimination.

4. Non-Tariff Barriers: The Chairman summarises some elements for reductions or elimination of non-tariff barriers.

The above components do not summarise elements of 'special & differential treatments', 'newly acceded members' and 'appropriate study and capacity building'.

Table 5.2: A Summary of Alternative Liberalization Proposals

"EU"	Initial tariffs under 2 per cent are eliminated, tariffs between 2 and 15 per cent are reduced by 50 per cent, tariffs between 15 and 25 per cent are reduced by 55 per cent with final tariffs capped at 15 per cent. No reductions in agriculture or services or in least developed countries.
"Korea"	For industrials, as specified by formula. No reductions in agriculture or services or in least developed countries.
"India"	50 per cent reduction in bound import tariffs in developed countries and 33.3 per cent reduction in developing countries for industrials. No reductions in agriculture or services or in least developed countries.
"China"	For industrials, as specified with B=1. No reductions in agriculture or services or in least developed countries.
"US"	All tariffs eliminated. No reductions in agriculture or services or in least developed countries.
"WTO" NGMA-CD	Tariffs reduced according to a Swiss formula with maximum coefficient equal to country average. Tariffs eliminated for electronics & electrical goods, fish and fish products, textiles, clothing, footwear, leather goods, motor vehicle, parts and components, stones, gems and precious metals. No reductions in agriculture or services or in least developed countries.

Note: **(Based on proposals, modified to take account of undefined LEMENTS)[1] Under the "WTO" simulation, the binding of developing country tariffs at double the applied rate follows the WTO proposal except that the WTO proposes to bind 95 per cent of tariff lines and imports. Obviously, it could be very important which lines are excluded.**

Source: **RIS based on Laird et al. (2003). Market Access Proposals for Non-Agricultural Products (Draft), Trade Policy Branch, UNCTAD, Geneva, 16 July 2003.**

Table 5.3: Bound and Applied Non-agricultural Tariffs before and after Application of Various Proposals

	Developed Countries		Developing Countries	
	Bound %	Applied %	Bound %	Applied %
Initial	3.0	2.8	14.6	8.3
Proposal				
EU	1.6	1.5	5.6	4.6
Korea	2.1	1.8	11.5	7.0
India	1.4	1.3	10.8	7.5
China	1.1	1.1	5.7	5.0
WTO NGMA-CD (B=1)	0.7	0.6	5.8	4.1
USA	0.0	0.0	0.0	0.0

[1] Brown, Deardorff and Stern (2001).

Source: RIS based on Laird et al. (2003). Market Access Proposals for Non-Agricultural Products (Draft), Trade Policy Branch, UNCTAD, Geneva. Derived from GTAP database, Comtrade, TRAINS and AMAD, 16 July 2003.

A comparative summary of the different proposals is provided in Table 5.2. Table 5.3 presents simulations of tariff reductions resulting from different proposals to get a comparative perspectives.

Keeping the priorities of developing countries, the following paragraphs give some pointed observations on NGMA-CD modalities:

The core modality is based on formula. The formula proposed in NGMA-CD is a modified version of Swiss Formula. Swiss formula does not incorporate the structure and average level of tariff rates of individual member countries, while the NGMA-CD proposed formula takes care of average tariffs of member countries. However, this formula (like Swiss formula) also depends upon the (*magic*) value of coefficient B. In the Tokyo Round, the value of B was taken as 14 (and 16 in some cases). In this modified formula of NGMA-CD we cannot take B=14 or 16; because it will not lead to deeper reduction as per guidelines of the Doha declaration. The draft proposal is silent on the value of coefficient B.

To understand the implication the NGMA-CD proposed formula, we have calculated post-development round binding tariff rates under alternate scenarios depending on values of B and average tariff (t_1). Figures 5.1-5.5 give select broad scenarios based on NGMA-CD proposed formula using alternate values of B = 0.25, 0.5, 1.0, 1.5, and 2.0, respectively; and average tariff rates of t_a = 5, 10, 15, 20, 25, and 30 per cent. One can notice from these figures that the post-development round bound rates for countries with average tariff of 5 per cent and B = 1.0 per cent (Figure 5.4), will be 70 per cent lower than the pre-development round. In case the uppermost tariffs is 50 per cent, the post-development round tariff will be around 4 per cent. This scenario is close to the tariff structure of a large number of developed countries. On the other hand, a scenario with average tariff of 25 per cent and B=1, will lead to reduction of around 50 per cent. In case peak tariff is 50 per cent in pre-development round, it will be reduced to 17 per cent in post-development round. This scenario is close to the countries whose average tariff is high. Basically it shows that the NGMA-CD formula can take care of (i) reduction of tariffs, (ii) peak and high tariff and (iii) structure of pre-development round binding rates. In other words, if the average tariff of a country is low the declining rate of peak tariff will be substantial.

The NGMA-CD formula is sensitive to co-efficient value of B. If the value of B is high (say 2) the reduction will not be significant (see figures 5.1-5.5). This can be illustrated through a case study. Let us suppose the average tariff of a country is 5 per cent. If we take B = 2, we can expect that it will lead to a decline from 10 per cent level (of a commodity) to 5 per cent level; and a B = 0.25 will lead to a decline from the 10 per cent level to 1 per cent level. Keeping these factors in view it is clear that the co-efficient value for developed and developing countries should not be unique. In fact the value of B for developing countries should be higher as compared to that of developed countries.

The zero-by-zero approach for tariff elimination of seven sectors, i.e. Electronics & Electrical goods; Fish & Fish products; Footwear; Leather goods; Motor Vehicle parts & components; Stones, Gems, & Precious Metals; and Textiles & Clothing; is similar to information technology agreement (ITA). Although the NGMA-CD talks about S&D treatment for implementation period in these sectors, it adds, however, very specifically that approach will be applicable to all the products of these sectors, even for developing countries. In other words, developing countries have to eliminate tariffs on all lines of these sectors. These sectors constitute a major share of developing countries' trade. As mentioned earlier, it is not easy for developing countries to accept the elimination of all tariff lines even in an extended time frame.

The NGMA-CD is completely silent on tariff escalation of non-agricultural products. The formula does indirectly capture it. In case the NGMA-CD formula is used, the rate of the tariff escalation may decline as compared to as that of Uruguay Round.[23] The 'supplementary modalities' of NGMA-CD may lead to increase in tariff escalation. This may not meet the priorities of developing countries. In this context the draft proposal for market access for agricultural[24] is very clear. The proposal says that "for developed countries "...... where the tariff on a processed product is higher than the tariff for the product in its primary form, the rate of tariff reduction for the processed product shall be equivalent to that for the product in its primary form multiplied, at a minimum, by a factor of 1.3". In other words, the proposal for market access for agriculture suggests that the binding rate of finished products should be reduced by more than 30 per cent as compared to that of raw-materials, if the pre-development round tariff of the final product is higher than that of the raw material.

The NGMA-CD proposal is very clear that all items whose duties are defined in the form of specific and complex forms should be included in negotiations. It says "... Non-*ad valorem* duties shall be converted to *ad valorem* equivalents (AVEs) according to the procedures..." The NGMA-CD proposal also mentions the formula for working out *ad-valorem*

Figures

Figure 5.1: NGMA Chairman Draft Formula for Tariff Reduction Proposed Tariff = (B*a*X)/(B*a+X), where B=2.0 and a= average tariff

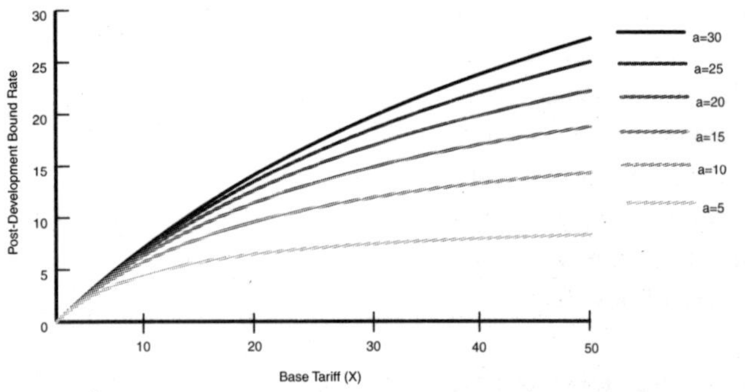

Figure 5.2: NGMA Chairman Draft Formula for Tariff Reduction Proposed Tariff = (B*a*X)/(B*a+X) where B = 1.5, and a = average tariff

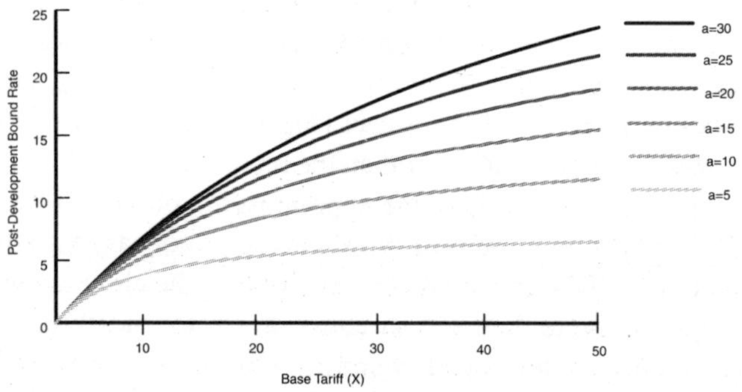

Figure 5.3: NGMA Chairman Draft Formula for Tariff Reduction Y=(B*A*X)/(B*A+X) where B=0.5, and a=average tariff

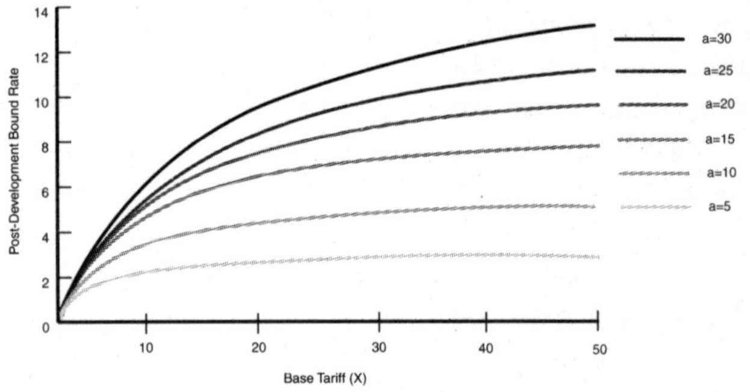

Figure 5.4: NGMA Chairmand Draft Formula for Tariff Reduction Proposed Tariff = (B*a*X)/(B*a+X) where B = 1, and a = average tariff

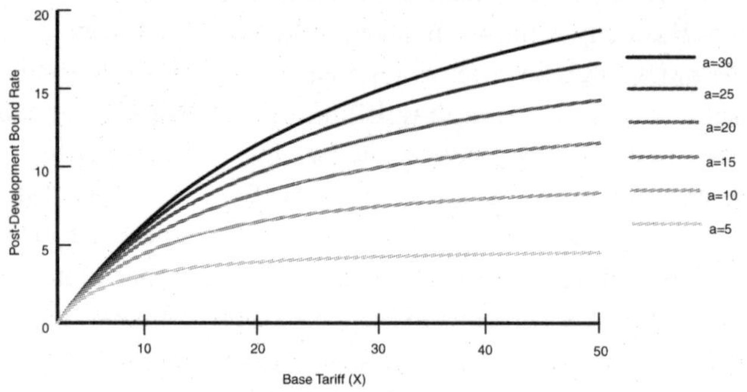

Figure 5.5: NGMA Chairman Draft Formula for Tariff Reduction Proposed Tariff = (B*a*X)/(B*a+X) where B = 0.25, a = average tariff

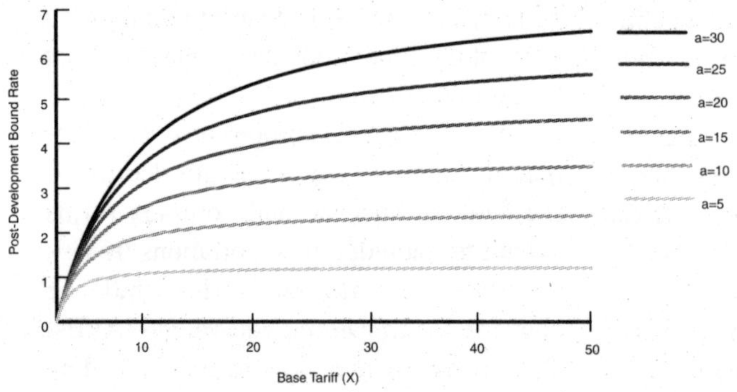

equivalence of specific duties using simple methods. However, it is well known how some of these specific duties are defined and it is very difficult to calculate *ad-valorem* equivalence of these duties.[25] The NGMA-CD proposes that in such case of "Non *ad valorem* tariffs for which AVEs cannot be calculated by the Secretariat because of the technical nature of the duties concerned shall be assumed to have an AVE equivalent to the tariff average (t_a) as used in the formula". India and developing countries should keep a close watch on this, because it has been noticed that the *ad valorem* equivalence of specific duties, indeed, is relatively very high as compared to those commodities whose duties are defined in the form of *ad-valorem* rates.

NGMA-CD is still not clear about coverage of NTBs to be dealt with. It is probably not very clear about how to deal with non-tariff barriers. It is still talking about (i) identification and examination of various types of NTBs, (ii) categorisation, (iii) collection of information and (iv) inter linkage with other bodies of WTO. It says that modalities could include request/offer, horizontal or vertical approaches. Developing countries should ask for clear interpretation of such steps towards NTBs.

The NGMA-CD proposal says that "for developing countries ..." up to 5 per cent of tariff lines may remain unbound provided that they do not exceed 5 per cent of the total value of a member's imports". Both these conditions of 5 per cent tariff lines and 5 per cent import value are very strict. The developing countries should demand either a 5 per cent tariff line or 5 per cent imports value.

A revised version the May 2003 Draft Modalities Paper by chairman, NGMA was issued on 19 August (TN/MA/W/35/Rev/1). In this revision, a number of provisions were changed. For instance, the flexibility offered to developing and least developed countries to keep up to 5 per cent of tariff lines unbound, provided they do not exceed 5 per cent of the total value of imports. This flexibility has been curbed by amending it to 5 per cent of tariff lines provided that no more than 1 per cent could be taken in one HS Chapter. Another change is the exception allowed to countries having binding coverage of less than 35 per cent from the reduction commitment provided they bind 100 per cent of tariff lines at 27.5 per cent or less.

Concluding Remarks

Market Access for non-agriculture products is one of the principal agenda items in the WTO negotiations. The basic mandate in the Doha Declaration under the category 'tariff and trade of industrial products' is both broad and comprehensive. Developing countries should concentrate on reduction in peak tariffs, and tariff escalations. They should also demand that all the countries should define their binding rates in the form of *ad valorem* rates, because it has been noticed that *ad valorem* equivalence of non-*ad valorem* duties are very high.

After the adoption of the Doha Agenda a number of proposals relating to 'modalities' were submitted by member countries to NGMA. The Chairman of NGMA submitted a draft proposal of modalities after a series of formal and informal consultations. The core modality/formula submitted by NGMA-CD does attempt to address: (i) tariff peaks, (ii) tariff escalation, and (iii) *non-ad valorem* duties. However, it also seeks drastic reductions in tariff rates in developing countries. It is not easy for developing countries to completely accept the tariff elimination in seven sectors, even in an extended framework. They should be either made 'zero-for-A", where A is a positive number; or alternatively, the coverage of lines in identified seven sectors should be 75 per cent of lines for developing countries. The thrust could be to grade the product tariff according to the developing countries' capabilities.

Keeping in view the prevailing level of development and their infrastructure in the developing countries, it needs to be appreciated that tariff is an important instrument for making domestic and trade policies. On the domestic front tariff elimination, it may be recalled, will lead to substantial reduction in customs revenue that is the main form of revenue receipt for the developing countries. The developing countries therefore, should be given full advantage of "less than full reciprocity".

Endnotes

1 See for example WTO. 2001. *US Trade Policy Review*, Geneva.

2 See, Mehta. 2001. WTO, Liberalisation and Industrial Sector: The Case of Market Access, *RIS Occasional Paper No. 63*.

3 See, Mehta. 2003. *Indian Industrial Tariffs: Towards, WTO Development Round Negotiations*, RIS.

4 UNCTAD. 1999-2000. The Post-UR Tariff Environment for Developing Countries: Tariff Peaks and Tariff Escalation, TD/B/COM/1/14/Rev/1, 14, September. Mehta (2001), ibid; Mehta (2003), ibid, UNCTAD (2003), Back to Basics: Market Access Issues in the Doha Agenda, UNCTAD/DITC/TAB/Misc.9, and Bacchetta, M. and B. Bora (2003), Industrial Tariff Liberalization and the Doha Development Agenda, *WTO Discussion Paper*.

5 Amount of value per unit of imported commodity.

6 See, for example, UNCTAD, CDROM TRAINS Winter 1998 and Mehta, R. and S.K. Mohanty (2001), *WTO and Industrial Tariff: An Empirical Analysis for India*, Reprint, RIS.

7 See Mehta, Rajesh and Mohanty, S.K. 2001. ibid. UNCTAD, ibid.

8 See Mehta, Rajesh and Mohanty, S.K. 2001. ibid. UNCTAD, ibid.

9 See Mehta, Rajesh and Mohanty, S.K. 2001. ibid.

10 Mehta, Rajesh. 2001. ibid.

11 See, UNCTAD. 1999-2000. ibid and UN, Market Access since UR, Implications, Opportunities and Challenges, Report prepared by UNCTAD and WTO, May 1998.

12 See UNCTAD. 1999-2000. ibid for instance.

13 Mehta and Mohanty. 2001. also prove this point using detailed data of five developed countries.

14 UNCTAD, ibid and Mehta. 2001. ibid in the recent past.

15 A number of proposals have been submitted by different countries. Among these proposals three submissions have been made by India.

16 TN/MA/W/20.

17 TN/MA/W/11/Add.1 and Add.2.

18 TN/MA/W/10/Add.2; suggestions for the treatment of unbound lines are beyond the scope of this document and have therefore not been included.

19 TN/MA/W/15.

20 TN/MA/W/6/Add.1.

21 TN/MA/W/18.

22 For details of Swiss Formula, see Hoda, A. 2001. Tariff Negotiations and Renegotiations under the GATT and the WTO, Procedures and Practices, Cambridge University Press, UK. and Mehta, R (2003), ibid.

23 Uruguay Round led to increases in tariff escalation particularly for products in which developing countries have export potential. See, Mehta and Mohanty (2001) and UNCTAD (1999/2000), among others.

24 WTO. 2003. Negotiations on Agriculture First Draft of Modalities for the Further Commitments, Committee on Agriculture, TN/AG/W/1/Rev.1, 18 March 2003.

25 See for example UNCTAD, TRAINS, Winter 1998; and Mehta and Mohanty (2001).

6

TRIPs, Public Health, Traditional Knowledge and Geographical Indications

Introduction

The international environment with respect to intellectual property has changed considerably with the conclusion of the TRIPs Agreement in the Uruguay Round. The TRIPs Agreement accommodates the demands of the industrialized countries for higher international standards of protection by mandating the extension of patentability to virtually all fields of technology recognized in developed country patent systems, by prolonging the patent protection for a uniform term of twenty years, and by providing legal recognition of the patentee's exclusive rights to import the patented products. The patent rights are enjoyable without discrimination as to the place of invention, the field of technology and whether products are imported or locally produced. All signatories to the Uruguay Round trade negotiations are, therefore, obliged to adhere to the minimum standards prescribed by TRIPs Agreement and to provide product patents for pharmaceuticals and chemicals. The coverage of the patent protection has also been expanded by the provision for patents on micro-organisms and protection of plant varieties either by patents or by an effective *sui generis* system or by any combination thereof.

Besides its wide-ranging adverse effects on the technological capability, balance of payments and economic growth of developing countries,[1] the implementation of TRIPs has raised three sets of negotiating concerns in recent times. Firstly, its impact on prices and availability of essential medicines caught attention from the huge differences between prices of HIV AIDS drugs sold by patent holders in South Africa and their generic substitutes. The controversy led the Doha Ministerial Conference of WTO to adopt a Declaration on TRIPs and Public Health, recognizing the supremacy of public health concerns over IPRs and allowing the members some flexibility.

Secondly, TRIPs Agreement created an anomalous situation where the knowledge created from traditional and communities innovation systems is left free for commercial exploitation without any compensation as against intellectual property resulting from formal innovation systems being protected from unauthorized commercial exploitation. This resulted in private enterprises obtaining patents on the traditional knowledge of particular communities/countries without the prior informed consent of the owners of knowledge. Developing countries which happen to be rich in genetic resources and traditional knowledge, have been seeking a redressal of this asymmetry. In recognition of this concern the Doha Ministerial instructed the Council for TRIPs to examine 'the relationship between the TRIPs Agreement and the convention on Biological Diversity, the protection of traditional knowledge and folklore', among other new developments.

Finally, the provision in the TRIPs Agreement for additional protection of geographical indications (GI) for wines and spirits under Article 23, has also created an anomalous situation as geographical indications for other products are not protected. The EU, Switzerland and India, among many others, have sought the extension of protection of GI for other products. The Doha Ministerial agreed to address the issue of extension of the protection of GI to products other than wines and spirits in the Council for TRIPs as an outstanding Implementation Issue under Para 12 of the Ministerial Declaration.

This Chapter examines these three TRIPs related issues from a developing country perspective. It is then concluded with some remarks for policy at the national and international levels to moderate the adverse effects of TRIPs.

TRIPs and Public Health

The recent controversy concerning the HIV AIDS drugs in South Africa, among other factors, has helped to focus attention of the international community on the possible adverse effects of the implementation of TRIPs Agreement on poorer countries. Over the past couple of years a number of international initiatives have been taken to deal with the matter. These include establishment of the Commission on Macroeconomics and Health by the WHO and Commission on IPRs by the British Government. WHO and WTO organized a Workshop on Differential Pricing and Financing of Essential Drugs at Hosbjor, April 2001. UNDP's *Human Development Report 2001* as well as World Bank's *Global Economic Prospects 2002* reports focused on the IPRs and their impact for developing countries. The Fourth Ministerial Meeting in Doha in November 2001 adopted a Declaration on TRIPs Agreement and Public Health. However, these initiatives are yet to lead to a concrete outcome addressing the many problems that are raised by the TRIPs Agreement.

Effect of TRIPs on Prices and Availability of Medicines

TRIPs Agreement is likely to affect the prices and availability of cheaper medicines in a number of ways, as summarized below:

Prices of Medicines and Loss of Consumer Welfare

A number of studies have examined the effect on prices of medicines after introduction of product patents and have simulated welfare losses for consumers in developing countries. It is widely believed that drug prices will go up upon introduction of product patents as happened in China which introduced them in 1993. Studies on India simulate that the increase in pharmaceutical prices could be either in the range between 26 per cent to 242 per cent with the introduction of product patents on 22 existing pharmaceutical products or in the range between 182 to 225 per cent as the case many be.[2] The increases in drug prices would have immense implications in terms of welfare losses. A study finds the welfare losses to 6 developing countries (Argentina, Brazil, India, Mexico, Korea and Taiwan) from introduction of product patents to be between US$ 3.5 billion to $10.8 billion depending upon the assumptions. The gains to the patent owners from such introduction would range between $ 2.9 billion to $ 14.4 billion. These findings thus suggest that introduction of product patents would affect prices of medicines significantly and unless new drugs are more efficient, there will be a decline in the health levels of population. The recent case of huge differences between prices of HIV AIDS drugs sold by patent holders in South Africa and their generic substitutes just provides a further evidence to the potential of price increases following the introduction of product patents. It may be argued that the vast majority of drugs are out of patent protection and hence will not be affected. Nonetheless the AIDS drugs controversy shows that effective treatment for many of scourges of the day such as cancer, cardiac failures, renal problems, among others, may be affected.

Impact on Global Innovative Activity and Availability of Drugs

One of the arguments in favour of a stronger IPR regime is based on the premise that expenditures on R&D were significantly determined by appropriability conditions. Hence, ensuring adequate appropriability with more stringent IPR protection was deemed to be a necessary condition for sustaining the pace of innovation in the global economy. The empirical literature, however, does not support this presumption as patent protection was found to be instrumental for only a small proportion of innovations. On the other hand, studies show that spillover effects of R&D activity of other firms to be a lot more important in inducing firms to undertake R&D compared to appropriability. The R&D outputs of other firms form valuable inputs for the R&D efforts of firms. Hence, tightening of IPRs is likely to affect innovative activity adversely by obstructing these spillovers.[3] Further, cross-country evidence suggests that substantial amount of technological learning took place under weak IPR regimes and the respective IPR regimes were often strengthened in developed countries as local technological capabilities matured (see Box 6.1).

Therefore, it is by no means clear that strengthening of IPRs will increase innovative activity even in the developed world especially for solving the problems

Box 6.1:
IPRs and the East Asian Miracle

The rapid and sustained growth and development in the East Asian economies, viz. Japan; South Korea, Taiwan, Hong Kong and Singapore (first tier Asian NIEs), Malaysia, Thailand, and Indonesia (second tier NIEs) and China, generally termed as the 'East Asian Miracle', has attracted a large volume of literature. The growth rate of *per capita* income over the 1960-90 for these economies averaged over 5.5 per cent, making it the fastest growing region in the world sustaining such rates of growth over such a long span of time. Japan and Asian NIEs have been able to expand their share in world exports from 8 per cent in 1965 to 13 per cent in 1980 and 18 per cent in 1990, suggesting that their exports have expanded much faster than any other region's. Their share in the world's manufactured exports has grown from 11 to 21 per cent over the same period. In particular rapid transformation of Korea and Taiwan from technologically backward and poor economies into affluent and relatively modern economies by the early 1990s has been truly remarkable. Some analysts have attempted to downplay the East Asian achievement as a result of factor accumulation along the production function. However, since then a number of studies have corroborated that a substantial proportion of East Asian growth was contributed by growth of total factor productivity (TFP) and it was not a result of merely factor accumulation. The total factor productivity growth in Japan, Korea, Taiwan, Hong Kong and Thailand has averaged from 2 to 4 per cent per year over 1960-89 thus contributing over a third of the growth of output!

A large volume of literature has also been concerned with the explanation of the rapid TFP growth in the East Asian countries. It is now widely accepted that the assimilation of foreign technology was a 'critical component of the Asian Miracle'. They provide econometric evidence suggesting that R&D expenditures in Japan, South Korea and Taiwan have contributed to TFP growth.

In particular, the soft intellectual property protection regime adopted by these countries in the period of duplicative imitation or reverse engineering has played an important role in facilitating the firm level technological learning.

The available evidence suggests that the East Asian countries, viz. Japan, Korea and Taiwan have absorbed substantial amount of technological learning under a weak IPR protection regime during the early phases. These patent regimes facilitated the absorption of innovation and knowledge generated abroad by their indigenous firms. They have also encouraged minor adaptations and incremental innovations on the foreign inventions by domestic enterprises and developed a patent culture through utility models and design patents. As local technological capabilities matured and the domestic industry sought stronger protection for guarding their own inventions, the IPR regime was strengthened in Japan in the mid-1970s. In the other two countries, the IPR regime had to be strengthened under US pressure.

Source: ***RIS Discussion Paper #25*****. 2002. "Intellectual Property Rights, Technology and Economic Development: Experiences of Asian Countries" by Nagesh Kumar, RIS, New Delhi.**

and diseases faced by developing countries. Furthermore, the research priorities of MNEs are determined by the purchasing power and very little R&D is currently done on tropical diseases. Unless some steps are taken by the international community, such as those discussed by the recent report of WHO's Commission on Macroeconomics and Health (CMH), the pattern is not likely to change significantly in the future.

Affecting Development of Cost Effective Processes

The provision of product patents on chemical and pharmaceutical products, for instance, would adversely affect the process of innovative activity of the developing country enterprises in the manufacture of chemicals covered by patents. The development of new chemical compounds is generally beyond the capability of most developing country enterprises in view of the huge resources involved. Therefore, they focus attention on process innovations for the known chemicals and bulk drugs. This imitative or reverse engineering activity is an important source of learning in developing countries. It has also led to development of cost-effective processes that have in turn led to reduction in prices of generic drugs in countries like India.

Implementation of the Agreement on TRIPs and Public Health

A 31 December 2002 deadline was proposed for signing of the proposed Agreement on TRIPs and Public Health in the Doha Mandate that recognizes the supremacy of public health over IPRs and grants flexibility to poorer countries, having no domestic capability to produce, from the provisions of TRIPs.

"We recognize that WTO Members with insufficient or no manufacturing capacities in the pharmaceutical sector could face difficulties in making effective use of compulsory licensing under the TRIPs Agreement. We instruct the Council for TRIPs to find an expeditious solution to this problem and to report to the General Council before the end of 2002." (Paragraph 6 of the Doha Declaration on the TRIPs Agreement and Public Health).

Despite long and intense negotiations, Members could not reach consensus on the 'expeditious solution' by the 31 December 2002 deadline. The US opposed the adoption of a draft Decision — put forward by TRIPs Council Chair Ambassador Eduardo Pérez Motta (Mexico) on 16 December 2002 — arguing that the solution should apply only to HIV/AIDS, malaria, tuberculosis and other infectious diseases of comparable gravity. The US resistance to the Agreement has stemmed from the intensive lobbying from its pharma industry (see Box 6.2).

Major bone of contention has been on the disease coverage. The 16 December 2002 draft text refers to paragraph 1 of the TRIPs and Health Declaration, i.e. "public health problems afflicting many developing and least developed countries, especially those resulting from HIV/AIDS, tuberculosis, malaria and other epidemics." The draft also covers active ingredients used in the manufacture of medicines, as well as diagnostic kits needed for their use, as proposed in particular by the African Group.

The US rejected the draft on the grounds that the disease coverage was too broad. In a last-minute attempt to reach a deal, the US had suggested the inclusion of a footnote that would expand its previously proposed list of diseases from three (HIV/AIDS, malaria and tuberculosis) to 23 and "other epidemics of comparable gravity and scale", including those that might arise in the future. Developing countries, however, rejected this proposal, arguing that it would restrict the mandate given by the Doha Declaration, which refers more generally to "measures to protect public health" (para. 4). They also opposed a proposal by the EU that the US could make a statement to the effect of its proposed footnote, which would then be supported by the TRIPs Council Chair as the framework for implementing the solution.

Two extensions of the 31 December 2002 deadline have failed to bridge the gap between the US and other Members. It is now left for the Cancun Ministerial to take a decision on the subject unless a last minute solution is found by the General Council.

Box 6.2: Campaign Funds Help Steer U.S. Stance on Drug Patents

Pharmaceutical companies shelled out more than $50 million to help Republicans win control of Congress last November. Days after the election, when international trade talks threatened their profitable drug patents, the companies sought help from Republicans. And they got it. More than two dozen Republican lawmakers signed letters opposing efforts to dilute the industry's international patent rights in order to make less costly drugs available to patients in poor countries. Sen. Bill Frist of Tennessee, a top election strategist who since has become Senate majority leader, phoned U.S. Trade Representative Robert Zoellick with the same message. Top While House aides phoned Mr. Zoellick's office to express concern as well.

On Dec. 20, the industry celebrated a victory when the U.S., alone among the 144-member WTO, blocked a proposal for distributing patented medicines to less-developed nations. Foreign diplomats and international relief workers say lobbyists' pressure led Mr. Zoellick to backtrack on an earlier U.S. commitment. U.S. trade officials deny that, insisting the administration merely prevented the WTO from expanding the scope of that commitment. But the episode makes one fact of American political life undeniably clear: After spending millions of dollars on campaign help in recent years, the pharma industry has accumulated powerful friends it can turn to in a pinch. Drug-company lobbyists began feeling squeezed in mid-November by unfavourable developments in follow-on negotiations to a 2001 agreement signed by WTO members in Doha, Qatar. The Doha agreement declared that poor countries could override patent protections and permit use of less costly generic copies of drugs to tackle acute health problems.

The Bush administration had believed the patent exception would apply only to epidemics such as AIDS, tuberculosis and malaria, according to a senior trade official. Representatives from other countries pressed the broader view that any "public-health problem" might justify overriding patents. A meeting was scheduled for December in Geneva to resolve the differences. So the drug companies turned to their allies in Washington to help squelch the broader interpretation, which they said would set a dangerous precedent and erode the value of their patents world-wide. Their lobbyists asked lawmakers to contact Mr. Zoellick's office, even suggesting specific language delineating the diseases and countries that would be affected.

As it happened, those were precisely the words that appeared in individual and group letters that 34 lawmakers signed and sent to Mr. Zoellick. One signatory was Republican Rep. Nancy Johnson of Connecticut, who survived a pivotal House race last November with help from more than $204,817 of drug-industry spending, according to the Center for Responsive Politics.

Mr. Zoellick, whose boss in the White house espouses a "compassionate conservative" approach to governing, moved to counter international critics by announcing a temporary moratorium on enforcing drug patents for poor nations facing epidemics. Separately, the president himself announced a $10 billion initiative to combat AIDS world-wide in his State of the Union Address last month.

But critics insist the patent-enforcement moratorium is a smoke screen for the administration's failure to agree to a long-term solution on the issue. "The U.S. is backtracking," says Faizel Ismail, who heads the South African delegation to the WTO. Nor has the AIDS funding quelled criticism of Mr. Zoellick by international health activists.

"Doha was not just about AIDS, but about access for the poor to a range of life-saving medicines in the future," says James Love, who monitors WTO talks for the Consumer Project on Technology.

Change of Heart

How the U.S. became wary of the Doha agreement:

November 2001: U.S. Trade Representative Robert Zoellick signs Doha agreement allowing countries to override drug patents to address health crises, such as AIDS and tuberculosis.

Summer 2002: In discussions over final language for the agreement, Mr. Zoellick learns many countries want to use Doha provisions to treat non-epidemics, "maybe even to provide Viagra" at low cost.

November: Nervous about the broader interpretation, U.S. drug companies begin lobbying the White House and Congress to oppose Doha if it isn't limited to specific epidemics.

Late November-early December: Top White House aides and Sen. Bill first call Mr. Zoellick, urging him to protect patents in a narrowly targeted Doha deal. Mr. Zoellick receives letters from two dozen drug-company CEOs and 36 members of Congress.

December 20: Mr. Zoellick becomes the only representative among 144 WTO nations to oppose the final Doha agreement. Instead, he proposes a temporary moratorium on patent enforcement for countries facing certain epidemics.

Source: *The Wall Street Journal*, February 7, 2003.

Biodiversity and Traditional Knowledge

The Doha Ministerial Declaration emphasized the importance of traditional knowledge (TK). It instructed the Council for Trade-Related Aspects of Intellectual Property Rights (TRIPS) "to examine, *inter alia*, the relationship between the TRIPS Agreement and the Convention on Biological Diversity, the protection of traditional knowledge and folklore, and other relevant new developments raised by Members pursuant to Article 71.1." (para. 19).

In the TRIPS Agreement, there is nothing that specifically prevents countries from developing systems to protect TK at the national level. However, the concerns about TK cover a wide range of issues (see Box 6.3). Developing countries have made a number of proposals to incorporate provisions related to the protection of TK and avoidance of misappropriation in the TRIPS Agreement. These relate to Articles 27.3(b), 29 and 71.1. These proposals include the following:

- To incorporate provisions in the TRIPS Agreement indicating that the State exercises sovereignty and inalienable rights over the biological resources within its national territory (*Cuba, the Dominican Republic, Honduras and Nicaragua).*[4]
- To make it obligatory in all patent applications for biotechnological innovations, to include the country of origin of the germplasm; to make it obligatory to indicate whether prior informed consent was obtained for the biological genetic resource or traditional knowledge so as to facilitate benefit-sharing arrangements (*India*).[5]
- To seek to harmonize Article 27.3(b) with the CBD and the International Undertaking, *inter alia* by allowing developing countries to implement sui generis law that can provide for the protection of the innovations of indigenous and local farming communities in developing countries (*African Group*).[6]
- To establish, on a mandatory basis, within the TRIPS Agreement, a system for the protection of intellectual property, with an ethical and economic content, applicable to the traditional knowledge of local and indigenous communities, together with recognition of the need to define the rights of collective holders (*Venezuela*).[7]

Traditional knowledge is essential to the food security and health of millions of people in the developing world. In many countries, traditional medicines provide the only affordable treatment available to poor people. Moreover, in developing countries, up to 80 per cent of the population depend on traditional medicines to help meet their healthcare needs.[8] However, it is only recently that the international community has started giving recognition to traditional knowledge. However, universally acceptable solutions for the protection and promotion of traditional knowledge have not yet emerged. In last couple of years, large number of disputes pertaining to traditional knowledge. As a result, the issue of traditional knowledge has been brought to the fore of the general debate surrounding intellectual property. These cases involve what is often referred to as "biopiracy". The examples of cases like turmeric and neem illustrate the issues that can arise when patent protection is granted to inventions relating to traditional knowledge which is already in the public domain. In these cases, invalid patents were issued because the patent examiners were not aware of the relevant traditional knowledge.

Owing to the result of these well known cases, many developing countries, holders of traditional knowledge, and campaigning organisations are pressing for better protection of traditional knowledge. Such pressure has led, for example, to the creation of an Intergovernmental Committee on Intellectual Property and Genetic Resources, Traditional Knowledge and Folklore in WIPO. The protection of traditional knowledge and folklore is also being discussed within the framework of the CBD and in other international organisations such as UNCTAD, WHO, FAO and UNESCO.[9] In addition, the Doha WTO Ministerial Declaration highlighted the need for further work in the TRIPS Council on protecting traditional knowledge.[10]

Box 6.3: Urgency to Conserve Protection of Traditional Knowledge

An International Seminar was convened with the participation of representatives from Brazil, Cambodia, Chile, China, Colombia, Cuba, Egypt, Kenya, Peru, the Philippines, Sri Lanka, Thailand, Venezuela and India at New Delhi from 3-5 April 2002. The Seminar was sponsored by India and UNCTAD, where, apart from national delegations, a number of international experts and inter-governmental organizations expressed their views. The range of issues covered included the commercialization of TK, exchange of national experiences of systems for protection of TK, including *sui generis* systems, and the international dimension of protection of TK.

Recognizing the serious and irreversible loss to bio-diversity at the global level, participants expressed a need for creating and strengthening systems for protecting biodiversity and its associated traditional knowledge (TK), innovations and practices. In this context, participants expressed the need for understanding the viability of various instruments including national *sui generis* systems of protection and their recognition at the international level. This issue has been the subject of debate in various inter-governmental forums including WTO, WIPO, CBD, UNCTAD and FAO. A number of countries expressed strong views on the need for identifying new means for protecting TK in the light of increasing globalization and its impact on local and indigenous communities. Participants expressed a strong view that apart from existing IPRs, suitable systems based on national experiences through customary laws and other means need to be fully explored.

Participants noted that traditional and local communities historically developed customary and other forms of protection over TK, which enabled its preservation and growth. Loss of biodiversity and its associated TK is in part due to increasing globalization. It is in part also due to misappropriation of TK *inter alia* through improper granting of patents and lack of rewards to TK holders in the patent system. These were discussed as some of the issues which need urgent redressal. To offset such impacts of globalization, *sui generis* systems have been developed at the national level to protect TK and reward TK holders. While these do provide the means for protection and growth of TK within national jurisdictions, the participants felt that national systems by themselves would not be adequate to fully protect and preserve TK. For example, the ability of patent offices in a national jurisdiction to prevent bio-piracy as well as to install informed consent mechanisms to ensure reward to TK holders, does not *ipso facto* lead to similar action on the patent application in other countries. A need was therefore expressed for an international framework for protecting TK. In this connection it was felt that the existing forms of IPR protection regimes may not sufficiently recognize the rights of TK holders. Similarly, benefit-sharing mechanisms installed through national legislation would need to be recognized in user countries.

Commercialization of TK based products and services, where appropriate, should be promoted with an emphasis on equitable benefit-sharing with local and indigenous communities and with their prior informed consent. Particular attention should be paid to the sustainable use and management of biological resources in the process. The participants expressed a view that the transfer, utilization and commercialization of TK should take place through fair and equitable terms and conditions, for which a set of guidelines should be developed with the help of relevant international intergovernmental organizations. Where commercialization of TK derived products takes place outside the country of origin, there is a need to establish mechanisms for ensuring equitable benefit sharing.

Discussions then focused on the process of identifying essential components of a framework for international recognition of various *sui generis* systems, customary law and others for protection of TK. Some of the possible components identified include (i) local protection to the rights of TK holders through national level *sui generis* regimes including customary laws as well as others and its effective enforcement *inter alia* through systems such as positive comity of protection systems for TK (ii) protection of traditional knowledge through registers of TK databases in order to avoid misappropriation (iii) a procedure whereby the use of TK from one country is allowed, particularly for seeking IPR protection or commercialization, only after the competent national authority of the country of origin gives a certificate that source of origin is disclosed and prior informed consent, including acceptance of benefit sharing conditions, obtained (iv) an internationally agreed instrument that recognizes such national level protection. This would not only prevent misappropriation but also ensure that national level benefit sharing mechanisms and laws are respected worldwide.

The participants recommended that countries would work together in various intergovernmental forums particularly CBD, FAO, WIPO, WTO and UNCTAD to develop an international framework for the recognition of national systems of protection of traditional knowledge, including diverse *sui generis* systems. This was found to be particularly relevant and urgent in the context of the ongoing work programme pursuant to the Doha Ministerial Declaration. Further work should also be undertaken by intergovernmental organizations including UNCTAD on protection and commercialization of TK with a view to promoting its sustainable use.

Source: **Report of the International Seminar on "Protection and Commercialization of Traditional Knowledge", New Delhi, 3-5 April, 2002. UNCTAD and Government of India.**

Developed countries do not, in general, contest the right of countries to protect TK. They generally hold the view that the TRIPS Agreement and the CBD are mutually supportive and object to the idea of disclosure requirement of genetic resources in the process of patent applications. Some developed countries such as USA, EU, Japan and Norway have said that the discussion in the TRIPS Council should wait for the results of work being done in the various international forums, such as WIPO. In contrast, some developing countries such as Brazil and India have underlined the need to explore *sui generis* systems for the protection of TK. The Commission on IPRs set up by the British Government has also endorsed the need for protection of TK and genetic resources of developing countries with electronic libraries and endorsed the requirement of prior informed consent and sharing the benefits of commercial exploitation.[11]

Geographical Indications

The provisions of the TRIPs Agreement covering geographical indications have attracted a considerable debate in the TRIPs Council. The additional protection has remained confined to wine and spirits. The EU, Switzerland and India among other countries have been highly critical of this approach because of its adverse trade implications. The issue was raised at the Doha Ministerial Conference. The Conference took note of these concerns. Accordingly, the Doha Ministerial Declaration refers to the issues related to the extension of protection of geographical indications provided for in Article 23, to products other than wines and spirits (paragraph 18). This is now to be addressed in the Council for TRIPs as an outstanding implementation issue.[12]

GIs and Developing Countries Proposals

The developing countries have submitted two major proposals at WTO on IPR issues where geographical indications have also been covered. Some of the recent patents at the US have triggered an intensive debate on linkages between IPR regime, traditional knowledge, and benefit sharing. Some of the patents are even based on GIs from developing countries; for instance, patents on basmati rice from India and jasmine rice from Thailand. After a patent on Basmati rice lines and grains granted by the USPTO to M/s. Rice Tec Inc. USA on September 2nd, 1997, India contested this patent. In a long litigation of almost five years, ultimately the title of the patent was changed in the year 2002. In order to avoid such situation, India has now set up a Basmati Development Fund, a watch agency to keep a worldwide watch for new trademark applications for Basmati Rice or its deceptive variations. The watch agency has identified a number of attempted registrations of which 15 have been successfully challenged and concluded in India's favour. They were largely in UK, Australia, France, Spain, Chile, UAE, etc. The remaining cases are being pursued by Agricultural and Processed Foods Export Development Authority (APEDA).

The Doha Ministerial Declaration had suggested considering extra protection, which WTO members already apply to wines and spirits, to other traditional high quality products that just deserve such recognition. The product list could include goods such as Indian saris, oriental carpets, specialty teas such as Darjeeling (India), Jasmine rice (Thailand), cheeses such as Parmigiano Reggiano (Italy), Jamon de Huelva (Spanish ham), art paper (China), porcelain from Limoges (France).

The discussion on GI extension has taken up a significant part of the regular TRIPs Council sessions. Switzerland on behalf of 20 developing, developed and transition economy countries, has proposed that the additional protection should apply to all GIs and that the multilateral register to be established should include GIs for all products.[13] These countries believe GIs can be used to promote the export of valuable products and prevent misappropriation. They also consider it a matter of fairness that such additional protection not be limited to alcoholic beverages. Those who oppose additional protection are mainly from the Americas plus Australia and New Zealand, all of which are bulk exporters of agricultural products.

As a result of the deep divergences in view points among Members on whether to begin negotiations on GI extensions, the TRIPs Council did not submit a report to the Trade Negotiation Community (TNC) on 'appropriate action' as mandated under paragraph 12. The deadlock is unlikely to be broken in the TRIPs Council. Several countries, including the EU, Switzerland and Bulgaria, have explicitly linked the GI discussions to the agriculture negotiations in both the TRIPs Council and the Committee on Agriculture.

Concluding Remarks and Policy Imperatives

The above discussion has summarised some the concerns that TRIPs Agreement has raised for developing countries. The challenge for development posed by TRIPs before developing countries has to be responded at national and international levels. In what follows we outline an inventory of these challenges for the national and international policy action.[14]

Policy Responses to be taken at the National Level

Incorporating the Provisions of Compulsory Licensing in the IPR Legislation

Developing countries should build adequate provisions for compulsory licensing in their IPR legislation in order to safeguard them from possible abuses of monopoly power obtained by patent owners. The compulsory licenses are permitted under Article 31 of the TRIPs Agreement. The Agreement does not limit the grounds upon which compulsory licenses may be granted and only sets forth the conditions to be applied in the case of granting. This includes specification of grounds of compulsory licensing and reasonable rates of licensing fees. Recent withdrawal of proceedings by the US against Brazil's compulsory licensing provisions show that intelligently crafted domestic patent laws can meet national objectives and yet be TRIPs compatible.

Incorporating the Research Exception

Developing countries could incorporate provisions allowing researchers to use a patented invention for research, in order to understand the invention more fully. Experimentation on a patented invention is clearly admissible as an exception to exclusive rights under Article 30.

Early Working Exception or 'Bolar' Provision

It is possible to make provision for allowing manufacturers of generic drugs to use the patented invention to obtain marketing approval without patent owner's permission and before the expiration of patent. This facilitates the generic manufacturers to market their products as soon as the patent expires. This provision is sometimes called the regulatory exception or Bolar provision under Article 8. The US, Canada, Australia, Israel and Argentina have adopted Bolar exception in their patent legislation.

Resisting the Attempts to Evolve TRIPs Plus Regime and Ever-greening of Patents

Developed countries are constantly putting pressure on developing countries to implement stricter patent legislation than required under TRIPs, exclude compulsory licensing, parallel imports provisions and include provisions that would result in increasing the life of the patent (ever-greening), as well as grant data exclusivity to them. The TRIPs Agreement, however, is clear that a new use for an old formulation does not constitute an inventive step (Art. 27(1)). Therefore, member countries are within their rights not to permit the practice of ever-greening of patents.

Allowing Parallel Imports or Grey-Market Imports

Since the 'exhaustion of rights' issue cannot be raised in the dispute settlement under the TRIPs Agreement, developing countries should allow parallel imports or grey-market imports. The experience of several countries suggests that substantial costs savings could result from such imports because of differential pricing strategy practised by MNEs depending upon the extent of competition in different markets.

Price Controls for Essential Drugs

To protect the poor masses from price increases following the introduction of product patents, governments may impose regulation of prices of essential drugs. To keep the price controls effective, transparent formula for evolving them could be made providing for a reasonable mark-up over the cost. Indian experience shows that price controls have proved to be effective means of keeping prices of life saving essential drugs under check. However, given the possibility of transfer pricing manipulation, there may be complications in administering price controls for imported drugs.

Competition Policy

The patent system grants temporary monopolies to the firms that introduce innovations. National competition or antitrust policies are needed to prevent the build up of excessive monopoly power of certain enterprises and to deal with possible abuse of monopoly power emanating from patent protection. The TRIPs Agreement (Articles 8 and 40, Section 8) explicitly provides for appropriate measures to prevent the abuse of IPRs or the resort to anti-competitive practices. Apparently in the US, 'compulsory licensing has been specified as a remedy in more than 100 anti-trust cases making available some 40,000 to 50,000 patents at reasonable or no royalties'.

Establish National sui generis *Systems for Protection of Traditional Knowledge*

Developing countries should take steps to establish *sui generis* systems for protection of traditional knowledge that protect the rights of knowledge holders. Steps should also be taken to set up TK databases or digital libraries in order to avoid misappropriation. They should also work with international community to evolve an international framework for protecting TK, as proposed later.

Incorporating Breeders Exceptions and Farmers Exceptions in sui generis *Plant Variety Protection*

TRIPs Agreement allows flexibility to member countries to exclude plant varieties from the scope of patent protection and instead opt for an effective *sui generis* system. In order to minimize the adverse effect on plant breeding programmes and protecting small and marginal farmers from buying seeds to save them for the next crop, developing countries could build provisions for exceptions for farmers and plant breeders. They should also participate effectively in the mandated Reviews of the Agreement under Article 27.3(b) to protect their interests.

Introduce Utility Models and Industrial Design Patents

The experience of several East Asian countries suggests that utility patents and industrial design patents could be effective means of encouraging domestic enterprises to undertake minor adaptive innovations and foster a innovation based rivalry among them. In any case, few developing country based enterprises will be able to generate inventions that can be patented in different countries. Utility models and industrial designs may encourage developing country enterprises, especially small and medium enterprises, to undertake minor incremental adaptations and innovations. The cumulative impact of these minor or incremental innovations on growth and total factor productivity improvement could be substantial. Besides Japan, Korea and Taiwan, they have been fruitfully employed by many countries. In Brazil, utility models helped domestic producers gain a significant share of the farm machinery market by encouraging adaptation of foreign technologies to local conditions. Developing countries could consider to introduce utility models and industrial design patents, tailored appropriately to their requirements.

Issues for Multilateral Negotiations

In what follows we summarize a few avenues for possible international cooperation action.

An International Framework for Protection of Traditional Knowledge

The protection of TK at national levels will not be complete until there is an international framework for use of TK outside the country of origin. The framework should establish a procedure that requires patent or other IPR applications to disclose the source or origin of TK or genetic resource used and enclose a certificate from a competent authority in the source country of prior informed consent and benefit sharing conditions. This would require an amendment in TRIPs Agreement.

Delivering the Doha Promise on Public Health

The developed countries, particularly the US, should accept the draft Agreement on TRIPs and Public Health of 16 December 2002. This would be of great symbolic value for developing and least developed countries who are feeling let down on the commitment made at Doha Ministerial.

Extending the GI Coverage to Other Products

Steps should be taken to expeditiously implement the extension of scope of protection of GIs beyond wines and spirits, which is an outstanding implementation issue from the Doha Ministerial.

Moratorium on Further Strengthening of IPR Regime

There is a tendency in some developed countries to treat the provisions of TRIPs as the minimum standards and are constantly attempting to evolve stronger norms through unilateral or bilateral approaches. A consensus needs to be built on the need to put a moratorium on such approaches for the next couple of decades or so.

Granting Flexibility to Developing Countries in Implementing the Provisions of TRIPs

Most of the adverse effects concerning TRIPs on poor countries arise not because of IPR regimes *per se* but from the attempt to harmonize them across countries at different levels of development. There is also a discussion whether TRIPs should fundamentally belong to WTO. However, the least that could be done is allowing flexibility to developing countries to implement the provisions of the Agreement as and when their level of development has reached a certain stage. This could be achieved if a consensus among developed countries is built on the differential need of developing countries for IPR regime.

Apart from this, a possible revision of TRIPs could incorporate a provision that grants developing countries the flexibility to implement the TRIPs obligations until they reach a certain level of development defined in terms of some objective criteria such as per capita income. One possibility in this respect is to adopt a threshold of US$ 1000 of per capita income as the Agreement on Subsidies and Countervailing Measures (SCM) adopted, as it would be easier to agree to, having been adopted in one of the WTO's Agreements. This would bring in an element of graduation in the treatment of countries as the preferential treatment would cease as they cross the developmental threshold. Another possibility could be to shorten the term of product patents applicable to low income countries. This way the Agreement would have incorporated development dimension.

Incorporating Specific Provisions for Transfer ofTechnology

Although transfer and dissemination of technology is an explicit objective of the TRIPs Agreement (Article 7), and provides for appropriate measures to prevent practices that adversely affect international transfer of technology (Article 8), the Agreement leaves the provisions for transfer of technology quite vague. The access to technology is increasingly becoming difficult for developing countries, as observed earlier. There is need for defining conditions, norms and practices for facilitating transfers of technology for production of essential drugs and other critical inputs. A review of the Agreement could address the important issue of transfer of technology and conditions under which technologically less advanced countries could seek transfer of technology from patent owners.

International Funding of R&D Activity in Low-Income Countries

One of the ways of compensating low income countries for the adverse effects of strengthened IPR regime is to provide increased technical assistance and R&D funding to local enterprises to help them build local capabilities. One possibility in this respect could be that governments of developed countries donate a sum equal to (or a substantial proportion of) technology license fees collected from low-income countries to a fund created in the respective countries to assist inventive activities of domestic enterprises. This provision will neutralize the adverse balance of payment effects of the additional income transfers resulting from strengthening of the IPR regime. In addition it will moderate the adverse effect on the local technological activity of domestic enterprises by providing additional financing for undertaking such activity.

Furthermore, there is need to address the issue of funding R&D on special problems and tropical diseases that concern low-income countries. It has been widely acknowledged that the global pharmaceutical industry has neglected research on tropical diseases. The CMH has recommended a donor commitment of $ 27 billion per annum for the health needs of low-income countries including $ 3 billion per annum for R&D for diseases of the poor. It is arguable that this funding of $ 3 billion could also help to moderate some adverse effects on the inventive activity in low-income countries if it is awarded to institutions and enterprises based in these countries. Therefore, an additional recommendation could be made in conjunction with those of CMH that the funds be allocated to eligible and competent institutions and companies of low income countries.

Endnotes

1. See for more details *RIS Discussion Paper #25,* "Intellectual Property Rights, Technology and Economic Development: Experiences of Asian Countries" by Nagesh Kumar, 2002, New Delhi.
2. See studies by May 2000, Lanjouw 1998, Scherer and Watal 2001, Panagariya 1999, Nogues (1993) Watal (2000), Subramanian (1994), Fink (2000) as summarized in RIS Discussion Paper #25, op. cit.
3. See for more details a review of empirical literature in RIS *Discussion Paper #25*, op. cit.
4. WTO document IP/C/W/166 of 5 November 1999 submitted by Cuba, the Dominican Republic, Honduras and Nicaragua
5. WTO document IP/C/W/198 of 14 July 2000 submitted by India on the "Protection of biodiversity and traditional knowledge"
6. WTO document IP/C/W/206 of 20 September 2000 submitted by the African Group
7. WTO documents WT/GC/W/282 of 6 July 1999 submitted by Venezuela
8. WHO. 2002. *Fact Sheet* No. 271, June 2002.
9. UNCTAD. 2002. "The State of the Debate on TK ", Background note prepared by the UNCTAD secretariat for the International Seminar on Systems for the Protection and Commercialisation of Traditional Knowledge, in particular traditional medicines, 3-5 April 2002, New Delhi
10. WTO. 2001. Paragraph 19 of Doha WTO Ministerial Declaration (WTO Document No. WT/MIN(01)/DEC/1) adopted on 14 November 2001
11. This section draws upon *RIS Discussion Paper #25* op. cit.
12. This section is based a *RIS Discussion Paper #35 India, the European Union and Geographical Indications (GI): Convergence of Interests and Challenges Ahead* by Sachin Chaturvedi, and *RIS Policy Brief #7* "Cancun Agenda: Geographical Indications and Developing Countries", July, RIS, New Delhi.
13. (IP/C/W/353)
14. This section draws upon *RIS Discussion Paper #25* op. cit.

7

Environmental Requirements and Market Access for Developing Countries: Implementation Related Concerns

Introduction

As the liberalization of tariff and quantitative restrictions on trade in agricultural, food and other products has progressed, there has been an increased concern in the developing countries about the impact of technical measures on the exports of these products. In this regard, one important concern of the South is the stringent environmental standards imposed by the North. Technical standards such as food safety regulations, labelling requirements and quality and compositional standards have proliferated. Though empirical evidence on this, in the literature, is limited, some developing countries have experienced losses in exports because of difficulties in complying with certain sanitary and phyto-sanitary (SPS) measures in the import markets. These requirements are termed as environment related trade barriers (ETBs).

ETBs generally cover all barriers that have been introduced by the importing country to protect the environment, as well as the health and safety of wildlife, plants, animals and humans. The developing countries have had to adjust their production processes in response to changing environmental regulations in the developed countries. Measures such as pesticide residue levels (MRL) permitted in foodstuffs, emission standards for machines, and packaging requirements have exerted pressure on the exporters. It is now widely believed that these technical measures impede trade of the developing countries, either implicitly or explicitly.

The WTO Agreement on SPS (Sanitary and Phytosanitary Measures) aims to ensure that these standards and regulations are not used for protectionist purposes thereby adversely impacting on trade. However, is considerable discretion available to importing countries to impose their own rules regarding these standards and other regulations such as inspection of imported products, specific treatment or processing of products, fixing of minimum allowable levels of pesticide residue, labelling and packaging requirements, good manufacturing practices, etc.

The Doha Ministerial Declaration while recognizing the rights of countries to take measures for the protection of human, animal or plant life or health, has argued against their application 'in a manner which would constitute a means of arbitrary or unjustifiable discrimination between countries where the same conditions prevail, or a disguised restriction on international trade' (Para 6). In addition, the Ministerial Conference in its Decisions on Implementation-related Issues and

Concerns adopted at Doha under Para 12 of the Declaration, included six points concerning SPS Agreement.

This chapter examines the concerns raised by the SPS Agreement for developing countries and the implementation related issues. It is concluded with some policy remarks.

Impact on Trade of Developing Countries

As observed earlier SPS Agreement allows importing countries to impose SPS norms that are higher than international standards, provided there is a scientific basis. This flexibility has been exploited by various countries to restrict market access of specific countries (Box 7.1).

A case in point is unmanufactured tobacco where Japan insists on a DDT residue level of 0.4 particles per million (PPM) Even though while the international standard is 6 PPM. Indian tobacco has a DDT residue level of 1-2 PPM which is well below the internationally permissible levels, Japan does not allow tobacco imports from India on phytosanitary grounds.

Very minute risk assessments are often used to justify imposition of these higher standards. For instance, adoption of a new aflatoxin standard in the European Union that would reduce health risk by approximately 1.4 deaths per billion a year. While there are not a billion people in the whole of EU, African exports of cereals, dried fruits and nuts to EU are expected to decline by 64 per cent as a result of adoption of these standard with an estimated loss of export earnings of the order of US$ 670 million. Even though international standards such as Codex are evolved by developed countries, they themselves do not adopt them.

Another problem is the wide variation in the standards adopted by different importing countries. Different countries follow different norms of aflatoxins and pesticide residue increasing the compliance cost for the exporting countries. The European Union countries have gone as far as to adopt a single currency. However, their standards with respect to pesticide residue vary widely, for instance, from 0.01 PPM in the case of the UK to 0.03 in the

Box 7.1: Emerging Non-Tariff Barriers and Multiplicity of Standards

Discussions with exporters provided a glimpse of the various hurdles they face. A case in point is the experience of an Indian company exporting seedless grapes, to a large chain of departmental stores in Europe. Before exporting this company had to fill an elaborate questionnaire, which covered issues like the status of their employees, facilities available to them, and the working conditions. Thus, exporters are supposed to meet certain social standards before they could start exporting what the importing company is calling as, '*Socially Responsible Trading*'. This department chain has actually come out with a code for its exporters which covers apart from social issues, building health centres and getting new sets of imported instruments for fire extinguishing and evacuation belts, etc. The RIS survey shows that the production cost would go up by 35 to 40 per cent because of compliance with this code.

Apart from this, grape exporters have to meet the various standards prescribed by *Eurepgap*, which would become mandatory by July 2003. The *Eurepgap* certification itself requires exporters to meet a number of conditions, in case of training, planning and preparations, pesticide record keeping, disposal and post harvest preparation. The European countries levy an import duty of additional 12.5 pre cent on Indian grapes, whereas a number of African countries are not levied any duty.

One of the major challenges Indian exporters are facing relates to multiplicity of products and other standards. Though international efforts have been made to harmonise standards across the board but lot has yet to be achieved. Recently, Italy and Germany have detained Indian spice consignments on the ground of pesticide residue. Both the above countries failed to convince Indian exporters on the changes they made on their existing regulations on microbial contaminations and contamination due to p esticide residue. This is a blatant denial of facilities offered under Article 7 of the SPs regulations and is causing not only difficulties for India in its regular exports but also leading to loss of opportunities elsewhere.

The efforts of European Spice Association (ESA) to lay down uniform standards and code of practices in collaboration with the spice trade associations of individual European countries are yet to find wider acceptance at EC levels. Until a common European regulation and code of practice is established, traders have to follow regulation of individual countries

Source: **Based on Primary Survey of Industries conducted by RIS (2001-02) and Kittu (2001)[1]**

Netherlands to 0.10 PPM in Germany for Aldrin and Dieldrin.

A broader indication of impact of SPS requirements on South Asian exports of agricultural and food products is provided by data on rejections of exports from this region. At present such data are available only for the United States. Table 7.1 shows that, over the period August 2000 to July 2001, there were significant rejections of imports from South Asia owing to microbiological contamination and filth. More than 40 per cent of rejections of exports from India were due to this reason. Food and Drug Administration of the US rejected about 36 per cent of Bangladesh's exports because of microbiological contamination. This shows the considerable problems that South Asian countries have in meeting basic food hygiene requirements. The table also shows that these countries also have a problem meeting the stringent labelling requirements of the United States. More than 15 per cent of total agricultural imports from India and Sri Lanka were rejected because of their failure to meet these requirements. Other than that inadequate food additives, presence of pesticide residues and heavy metals and low acid canned foods are commonly cited reasons for contravention. Out of 18 import detentions of Sri Lanka, 9 detentions are because of low acid content in canned food. More sophisticated monitoring and testing facilities, and therefore more costly procedures, are required for meeting these regulations. On top of that, the cost of rejection at the border can be considerable, as it includes loss of product value, transport and other export costs and product re-export or destruction.

Many of these environment related standards are imposed in a less than transparent manner and sometimes are accompanied by other requirements such as Good Manufacturing Practice. There are cases of detention of consignments of Indian spices in Spain, Italy and Germany without any satisfactory explanation forthcoming on the changes made in their regulations on microbial contamination and pesticide residue, despite transparency

Table 7.1: Number of Contraventions cited for US Food and Drug Administration import detention from South Asia, August 2000-July2001

Reasons for contravention	India	Pakistan	Sri Lanka	Bangladesh	Nepal
Food Additives	159 (7.4)	12 (1.3)		1 (3.0)	
Pesticide Residues	41 (1.9)				
Heavy Metals	13 (0.6)	4 (0.4)			
Mould	9 (0.4)				
Microbiological contamination	329 (15.3)	49 (5.5)		12 (36.4)	
Decomposition	7 (0.3)				
Filth	568 (26.4)	12 (1.3)	2 (11.1)	12 (36.4)	
Low acid canned foods	87 (4.1)	25 (2.8)	9 (50.0)	3 (9.1)	
Labelling	338 (15.7)	50 (5.6)	3 (16.7)	1 (3.0)	
Others	597 (27.8)	744 (83.0)	4 (22.2)	4 (12.1)	1
Total	2148	896	18	33	1

Note: Parenthesis gives the percentage share.
Source: US Food and Drug Administration Import Detention Report, 2001.

obligation under Article 7 of the SPS Agreement.

Sometimes additional standards are just imposed informally by the importing countries on their exporters as pre-conditions for doing business. Often importers use these standards to depress prices of imports. For instance, foreign buyers reportedly paid lower prices for leather products from Bangladesh because of the poor environmental conditions in the tanning sector in Dhaka. The experience of India in the case of export of flowers to Japan is also similar.

Another important issue is that the cost of compliance is substantial and often beyond the competence of many of the developing country enterprises especially the smaller ones. A rough estimate for setting up a moderate lab for testing and analysing samples of spices comes to about US $ 100,000. Furthermore, in a number of cases the technology for compliance with the standards may not be available easily in developing countries.

Many developing countries have experienced losses in exports because of difficulties in complying with these emerging standards and regulations. South Asian countries, in particular, are affected badly as some major items of their export interest such as textiles, marine products, spices, among others, are affected by these barriers. There is an urgent need to respond to this challenge. Besides the policy responses at the national level, actions at the international and at the regional levels would often be necessary for mitigating the adverse effect of these emerging trade barriers on developing countries.

Outstanding Implementation Concerns

The implementation issues, as is commonly referred to in the WTO literature, are those negotiated obligations agreed upon as part of Uruguay Round Agreements but have created imbalances in reaping meaningful and lasting benefits of multilateral trade by the developing countries. Needless to say, these imbalances are rooted in the lack of implementation of many commitments and obligations, in large measures, on the part of developed countries. Realizing primacy of these difficulties being faced by the developing countries, the Doha Ministerial frontally addressed a series of such outstanding implementation issues for speedy resolution.[2]

The work programme mandate under Para 12 of the Doha Declaration on "Implementation-related issues and concerns", in fact, laid out the detailed six point action plan for implementation of SPS measures. The implementation points are:

(1) Longer time-frame for developing countries to comply with other countries' new SPS measures.

(2) "Reasonable interval" between publications of a country's new SPS measure and its entry into force.

(3) Equivalence (Article 4) – Steps to make it easier.

(4) Review of SPS Agreement.

(5) Developing countries' participation in setting international SPS standards – special emphasis to least developed countries.

(6) Financial and Technical assistance focussed on least-developed countries.

All of these six issues were expected to be implemented immediately under the two-track solution as elaborated in Para 12 (a) and (b). However, a close look at these issues does indicate their procedural nature. For instance, it is claimed that Point Nos. (1), (2) and (4) have been implemented immediately under track-I. The stipulation in this resolution, i.e., Track-I, specify the process in principle (Para 12(a)). Accordingly, such outstanding items should be addressed in the relevant negotiating body established by the Trade Negotiations Committee (TNC). Point No. (3), as we shall see below, much to the consternation of the developing countries, has got entangled into procedural as well as substantive maze. On the other hand, Point Nos. (5) and (6) appear to be the common theme in many other Doha mandated issues and are constrained by the budgetary considerations as well as available capacities in countries and international organizations.[3] These issues though reported resolved, many glitches still remain at the procedural level and the developing countries undoubtedly appear at the receiving end. In the following section these concerns have been taken up for a detailed analysis.

What is Implemented?

For clarification, it needs to be recalled that the first two points pertain to the transparency clause (Article 7 and Annex B) of the SPS agreement. It is an obligation of WTO member countries to *publish* all sanitary and phytosanitary measures and *notify* changes in SPS measures. The development challenge indeed appears to be the ambitions expressed in standards escalation and standards divide. But the linking mechanism to these challenges is through the time period allowed to the developing countries for implementation.

(a) Time-frame and Reasonable Interval

The implementation decision as referred above on the longer time frame for developing countries is six months and the decision on 'reasonable interval' between publication and entry into force is six months. Both these time periods require to be benchmarked with SPS related notifications issued after the Doha Declaration came into force, say January 2002.

The available information does not provide any evidence of positive implementation of these decisions. For instance, US notified about 323 SPS proposals during the years 2000 and 2001. About two-third of these were concerned with revisions of pesticide residue limiting measures. And, since it was a revision of the existing measure already in force, the implementation decisions are inoperative.

Against this backdrop we find that during the year 2002 (January-December) USA submitted a total of 221 notifications, largest number by any member of WTO. Out of this, 125 (55 per cent) were routine notifications either for information or comments of the members. The average time, if allowed, was a mere three weeks. Remarkably, 96 (45 per cent) of these proposals did not require to be allowed any reasonable time as they were either Addenda, Corrigendum, Revisions of the already existing rule in force or could be due to some Emergency measures warranted by exigencies. Similarly, the European Union, another major group credited with larger notifications, did not allow in about 49 per cent cases any reasonable time period as per the decision on the SPS implementation concerns mentioned in the Doha Declaration.

As a further illustration of the confusion on these decisions, US submitted a notification entitled "Food Security Guidance".[4] Since this was an *announcement* regarding the "*Availability*" of guidance documents on food security issues the *proposed date of adoption* and the *proposed date of entry into force* were mentioned as *"to be determined"*. Subsequently, it has been announced that "Food Security and Bioterrorism Act" will become operative from December 2003 (24-25 June 2003: twenty-seventh regular SPS committee meeting agenda notes). Thus we find that the implementation decisions on *time frame* and *reasonable time interval* are, in fact, going in a circular direction without any concrete outcome. Such absence of tangible and genuine efforts at engagement with the ground level realities of the developing countries requires to be factored in during the stock taking of Doha mandates at Cancun.

(b) Equivalence

The SPS Committee consciously adopted a 'Programme for Further Work' regarding the implementation of Equivalence (Article 4).[5] In that respect, the issue of equivalence (Article 4), being substantive in addition to procedural, still holds out for a lot of discussion.

Again taking the illustration of USA, we found that about 1080 establishments were granted equivalence in 2002 for "meat and poultry" product imports into US. Most of the countries, except, Japan, belonged either to the NAFTA grouping (92.5 per cent) or the Western Hemisphere (7 per cent) or the Pacific region. No Asian, of course with the exception cited above, or African countries managed to get equivalence for exporting "meat and poultry" products to USA. Even in the case of Japan only four establishments were granted equivalence in 2002. Perhaps these figures explain why the concerns on equivalence has remained to be a live and yet vague even at the crossroads to Cancun.

The sum total of this *ad referendum* is two-fold. First, members have to get into a close consultation process with the three international standards organization, namely, Codex, OIE and IPPC. Secondly, in case of a difference in objectively assessing equivalence based on the guidelines, the importing member is expected to resolve this difference *independently* of the procedures laid down for determination of equivalence.

It is important to recall that most of the food safety standards in the developed importing countries are higher than those recommended by the international agencies (Codex, OIE, IPPC) and that OECD countries have submitted two out of every three notifications between the period the SPS agreement came into force in 1995 and end 2001.[6] Thus, the implementation issue of equivalence (Article 4) gets linked to the notification of SPS measures (Article 7) as well as the participation of the developing countries in standard setting exercise. However, when procedure for determination of equivalence is to be independently resolved, the leverage to be gained by the developing countries is not a matter of speculation.

(c) Remaining three implementation issues

It was decided that a review of SPS agreement would be carried out every fourth year or earlier if the members through the Ministerial desired so. The first review was carried out in 1999. With reference to the participation of developing countries in standard setting and the financial and technical assistance, some problems of seams between various bodies is emerging to be a major constraint. A case in point is the problem of inter-agency coordination.[7] Be that as it may, a focussed attention to these two issues is not visible. Thus it has become one of the important factors in the development challenges.

In this respect it is interesting to mention that the Doha Development Agenda Trade Capacity Building Database (TCBDB) was launched by the WTO and OECD Secretariats in November 2002. With this as the apex body with the DG, WTO as the main pivot, seamless Trade Related Technical Assistance and Capacity Building (TRTACB) activities have been built up. The SPS related Technical Assistance and Capacity Building (TACB) activities come under the broad group Trade Policy and Regulation in TCBDB. The data indicate that TBT and SPS related TACB activities though increased in 2002 to 237 from 143 in 2001, the value declined to US$ 58 million in 2002 from US$ 127 million in the previous year. The decline perhaps is attributable to the periodicity of the programming cycle of IDA loans.[8]

The challenges before the developing countries therefore are manifold as they approach the Cancun Ministerial. At the outset, it has become clear that active participation in both SPS Committee as well as standard setting international organizations is not only essential but financial provisions for subject matter specialist be provided for, as well. The moot point is how many developing country members can afford this in spite of the emphasis on technical assistance and capacity-building efforts.

Secondly, the *ad referendum* refers to "independently" resolving the difference between the importing and exporting member countries in case protocol laid down by the international organization fail to establish the equivalence of standards. Here, it is not clear what is meant by "independently". Perhaps, it could be either the DSB or any other body. Nonetheless it is important to recall the resources that need to be expended to reach any logical conclusion. For instance, the SPS related disputes in the DSB provide a good example of how many issues of "scientific merit" and other legal complexities gets weaved into the arguments of both the exporting and the importing countries.

Notably, there are 84 SPS related disputes that have been reported in the WTO between October 1995 and July 2003. Amongst these the classic cases are the dispute between Japan and USA on importation of Apples from USA to Japan; fresh fruits and vegetables imports into Australia from the Philippines, Rice imports into EC from India, etc.

Further, prevailing situations in the developing countries can be gauged from the fact that between 2001 and 2002 a record number of new SPS specific trade concerns have been raised. Interestingly, out of the 154 trade concerns related to SPS raised between 1995-2002, only 28 meaningful solutions have been reported.[9] There are at least 70 trade concerns that are a year or more old and an amicable solution is yet to be reached.

Concluding Remarks and Policy Imperatives

In what follows we have given is an inventory of policy lessons which cover some issues for action at the level of national governments that are likely to prepare the exporters in these countries to face the emerging challenges more effectively. These are also issues that need to be addressed at the international or WTO level. These will help in moderating the incidence of these new standards on the developing countries. Areas in which regional cooperation would be fruitful have also been identified.

Issues for Action at the National Level

It is quite clear that governments do have to play an important role especially when the exporters are small and medium enterprises (SMEs) are the exporters and it may be beyond their capacity to comply with the new standards.

Information Sharing

Governments should create mechanisms for disseminating information on the new emerging standards adopted by different countries to the exporters, especially the SMEs. This information dissemination could help in reducing the rate of rejections of export consignments and thus help avoid the costly process of bringing them back or destroying them.

Capacity Building for Compliance

Given the high cost of compliance which may be beyond the capacity of smaller enterprises, it may be of critical importance to create common infrastructural facilities such as test laboratories with international accreditation. Government agencies may assist the smaller enterprises complying with the new standards through provision of technology and necessary raw materials. Capacity building could also include

Box 7.2: Export of "Egg Powder" from a Developing country to Developed Countries: Case of EU Enthusiam

The case study of Egg Powder export is illustrative of the fact how the six implementation issues have been addressed in the last one year when associated activities in respect of the Doha mandate attained pace. An Indian consignment of "Egg Powder" was rejected in the EU because the destination market included additional element known as MRPL or "minimum required performance limit" in May 2003. The Indian establishment did not know the rejection based on this additional criterion, MRPL. Obviously, here the questions of *time frame* and *reasonable time interval* between the announcement and the adoption/coming into force do arise. On investigation it was revealed that in March 2003 a decision for establishing minimum required performance limits (MRPL) of analytical methods was amended by Decision 2003/181/EC. Thus establishing criteria and procedures for the validation of *analytical methods* to ensure the *quality and comparability of analytical results* generated by official laboratories came into force immediately. Since the Revisions, Corrigendum, Addendum or Emergency follows the original notifications, all variants come into force immediately unless bilateral consultations are requested.

The establishment whose consignment was rejected had a valid equivalence issued by the EU. And yet there was a "Rapid Alert' issued in EC as a routine that went to all importing countries. However when the consignment was declared to be meeting the additional element of MRPL, the 'Rapid Alert' was neither withdrawn nor importing countries de-alerted. The loss of reputation and increases in costs both implicit and explicit in this whole episode is going to take a long time to recover.

Source: **Forthcoming *RIS Discussion Paper* on *"Implementation Issues in SPS: A Developing country Perspective for Development Agenda on the Meandering Pathways from Doha to Cancun"* by Rajesh Mehta, and J. George (2003).**

organization of extension programmes which cover training of entrepreneurs, managers and different levels of workers in compliance of the required standards. Governments could also facilitate formation of cooperatives or voluntary associations of exporters so that they could share costs and create common facilities such as test laboratories, water treatment plants, effluent treatment plants besides information dissemination.

The patterns of clustering or agglomeration of exporters specialized in one product in certain areas that exist in the region (e.g. knitwear makers in Ludhiana) suggest that formation of these self-help groups/cooperatives could be effective. Furthermore, the governments have a role to play in ensuring the availability of all necessary raw materials for compliance with specific standards. For instance, a case study shows, non-availability of non-azo dyes for the carpet industry in Nepal impedes the compliance with ban on azo dyes imposed in the European Union. So governments have to make sure that substitutes of azo dyes are available to the carpet manufacturers. The concerned government could consider setting up Exporters Assistance Centres as one-stop shops to cover all different tasks such as dissemination of information, creation of test facilities, the provision of technical assistance and training, etc.

Evolve National Standards

As a result of the liberalization of trade regimes, the South Asian economies have become increasingly open to import of goods from abroad. In particular, a lot of imported fruits and vegetables are finding their way to the South Asian markets. There is a fear that these imports might become carriers of new pests and other harmful germs to the region. It is important for the governments to evolve their own environmental standards and quarantine regulations which should be strictly enforced.

Effective Participation in International Standards Setting

The experience of past years suggests that the international standards such as those in Codex Commission are evolved with very little participation of developing countries. Therefore, proposals of developed countries get approved by default on international standards setting. The developing countries need to participate in these events effectively with their own preparation of implications and other issues and concerns of alternative standards.

Generating Consciousness about Environmental Concerns in the Industry

Governments can play an important role in generating consciousness of environmental considerations in industry through media and by other means. The Indonesian example of colour grading of the companies on the basis of the environmental responsibility is a case in point. The increased environmental consciousness generated through the media of this scheme has led to a significant decline in market valuation of the companies that were labelled as relatively poor (black) in terms of environmental standards. It suggests that such schemes could build considerable pressure on companies to become environmentally more conscious.

Databases of Experiences

A variety of experiences of the imposition of environmental standards by importers on exporters exist, sometimes in an informal manner and often under the guise of good manufacturing practices. It is important to compile a database of such experiences so that necessary redressal could be sought through WTO Dispute Settlement if certain regulations imposed are not consistent with SPS and TBT norms.

Exploiting Opportunities for Environmentally- Friendly Goods and Services

Developing countries should take advantage of the growing environmental consciousness in the developed world by pushing exports of environment friendly goods and services. Some of these countries have a natural advantage in organic farming which should be exploited fully. The use of organic dyes in textile industry can tactfully avoid various environmental restrictions on dirty goods imposed by importing countries. For instance, the South Asian region has used vegetable dyes such as indigo for centuries in the textile industry. It may be fruitful to create a brand in the Western world on the basis of the use of vegetable dyes. Similarly, exports of herbal medicines, cosmetics, eco-tourism among other environmentally friendly goods and services could be pushed. Bangladesh has rapidly got an eco-label for its jute-packaging bag which has enhanced the sales of these bags significantly.

Diversification of Export Commodities/ Markets

Most developing and least developing countries are heavily dependent on exports of few commodities and on few markets. For instance, Nepal's dependence on carpet exports, Bangladesh's dependence on garments, marine products and leather goods. Even though, India's exports structure is more diversified, the share of textiles and garments in India's exports is quite substantial at 33 per cent. Similarly, there is a high dependence on specific markets. For instance, Germany accounts for 80 to 90 per cent of Nepal's exports of carpets. The dependence on a few products and markets for exports makes these economies highly vulnerable. Therefore, in medium to long term, the objective of government policy should be to diversify the composition of exports as well as expand the coverage of markets.

Issues for International Negotiations

A number of issues which have to be taken up at the WTO and other international fora, are as follows:

Effective Technical Assistance

Both SPS and TBT Agreements in WTO contain provisions for technical assistance to be provided by the importing countries to assist developing country and LDC exporters in their compliance with the new standards imposed by importing countries. The SPS Agreement under Article 9 includes 'provision of technical assistance to other Members specially developing country Members... in the areas of processing technology, research and infrastructure, including in the establishment of national regulatory bodies and may take the form of advice, credits, donations and grants including for the purpose of seeking technical expertise, training and equipment to allow such countries to adjust to and comply with sanitary and phyto-sanitary measures necessary to achieve the appropriate level of sanitary and phyto-sanitary protection in their export markets'. Furthermore, the SPS Agreement provides 'where substantial investments are required in order for an exporting developing country Member to fulfill the sanitary and phyto-sanitary requirements of an importing Member, the latter shall consider providing such technical assistance as will permit the developing country Members to maintain and expand its market access opportunities for the product involved' (Art. 9.2). Similarly, the TBT Agreement under Article 11 provides for advice and technical assistance, if requested, on mutually agreed terms and conditions.

However, there is little evidence of the promised technical assistance forthcoming. Following the ban imposed by the European Commission on exports of fisheries products originating in Bangladesh in 1997 due to deficiencies in the infrastructure and hygiene in fisheries establishments in the country, Bangladesh Frozen Foods Exports Association had sought technical assistance from European Union experts. Even though assistance was provided, the Association had to pay for it from its own resources. It is clear, therefore, that the obligation for technical assistance has not been fulfilled by developed countries in an adequate manner.

In this light, it may be useful for developing countries to seek mandate on implementation of standards that are different from international norms only after technical assistance has been provided.

Restricting the Discretion to Follow International Norms

Developing countries may consider seeking review of the Agreement on SPS at the WTO Committee on Sanitary and Phyto-sanitary Measures to reduce the discretion and flexibility available under the Agreement that is being misused, the universal application of international standards, and to bring about greater transparency in the imposition of standards, good manufacturing practices and all other regulations. Countries wishing to adopt higher than international standards should undertake to financially compensate potentially affected developing countries.

Substantive Special and Differential Treatment

Like other WTO Agreements, S&DT in the case of SPS and TBT Agreements has also been reduced to a longer transition period for developing especially the least developed country Members. However, the longer transition period provided under these Agreements is of hardly any use because the importing enterprises insists on new product standards owing to high consumer consciousness for these standards. Therefore, the S&DT has to be of a more substantive type. It could be, for instance, in the form of additional financing (along with technical assistance) to cover the costs of compliance by the developing country exports with the new standards within a relatively shorter period of time.

Compulsory Licensing ofTechnology

Sometimes the compliance with new standards is constrained by non-availability of technology owing to the strengthening regime of IPR protection. The TRIPs Agreement should provide for compulsory licensing on environmental grounds.

Enhancing the Scope of 'Standards and Trade Development Facility'

In light of the extremely vocal criticism from the developing countries about the health and environment related standards and the difficulties the developing countries are facing in meeting the disease and contaminant related standards for their food exports to richer countries' markets, the WTO and the World Bank have launched a new fund called Standards and Trade Development Facility. The World Bank has proposed an initial US$ 300,000 to establish the new fund, and the WTO will allocate funding from the Doha Development Trust Fund to launch the Facility.

At present the facility only proposes to help developing countries for better implementing the food safety and plant and animal health measures in the area of sanitary and phytosanitary (SPS) regulations. The developing countries have been finding it difficult to implement stringent standards being implemented by the developed countries. However, one of the factors behind this failure of developing countries in meeting these standards was their lack of participation in the existing institutional mechanisms for setting global standards like Codex Commission and other food safety standards-setting organizations, run jointly by the FAO and WHO. The scope of this facility should be enhanced to facilitate the participation of developing countries in the meetings of such organisations as well. Apart from providing the first hand information to the developing countries this will also ensure the long needed rationalisation of standard setting exercise itself.

Trilateral Cooperation

Very often the appropriate technical skills for providing technical assistance are not available in developed countries. For instance, skills for dealing with dairying in tropical countries. Such skills are more likely to be available in other developing countries. To make technical assistance effective, trilateral programmes could be evolved which involve resources from a developed (donor) country combined with skills of a developing country to assist another developing country.

Issues for Regional Cooperation

There are a number of areas where a regional approach could be fruitful as we see below.

Coordination in International Negotiations

Developing countries or countries within a particular region export many products that are common to all. Their concerns are quite similar. Hence, a region-wide coordination in international standards setting events and in the WTO Committees on SPS and TBT and other negotiations would be serving their interest better.

Cooperation in Compliance with the Emerging Environmental Standards

Regional cooperation could be effective in sharing costs of compliance with the emerging environmental standards. Regional cooperation could cover joint development of products which meet the new regulations and hence involve sharing the costs. In this context, a case in point is a highly successful project for development of Aflatoxin risk free groundnut jointly conducted by the Indian Council of Agricultural Research and the UNDP. This Project successfully brought down the Aflatoxin levels to 0-5 PPB in 80 per cent of the samples at the end of a three-year term of the project in a high risk area of Andhra Pradesh, India against the permissible limit of 15 to 20 PPB in developed countries such as Australia, Canada, USA. Such projects could be fruitfully undertaken at regional level. Regional cooperation could also cover creation of regional institutional infrastructure such as test laboratories, where the costs are high, and even translations of standards are done in the local language. The geographical contiguity in the region would facilitate the optimal utilization of such infrastructure. Joint training programmes and other measures to build local capacity would also be fruitful.

Regional Eco-labels

Another area of regional cooperation could be promotion of regional eco-labels which might be more acceptable and popular than national eco-labels. For instance, a number of South Asian countries including India have tried to launch their own eco-label programmes. However, these programmes have had limited success.

Evolving Regional Standards for Products of our Export Interest

Another area of fruitful regional cooperation could be to evolve regional standards especially for products of our export interest and have them accepted globally. Similarly, it would be fruitful to define environmentally sensitive goods from a regional perspective.

Endnotes

1. Kittu, C. 2001. "Issues on SPS and Environmental Standards for India", paper presented at the UNCTAD/World Bank Conference on 11-13 January.
2. This section is based on forthcoming *RIS Discussion Paper* on *"Implementation Issues in SPS: A Developing country Perspective for Development Agenda on the Meandering Pathways from Doha to Cancun"* by Rajesh Mehta, and J. George (2003).
3. WTO. 2002. G/TBT/W/172-27 February (02-0972).
4. G/SPS/N/USA/541- 02-0179 dated 15 January 2002.
5. WTO, G/L/592.
6. OECD. 2002. "Sanitary and Phytosanitary Measures and Agricultural Trade: A Survey of Issues and Concerns Raised in the WTO's SPS Committee", Joint Working Party on Agriculture and Trade (JT00129244). Com/TD/AGR/WP(2002)21/Final.
7. WTO. 2002. G/SPS/GEN/332-24 June (02-3478).
8. http://www.wto.org/english/tratop_e/devel_e/teccop_e/wto_oecd_report03_e.doc.
9. G/SPS/GEN/204/Rev.3.

8

Issues in Disputes Settlement Understanding: Developing Countries Perspective

Introduction

The Dispute Settlement Understanding (DSU) is the most important development in the World Trade Organization (WTO). Although the conflict resolution provision existed in the GATT, the DSU introduced number of other effective provisions for the setting up of trade disputes. The DSU under the WTO contains three salient features that are absent from the dispute settlement provisions of most international legal instruments such as (i) panel to examine complaints from Member countries (Art 6); (ii) appellate review of panel decisions (Art 17); and (iii) the ability to render binding decisions (Art 20).[1] Specifically, DSU is more clear and lays extra stress on the provisions concerning procedural matters to its predecessor (GATT). Though the DSU mechanism has gained credibility among the Member Countries, only a few developed countries continue to be major users of the system due to some existing lacunae in current dispute settlement procedure. The participation of developing countries, especially least-developed countries, in the DSU has still not improved. For example, the lack of effective sanction in DSU System results in a complaining party being largely left alone in their struggle against violator. Consequently countries that are economically and politically weak stand at relatively disadvantageous position in the WTO.

It is a recognized fact that the current system of DSU is a rule-based multilateral trading system and is a principal tool which will help developing countries protect and promote their interests. However, doubts have emerged regarding the possibilities of the developing countries to use the system effectively.

The purpose of this chapter is to discuss the role of the DSU for developing countries and find out whether procedure that are provided in the DSU allow these countries to defend their interests against developed nations. Although developing countries have already submitted a number of reasonable proposals to the dispute settlement body (DSB) in this regard, to defend and follow up proposals forcefully and collectively are the only ways that can lead to improvements they desire in the system. Indeed, the aim is to suggest some points for improving the use of the WTO dispute settlement understanding based on developing countries' past experiences.

Objectives of the DSU

The DSU contains rules and procedures whereby an aggrieved Member country can make a request for consultations and initiate a dispute proceeding if another Member's trade measures are inconsistent with any of the WTO agreements.

Article 3.2 of the DSU contains the main principle underlying the WTO dispute settlement system. It provides that "the dispute settlement system of the WTO is a central element in providing security and predictability to the multilateral trading system." As stated in Article 3.3 of the DSU, WTO Members recognised the importance of "the prompt settlement of situations in which a Member considers that any benefits accruing to it directly or indirectly under the covered agreements are being impaired by measures taken by another Member is essential to the effective functioning of the WTO." Further 'the aim of the dispute settlement mechanism is to secure a positive solution to a dispute' which is "a solution mutually acceptable to the parties to a dispute and consistent with the covered agreements is clearly to be preferred."[2]

The DSU introduces some fundamental changes concerning the rules and procedures of dispute settlement under the GATT. The key changes under the DSU include stricter time limits at each stage of the dispute resolution, automatic establishment of panels, automatic adoption of panel reports, appellate review, limits on unilateral action, automatic authorisation for suspensions, and separate treatment of non-violation complaints.[3]

The DSU and Developing Countries – Some Trends

The latest available data show that 297 cases were brought to the WTO dispute settlement procedure till 14 July 2003. Table 8.1, by breaking down these figures by category of country (developed/developing), shows that out of 297 cases for resolution 180 were presented by developed countries (113 against other developed WTO Members and 67 against developing Members). The developing countries filed 106 claims, with 57 against developed country members and 49 against developing countries. An agreement-wise break-up reveals another interesting dimension of dispute settlement process. The maximum cases that have been registered, measuring by the obligation enforceable by the DSU, pertain to industrial products (more than 99 disputes submitted to the DSU). This is followed by 62 in Anti-dumping and 50 cases in agriculture.

In addition, there has been an increase in the number of disputes involving developing country Members (complainant/respondent or third party) during the last five years. Despite the foregoing, it is to be noted that the actual relates to the basic objective of procedural fairness and due process accorded to developing country Members. Moreover, the question arises that despite the increase in the number of cases involving developing countries, they are still skeptical about the use of DSU. The observed asymmetries also indicative of gaps in legal power and economic capacities of developed and developing countries.

Constraints Faced by Developing Countries in the Functioning of the DSU

The past seven years experience of developing countries has shown that there are number of constraints with regard to the implementation of the DSU. These constraints can broadly be categorized as follows:

- Too Legal an Approach to Dispute Settlement;

Table 8.1: Comparison of Participation by Developed and Developing countries in the WTO Dispute Settlement Process up to 14 July, 2003

Cases Filed by Developed Countries		Cases Filed by Developing Countries		Cases jointly filed by developed and developing countries
Total	Against Developing Countries	Total	Against Developed Countries	Total
181	67	106	57	10

Source: Based on the information posted on the WTO web site (http://www.wto.org)

- Non-effective implementation of provisions on special and differential treatment in favour of developing countries;
- High litigation costs in the recourse to the dispute settlement procedure; and
- The recourse to effective implementation regarding cases brought by developing countries against developed countries and the related issue of compensation/retaliation

Too Legal an Approach to Dispute Settlement

The WTO dispute settlement system has started adopting an exceptionally high legalistic approach to trade disputes involving developing countries members. For example, in the US S.301, the panel overdraws the issue of whether or not US S.301 is in compliance with WTO Agreements. The panel report, instead of giving a finding on the basis of the law, has discussed various other non-relevant issues such as the US administration's expression of intent on how it would administer the provisions in reply to the US statements before the panel.[4]

On the other hand, in the dispute raised by the US against India over the latter's TRIPS obligations, the panel and the Appellate Body ruled out the expressed intention of the Indian government to implement the transition provisions through administrative order. Both the panel and the Appellate Body insisted that only a legal provision could be considered adequate.[5]

In fact, most of the complaints filed with the WTO are basically "violation complaints" in which one Member alleges the other for violation of WTO agreement. In the case of a developing country Member's complaint against any developed country Member, the burden of proof lies on the former to prove a prima facie case of violation with the provisions covered under WTO agreement. This is a difficult situation as regard to developing countries, especially in case of uncertainty. In event of all the evidence and arguments against and in favours of the case cannot make any headway, a Panel may "give the benefit of doubt" to the defending Member.[6]

Owing to this exceptionally legalistic approach and burden of proof to establish a prima facie case, many developing countries are virtually at disadvantage in participating in dispute settlement mechanism.

DSU and S&D Provisions favoring Developing Countries

There are a number of provisions in the DSU that accord Special and Differential treatment to developing country members. However, the implementation of many of these provisions has proved to be difficult. The various provisions regarding special and differential treatment in the DSU have not been implemented with equal effectiveness. In what follows is a discussion on some of the S&D provisions important from the developing countries' point of view.

Even though in consultations provision its states that 'Member should give special attention to the particular problems and interests of the developing country Member'(Art. 4.10), the elements of "special attention" to be given to the problems of developing countries during consultations are not specified. Hence there are no means to assess the level of compliance by WTO Members with respect to this provision. India on behalf of various other developing and least-developed countries has already submitted a proposal regarding the language of this provision to be amended from "should" to "shall" in order to emphasise a mandatory duty that WTO Members owe.[7] However, this issue can be considered part of a wider problem in the sense that a large number of S&D provisions in various WTO Agreements, owing to the non-mandatory nature, have not been of any practical use for developing countries.

For Panel Reports (Art 12.11) where one party is a developing country Member, the panel shall take in to account the Special and Differential treatment for a developing country while giving its report.[8] However, there has been hardly any panel report which has explicitly mentioned this particular provision.

On implementation, attention should be paid to the measures affecting the interest

Box 8.1:
United States - Restrictions on Imports of Cotton and Man-made Fibre Underwear, Complaint by Costa Rica

In this case, the panel found that the US restrictions imposed on imports of underwear from Costa Rica were not valid because the United States had not 'demonstrably' shown that serious damage was caused by the increased level of imports as required under the Agreement on Textiles and Clothing (ATC) and also because the United States failed to make an adequate attribution of serious damage to Costa Rican imports, as distinct from other imports.

The panel also concluded that the United States violated the ATC because it retroactively applied the restriction starting from the date of the request for consultations. In the panel's view, the quota period should have started from the date of the official publication regarding the request. The panel recommended that the United States bring the measure challenged by Costa Rica into compliance with its obligations under the ATC. The panel further suggested that the United States bring the measure into compliance by immediately withdrawing the restriction. Costa Rica appealed the panel's conclusions relating to the permissible effective date of application of the US transitional safeguards. In February 1997, the Appellate Body allowed Costa Rica's appeal. It concluded that the ATC does not permit the retroactive application of transitional safeguard measures. Thus, the United States could not apply the restriction prior to 60 days after the date it requested consultations.

This case is significant as it involved the textiles sector, a major issue of conflicts between many developed (importing) countries and developing (exporting) countries. This was the first successful challenge under the DSU against invocation of the transitional safeguard mechanism under the ATC and greatly influenced later practice in the WTO.

Source: **The report of the Panel on United States - Restrictions on Imports of Cotton and Man-made Fibre Underwear (WT/DS24/R) adopted on 25 February 1997. (http://www.wto.org)**

of developing countries (Article 21.2). This provision is rather vague and it is difficult to assess the level of compliance by WTO Members. For cases such as *United States - Restrictions on Imports of Cotton and Man-made Fibre Underwear* (see Box 8.1) and *Indonesia – Measure Affecting the Automotive Sector* (see Box 8.2) illustrate that the Panel deliberately ignored the measures that are specially affecting the interest of developing countries (specifically application of transitional safeguard measures and TRIMs requirement in these cases).[9]

It is also stated that special assistance and advice will be made available to developing countries in disputes, but again it is very limited in nature and has hardly

Box 8.2:
Indonesia - Certain Measures Affecting the Automobile Industry, complaints by the European Communities, Japan and the United States

This case concerns Indonesia's national car programme. Under a presidential decree issued in February 1996, only one company was designated a "pioneer" company and only "national cars" manufactured by this company were made eligible for special tax breaks under certain requirements including local content requirement. Complaining parties alleged that this and other related measures were in violation of the WTO rules. A single panel to hear all the complaints was established in June 1997. The panel report, which was circulated in July 1998, found that the contested measures were in violation of Indonesia's obligations under GATT Articles I:1, III:2, III:4 and X:3(a), as well as Article 2 of the TRIMs Agreement and Article 5(c) of the SCM Agreement.

While the panel procedures were in process, due to the changed economic environment in Asia, Indonesia's economy slid into a critical condition, necessitating emergency assistance from the International Monetary Fund (IMF). As part of the deal with the IMF, the Indonesian government announced the termination of the national car programme. In the light of these developments, Indonesia did not appeal the panel's findings, and the panel report was adopted by the DSB in July 1998.

The outcome of this panel report is of great interest to many developing countries because it deals with the important question of trade and investment. The similar case was also brought against India by US and EC (WT/DS146/R).[10]

Source: **Indonesia - Certain Measures Affecting the Automobile Industry (WT/DS54/R) adopted on 2 July 1998 (http://www.wto.org)**

proved significant to the developing country Member. Likewise, various other Articles provide special and differential treatment to the developing countries and the LDCs. However, the implementation of these provisions has not been effective owing either to the fact that such provisions are of a non-mandatory nature and have no implementation modalities, or to the fact that developing countries have failed to use them effectively.

Cost of access to the dispute settlement process

The DSU settlement process is very costly for developing countries, as considerable human and financial resources are required to prepare and follow up a case through the consultation to the appeal stage spanning a lengthy period of close to three years. Owing to the lack of legal expertise needed to go through this increasingly complex and lengthy legal process, many developing countries have no option but to hire professional legal experts from developed countries and pay them hefty amount of fee.[11] On the other hand major developed countries have their permanent in-house resident missions at WTO with required human resources and legal experts to effectively tackle any trade disputes against them.

Developing countries are also wary of the expenses and not sure of the benefits of the outcome of the case. Hence they resort to seeking legal remedies very carefully even though they may be convinced that their rights have been infringed upon or that another WTO member has not discharged its obligations towards them. In addition, smaller developing countries also take into account the possible hidden political cost if the country infringing their rights happens to be a major developed country. This can create an imbalance of rights and obligations in the system.

Issues of implementation of decisions and compensation

The current system of DSU has some major weaknesses as regards the implementation of decisions and awarding of compensation in the trade dispute. The WTO Agreement allows a complaining party to suspend concessions where a defending party has failed to comply with the decision of a dispute settlement panel or the Appellate Body. However, the text of the Agreement is vague on two important points. First, it is with regards to the authority determining wether a defending party has failed to comply; and when the right to retaliate would arise. Second, it is the lack of effective sanctions in the WTO dispute settlement system. As a result, the complaining country are largely left alone in their struggle against the violator, and consequently developing countries and especially least developing countries, which are economically and politically weak, stand at a relatively inconvenient position in the WTO.[12] Developing countries face at least three major problems so far as the implementation of decisions is concerned:

(i) It may take up to three years from the start of the dispute settlement process until the withdrawal of the offending measure. Meanwhile, the export opportunities for the complaining developing country in the developed country concerned may suffer irreparably during this time. Indeed, there is no retrospective relief from the time the incorrect measure was applied by the respondent Member country. In the case of a developing country as a complainant, this gap of time-period in relief may be very costly.

(ii) There is substantial export loss to the developing country during the dispute settlement period, but there is hardly any provision for compensation for this loss even when the measure in question is found to be in contravention of the WTO rules or frivolous. This can be particularly damaging for smaller developing countries which are highly dependent on a limited number of export products/markets.

(iii) Retaliation is the final remedy to allow the complaining country to take action against the defending country. As for developing countries, it is difficult to take any retaliatory action against a developed country. This is owing not only to political considerations but also to the unequal economic relationship with developing countries being more dependant on continuing the relationship with developed countries for their economic growth and development.[13]

Facilitating Developing Countries Participation in DSU

The DSU, to some extent, has generated faith among developing countries as a rule-based system and improved their participation in the dispute settlement. However, there is a greater need to ensure a level playing field and enhanced participation of developed and developing countries in the DSU. As discussed above, many proposals have already been submitted by developing countries to the WTO to achieve this objective. These proposals, as well as others that may be submitted in this regard in future, must seek to improve the system of redressal taking into account the following important respects.

Adjustment of time-period

At present the period between the start of a dispute and its final determination may be go up to three years. This period is too long for complainant developing countries as their capacity to absorb the adverse effects of measures taken against them is considerably low. This can be improved by making suitable amendments in the time-frame of the relevant provisions of Articles 4, 5, 6 and 12 of the DSU, especially in all the complaints brought by a developing country against a developed country.

Provision of compensation for loss during the pendency of the dispute

Developing countries that are dependent on a limited number of export products/ markets can suffer heavy trade losses during the course of a dispute regarding a measure taken against them by a developed country. The damage is not limited to foregone exports. The market may be lost permanently to competitors and substitute products. Article 22 (Compensation and the Suspension of Concessions) of the DSU can be expanded to provide compensation for the loss suffered by a complainant developing country during the pendency of a complaint against a developed country. The panel should be mandated to determine the amount of compensation in all cases where measures by developed countries against developing countries are found to violate the WTO rules. This will help prevent the initiation of trade-related measures on frivolous grounds by developed countries, and hence will serve an important objective of the dispute settlement process, that is, the prevention of trade disputes.

Implementation of decisions

A developing country is hardly in a position to take retaliatory action against a developed country even if it is authorized to do so by the DSB. This problem can be tackled by amending the text of the DSU by incorporating following two options especially in the cases brought and won by developing countries against developed countries:

(i) to pay sufficient compensation to the developing country or joint retaliatory action by all WTO members against the offending member; or

(ii) mandatory removal of the measure violative of WTO rules. (This will reduce the options of the defendant developed country.)

Making S&D Provisions Effective

The review of the existing S&D provisions should also involve a comprehensive analysis of the implementation of all S&D provisions. This thorough analysis would serve the following broad objectives:

(i). It should lead to the elaboration of an implementation mechanism wherever such a mechanism is missing in the present provisions. For example, the "special attention" mentioned in Article 4:10 may be interpreted to mean, *inter alia*, that consultations initiated against a developing country by a developed country are held at a place convenient for the developing country concerned. This would certainly help the developing country because owing to financial constraints they are often unable to bring experts from their countries during the consultation period.

(ii). It should identify the reasons as to why certain special and differential treatment provisions, for example, Articles 12.10, 12.11, 21.7, 21.8 (panel procedure and surveillance of implementation), have so far not been used by developing countries. Such an analysis will also enable improvements in the current understanding of constraints and would eventually lead to a more extensive use of these provisions by developing countries.

Legal and Financial support to Developing Countries

It is important to ensure that the costs associated with using the dispute settlement process do not act as barriers for gaining access to the process for the developing and especially the least-developed countries. It will require making provision for adequate legal assistance to both the complainant and defendant developing countries by strengthening and expanding the coverage of present Article 27.2 of the DSU. The Advisory Centre for WTO law has recently been set up by WTO. It is, however, yet to be used effectively by developing countries. Besides increasing the number of consultants, setting up an independent legal unit within or outside the Secretariat, appointment of a permanent Defence Counsel, or establishment of special arrangements with private lawyers, adequate financial resources, etc. should be made available.

Strengthening the existing Legal Provisions in the various WTO Agreements

It is also worth mentioning here that many provisions in the various agreements are very lenient owing to which these can be used by the developed country Members for protectionist purposes. For example, to review the standard provided in Art 17.6 of the WTO Agreement on Anti-dumping, along with a remedy which in practice hardly goes beyond the recommendation-stage, makes it impossible to prove Anti-dumping illegal in DSU. Due to this, major developed country Members use Anti-dumping as a means for protectionist purposes towards developing country Member.[14]

Owing to the asymmetric legal powers and economic capacities of developed and developing countries, the former may bring a large number of disputes, some even on frivolous grounds, against the latter. There have also been instances where developed countries brought repeated cases, on the same grounds, against developing countries. (EC against India - *Patent Protection for Pharmaceutical and Agricultural Chemical Products* - WT/D579 and EC against Argentina - *Measures Affecting Textiles and Clothing* - WT/D577)

The proposals to address these issues should include:

(i) The complainant developed country may be asked to pay the cost of the dispute incurred by the defendant developing country, if the case brought by the former is not maintained by the panel/Appellate Body.[15]

(ii) WTO members may be prohibited from bringing cases against a developing country member once a case on similar grounds involving the same developing country has been decided by a panel/ Appellate Body.

(iii) The panels and the Appellate Body should be directed to give, to the extent possible, transparent and clear rulings that are less prone to conflicting legalistic interpretations so that once the case is decided it should not be appealed against on the similar grounds again.

Endnotes

1 Peter Van Den Bossche. 1998. World Trade Ongranization Dispute Settlement In 1997 (Part-I), Journal of International Economic Law, Vol. 1, No. 1.

2 WTO. 2001. The WTO Dispute Settlement Procedures: A Collection of Relevant Legal Texts. Second Edition, Cambridge University Press at pp 2-3.

3 Ibid.

4 Report of the Panel on United States – Section 301-310 of the Trade Act of 1974, WT/DS152/R, adopted on 27 January 2000 at para 7.117 & 7.121 at pp 330-331.

5 Report of the Appellate Body on India – Patent Protection for Pharmaceutical and Agricultural Chemical Products case (WT/DS50/AB/R) adopted on 19 December 1997.

6 Report of the Appellate Body in US – Woven Wool Shirts and Blouses case (WT/DS33/AB/R) adopted on 23 May 1997, at pp 14-16.

7 Although there has already been a proposal submitted by India (TN/DS/W/19) regarding the language of this provision be amended from "should" to "shall" in order to emphasise a mandatory duty that WTO Members owe.

8 Article 12.11 of the DSU, supra note 2, reads as " Where one or more of the parties is a developing country Member, the panel' report shall explicitly indicate the form in which account has been taken of relevant provisions on differential and more-favourable treatment for developing country Members that form part of the covered agreements which have been raised by the developing country Member in the course of the dispute settlement procedures".

9 Report of the Panel on India – Measure Affecting the Automotive Sector (WT/DS146/R) adopted on 21 December 2001, and Report of the Panel on Indonesia – Certain Measures Affecting the Automobile Industry (WT/DS54/R) adopted on 2 July 1998.

10 Debra P Steger and Susan M Hainsworth. 1998. 'WTO Dispute Settlement: The First Three Years', Journal of International Economic Law, Vol. 1, No. 2, at pp 220. Another highlight in this case was the participation of private counsel, should be noted. This is the first WTO case where a principal party in the dispute opted for a private counsel in its delegation to plead before a panel.

11 WTO . 2002. Proposal on DSU submitted by India on behalf of the Cuba, Honduras, Indonesia, Malaysia, Pakistan, Sri Lanka, Tanzania and Zimbabwe (TN/DS/W/19) on 9 October 2002 at pg 2.

12 McGivern, Brendan P. 2002. 'Seeking Compliance with WTO Rulings: Theory, Practice and Alternatives', The International Lawyers, Vol 36, Spring 2002 at 141-157.

13 Mukerji, Asoke. 2000. 'Developing Countries and the WTO: Issues of Implementation' Journal of World Trade, Vol. 34, No. 6 at pp 33-74.

14 Horn, Henrik & Mavroidis C. Petros. 1999. 'Remedies in the WTO Dispute Settlement System and Developing Country Interests', Institute for International Economic Studies and University of Neuchatel, at pg 29.

15 Supra, note 10.

9

Issues in Special and Differential Treatment

Introduction

Special and Differential Treatment (S&DT) has been an integral part of the multilateral trade rules right from the Havana Charter. GATT system provided special provisions for developing and least developed countries (LDCs) so as to ensure their enhanced participation in the international trade. Some of the trade rules were framed in such a way that they played a supportive role for the developing countries. These countries were also exempted from compliance of some others.

In the Uruguay Round, however, the S&DT provisions were considerably diluted. The concept of S&DT changed from one of providing a range of flexibilities and additional policy spaces based on economic measure to one essentially consisting of time-bound derogations from the rules, with more favourable treatment to developing and least-developed countries. However, the discontentment has grown among developing countries with the provisions of S&DT in the post-Uruguay Round years.

The submissions by developing countries have expressed concerns about the non-mandatory nature of most of the important provisions, lack of specificity and also over the rigid nature of some provisions which fail to take into account the specific needs of these countries. The developing countries have also sought creation of new instruments for making S&DT more effective.[1] The Doha Ministerial attempted to address some of these concerns of the developing countries. However, the progress on the Doha mandate has been for from satisfactory. In that context this chapter reviews the evolution of S&DT provisions in the world trading system and reviews the S&DT provisions in different WTO Agreements. It is concluded with some remarks for future action.

The Evolution of S&DT in GATT and WTO

The Special and Differential Treatment (S&DT) provisions in GATT were incorporated following the recognition of inherent inequality between players in the multilateral trading system and the special needs and development concerns of the developing countries. These provisions figured for the first time in the Havana Charter of the GATT. S&DT has been an integral part of the multilateral trading system. The developing countries are at different stages of economic, financial and technical development and therefore have entirely different capacities as compared to the developed countries in taking on multilateral obligations. Hence, they need special advantages and flexibilities to adopt appropriate national policies to pursue their development policy objectives. In 1954-55, the Article XVIII of GATT was amended to include

Article XVIII-B, allowing developing countries to use quantitative restrictions for balance of payments purposes.

In the mid 1960s, there was a lot of discussion on the special problems of developing countries following the observations by Prebisch-Singer. The Prebisch-Singer hypothesis in the light of evidence on secular decline in the Terms of Trade of developing countries, emphasized on the critical role that external factors play in the development process and argued that the developing countries need to industrialise rather than continue to be dependent on production of primary commodities. The culmination of these ideas was establishment of UNCTAD in 1964 to analyse the implications of trade for development. In the same year the Committee on Trade and Development was created in the GATT. A major development in 1965 was the addition of Part IV on Trade and Development to the GATT, 1947. This additional chapter GATT required developed countries to accord high priority to the reduction of trade barriers to the products of developing countries. The Committee on Trade and Development was to oversee the operation of the new GATT provision. The Part IV on Trade and Development covered three new Articles XXXVI to XXXVIII providing a framework for under which contracting parties are to provide "in the largest possible measure more favourable and acceptable market access conditions for products of export interest to the developing countries notably primary products, processed or manufactured products". Paragraph 8 of the Article XXXVI provides for the principle of less-than-reciprocity by specifying that developing country members "should not be expected" to make contributions which are inconsistent with their level of development in the process of trade negotiations.

Another important milestone was the adoption of Enabling Clause in 1979 in the Tokyo Round of the GATT providing for a further basis for the non-reciprocal trade preferences to developing countries under the GSP, Lome Convention and also giving developing countries the right to establish outside of Article XXIV, regional or global trade arrangements between themselves.

Although the Final Act of the Uruguay Round establishing the WTO signed in 1994 in its preamble in Marrakesh, recognized the "need for positive efforts designed to ensure that the developing countries and specially the least developed among them, secure a share in the growth in international trade commensurate with the need of their economic development", the Uruguay Round marks a departure from the approach followed towards S&DT in the previous rounds. This probably was the result of growing criticism of S&DT by developed countries in the early 1980s leading to the appointment of a special committee at the GATT. Leutwiler Report resulting from the Committee in 1985 concluded that the S&DT was of limited value and emphasis should be on complete integration of developing countries in the world trading system with appropriate rights and responsibilities (See Box 9.1).

The Uruguay Round Agreements shifted thrust from enhanced market opportunities for developing countries to transition periods and technical assistance. Furthermore even the transition period granted to developing countries has often been diluted. A case in point is the TRIPs Agreement, where during the 10 years transition period given to developing countries for implementing the product patent regime, these countries are expected to provide pipeline protection to the applicants of product patents in the form of exclusive market rights (EMRs).

The longer transition period is often of not much value where in the case SPS and TBT Agreements, where the consumers begin to demand goods produced according the newly adopted standards. The few years of additional transition period allowed to developing countries for implementing the commitments does not cover the wide development gap between developed and developing countries. For instance, developed countries have extensively imposed trade related investment measures, such as local content requirements, as part of their industrial policies, during their period of development. Under TRIMs Agreement,

Box 9.1: Leutwiler Report

One of the major critiques of S&DT came up in form of the Leutwiler Report (GATT 1985), which was commissioned in November 1983 by the then Director-General of the GATT, Arthur Dunkel. In order to meet the 'present crisis in the trading system', the Report recommended 15 specific, immediate actions, one of which addressed the problem of trade and development. This recommendation reads:

'Developing countries receive special treatment in the GATT rules. But such special treatment is of limited value. Far greater emphasis should be placed on permitting and encouraging developing countries to take advantage of their competitive strengths and on integrating them more fully into the trading system, with all the appropriate rights and responsibilities that this entails' (The Leutwiler report, GATT 1984:44).

however, developing countries are allowed only three additional years compared to developed countries to phase out the trade related investment measures. Obviously, the vast gap between the levels of development between developed and developing countries could not be bridged in the three additional years.

The experience suggests that the technical assistance offered under the Agreements has also not been adequately provided. As observed in Chapter 7, the experiences of developing countries with respect to Agreement on SPS suggest that the technical assistance is either not adequate or is provided too late, while the damage to export prospects of developing countries is already done.

Therefore, the S&DT provisions in the Uruguay Round Agreement generally do not go beyond best endeavour clause and are not legally binding. The lack of a mechanism to ensure effective implementation of S&DT provisions in the WTO has been a major area of concern for developing countries. A Group of 12 developing countries, including, Malaysia, Pakistan, India, Indonesia, Sri Lanka, Kenya, Tanzania, Uganda, Zimbabwe, Domanican Republic, Honduras, and Cuba gave a joint submission to the General Council in September 2001. They sought a thorough review of S&DT in the context of its basic objective of creating a "level playing field for unequal players in the multilateral trading system" and establishment of a concrete and binding S&DT regime, responsive to the development needs of the developing countries.[2] They also argued that liberalization of trade is not an end in itself but means for promoting economic growth and development and countries at different levels of development require different sets of policies to achieve economic development. Further, they drew attention to the flexibility and differential treatments enjoyed by developed countries during their earlier periods of development and even currently in the areas such as textile and clothing and agriculture. Emphasis was also placed on the interdependence in the global economic system where long term prospects of developed countries depended upon the economic development of developing countries. Therefore, they sought from the Doha Ministerial Conference a recognition of the importance of the issue and a mandate for negotiation of a Framework Agreement on S&DT which would make them mandatory and legally binding through dispute settlement system of WTO (see Box 9.2).

The Doha Ministerial Conference taking note of the submission by 12 developing countries attempted to address their concerns by reaffirming 'S&DT provisions are an integral part of the WTO Agreements and agreed that all S&DT provisions 'shall be reviewed with a view to strengthening them and making them more precise, effective and operational' (para 44). In addition, Ministers in their Decision on Implementation–Related Issues and Concerns adopted at the Doha Conference agreed to consider converting non-binding S&DT provisions into mandatory provisions and report to the General Council for decision, examine additional ways in which S&DT provisions can be made more effective, and how they could be incorporated into the architecture of WTO rules (para 12).

Box 9.2: Proposal for a Framework Agreement on Special and Differential Treatment

Communication from Cuba, Dominican Republic, Honduras, India, Indonesia, Kenya, Malaysia, Pakistan, Sri Lanka, Tanzania, Uganda and Zimbabwe.

9. The Uruguay Round Agreements shifted the thrust from enhanced market opportunities to grant of transition periods and technical assistance. The developing countries could hardly benefit from the almost 145 S&D provisions (in the Uruguay Round Agreements) which mostly do not go beyond a best endeavour promise and therefore are not legally enforceable. Lack of any mechanism to ensure effective implementation of S&D provisions in the WTO has been a major area of concern for developing countries.

10. It is imperative to undertake a thorough review of the concept of S&D as its basis objective is to create a level playing field for unequal players in the Multilateral Trading System. This should seen in the establishment of a concrete and binding S&D regime which is responsive to the development needs of the developing countries. There is an urgent need for such S&D regime which mainly focuses on enhancing market access opportunities (for developing countries) and provides policy options aimed at unlocking their growth and development potential. The guiding basis, therefore, should be that;

(i) the liberalization of trade is not an end in itself but the means to an end, that is, economic growth and development of all Members; and

(ii) different levels of development achieved by members require different sets of policies to achieve economic growth and development.

11. First, because developed countries, too, have enjoyed such flexibility and differential treatment during their earlier periods of economic development. In fact, some of them are still getting such treatment, particularly in areas such as textiles and clothing, and agriculture. Second, in this age of interdependence, the long term prosperity of developed countries depends on the economic development of developing countries. S&D treatment that facilitates developing countries to grow and develop will ultimately benefit all not just in terms of more and affluent markets but by ensuring a more peaceful world.

12. The system and the rules should ensure equal participation by, and equal benefits to, all. In the immediate/short term, all the existing S&D provisions in various WTO agreements should be fully operationalized/implemented. The implementation should go beyond technicalities and include operationalization of provisions that presently lack operational modalities.

13. In the medium term, the agreements should be suitably amended in the light of the experience by the developing countries that these provisions fall short of providing necessary flexibility to pursue appropriate policies and facilitate economic development in the developing countries. The WTO must demonstrate sensitivity to developmental objectives of majority of its Membership and to sustain credibility. Many of the Implementation proposals submitted by developing countries, in the backdrop of, uneven growth and development in the years following the establishment of WTO, can be viewed as an initial endeavour for extension and elaboration of enhanced, effective and a binding S&D regime.

14. In order to institutionalize and rationalize the adoption and application of S&D provisions in various WTO Agreements, WTO Members should elaborate a framework/umbrella agreement on S&D treatment which should include provisions reflecting the objectives and principles of S&D treatment for developing countries, as outlined above. The Doha Ministerial should recognize the importance of this issue and agree to the negotiation of such a "framework" agreement on S&D.

15. Some of the elements which can form part of the Agreement on S&D could be as follows:

- Special and Differential treatment shall be mandatory and legally binding through the dispute settlement system of the WTO (including notification requirements and inclusion of these commitments in country schedules).

Source: **WT/GC/W/442 dated 19 September 2001.**

All these decisions were to be completed by July 2002 and reported to the General Council. However, there has not been any progress on these mandates, despite the extension of the deadline two times, first to December 2002 and then to February 2003.

The developed countries have been resistant to operationalize the S&DT provisions beyond a longer transition period. The European Community, for instance, in its communication has mentioned that it is not very clear whether problems identified are attributable to shortcomings in S&DT provisions, or whether they are due to other factors such as domestic policy shortcomings or weaknesses inhibiting developing countries' fuller integration into the trading system.[3]

S&DT Provision in Different WTO Agreements

Different WTO Agreements include some 155 S&DT provisions. The developing and the least developed countries have submitted almost 85 proposals to strengthen the main S&DT provisions made in the various WTO Agreements. Several of these proposals are similar in nature, scope and converge in terms of their suggestions. This section attempts to summarise these positions with brief account of S&DT provisions in major WTO Agreements.

Agreement on Agriculture (AoA)

The Preamble of the Agreement on Agriculture suggests provisions to increase trade opportunities for developing countries. Accordingly, the schedules of developed country members exhibit greater than average reductions in tariffs on a range of products particularly of interest of developing countries. Article 15.2 makes specific reference to S&DT provisions for developing countries and LDCs. Developing countries have been given flexibility to implement reduction commitments over a period of up to 10 years while LDCs have been exempted from reduction commitments. The least developed countries (LDCs) were also exempted from making commitments to reduce export subsidies and domestic supports. Then there are certain provisions (precisely 9) which provide flexibility of commitments, of action and opportunities for usage of various policy instruments to protect agriculture. For instance, Article 6.2 provides that investment subsidies which are generally available to agriculture in developing country members and agricultural input subsidies generally available to low income producers in developing countries would be exempted from domestic support reduction commitments and subsequently from the calculation of AMS. Similarly, there is a provision which allows governmental stock holding programmes for food security purposes at administered prices, provided that the difference between the acquisition price and the external reference price is accounted for in the AMS.[4]

In the light of S&DT provisions in AoA, LDCs have put forth a combined proposal. The LDC proposal has come forward from Uganda.[5] According to the proposal the LDCs should be exempted from undertaking reduction commitments, as provided in Article 15.2. The proposal also demands that the international financial institutions should recognize LDCs' rights to adjust their applied tariffs within the bound levels or provide domestic support to agricultural producers, in order to meet the needs arising for the purposes of agricultural development for long-term food security. A demand for policy coordination has also been made for the WTO Working Group on Trade, Debt and Finance, which should regularly examine the coherence between WTO rules and national commitments under financial assistance from international financial institutions.

The Food and Agriculture Organisation (FAO) in its Geneva Round Table on S&DT in the context of Agriculture recommended that the enforceability of positive support measures to the food insecure countries could be made in one of the two ways.[6] The first, which may prove infeasible, is to endow the WTO with a financial facility. The other is to make final agreement on the AoA conditional upon appropriate decisions being made in the multilateral and bilateral bodies that have the relevant portfolio responsibilities and financial resources. The FAO proposal further suggests that it is also important to identify more clearly the types of domestic action that can be justified for food insecure states both in order to focus attention on the need to support them and to ensure that the freedom of manoeuvre of food insecure states is not limited by future rules. In this context it is also necessary to make existing declarations enforceable.

Agreement on Import Licensing Procedure

The provision under the Agreement on Import Licensing Procedures helps in preventing trade distortions that may arise from an inappropriate operation of these procedures. The Agreement (Article 1.2 General Provisions) suggests to take into account the economic development, financial and trade related needs of developing countries under the S&DT provisions. Article 3.5A (IV) provides exemption to developing countries to incur any additional administrative and financial expenditure on account of collecting imports statistics. Since import licences have to be allocated, it has been recommended that special consideration should be given to those importers importing products originating in developing and LDCs (Article 3.5J). In addition to these provisions Article 2.2 allowed a delay in the implementation of import licensing agreements by two years. There are also special arrangements for Least Developed Countries covering the allocation of quotas administered under import licensing agreements.

In the area of Import Licensing, two proposals have been received from India and Thailand regarding the non-mandatory provisions provided in Agreement.[7] According to the proposals, there is need for making S&DT provisions mandatory under Article 3.5(a) and 3.5(j) to enable the products originating from developing countries to benefit from this clause. According to the proposal submitted by India, this could be done either through an authoritative interpretation or by replacing the word "should" in the last sentence by "shall". In the context of Article 3.5 (j) of the Agreement, making the last section mandatory, would help developing countries, especially the least-developed ones, to increase their share in exports. The proposal lays stress on uniformity in the administration of Tariff Rate Quotas (TRQs). In the proposal from Thailand it is mentioned that in providing the import statistics, there is room for flexibility for developing country Members not to take an additional administrative and financial burdens. However, in view of the word "would" appearing in the last sentence of the provision, there is some doubt as to the mandatory nature of the provision. In the context of Article 3.5(a), developing country Members are required to provide all relevant information pertaining to the products of concern to any Member, having an interest in the trade of the product. Where Members provide such information to the Member making a request, there may be certain administrative and financial costs involved. These relevant costs should be deemed as necessary and sufficient for Members, especially the developing country Members. The proposal is that the word "would" be replaced by "shall," so that the sentence reads "Developing country Members shall not be expected to take additional administrative or financial burdens on this account."

Technical Barriers to Trade

The Agreement on Technical Barriers to Trade contains S&DT provisions which may be classified under five different categories. Article 12.2 suggests that interests of developing countries would be taken into account while implementing Agreement on TBT with a view to ensuring that such technical regulations, standards and conformity assessment procedures do not create unnecessary obstacles to exports from developing countries. Article 12.5 suggests broader participation of developing countries in international standardizing bodies and international systems for conformity assessment. The Article 12.8 provides time limited exemption from the application of technical regulations, standards etc. on the specific request from the developing countries. The developing countries are also supposed to get technical assistance to strengthen their abilities for regulating and enforcing technical standards (Article 11.3). Article 11.6 extends the scope to cover establishment of institutions and legal framework which would enable developing countries to fulfil their obligations. In all these articles it is suggested that priority should be given to the LDCs.

In this regard, a joint proposal was made by 12 countries[8] (including both developing and LDCs) regarding specific problems of inadequate technology and infrastructure in complying with the technical regulations and standards of an importing developed country. The proposal suggests that developed countries shall provide to the developing country and LDC Members with relevant technology and technical facilities on preferential and non-commercial term, preferably free of cost keeping in view the development, financial and trade needs of the exporting developing countries and LDCs. On this the African Group suggests that where the importing Member does not actually provide such technical assistance, Member shall withdraw the measures immediately and unconditionally; or the importing Member shall compensate the exporting developing country Members for loss resulting directly or indirectly from the measures.

Agreement on SPS Measures

In the Agreement on Sanitary and Phyto-sanitary Measures Articles 9 and 10 cover the S&DT provisions. It is suggested that members shall take account of the special needs of developing and least-developed country Members while formulating SPS measures (Article 10.1). In the process the participation of these countries would be especially encouraged (Article 10.4) and wherever possible phased introduction of new measures, longer time frame for compliance would be accorded on products of interest to the developing countries (Article 10.2). The SPS Committee, on requests from members, may grant specified time limited exceptions in whole or in part from obligation under this Agreement (Article 10.3). In the process of compliance to standards, the exporting countries may seek technical assistance as will permit the developing country members to maintain and expand market access opportunities (Article 9.2).

The developing and least-developed countries have demanded several changes in the way S&DT provisions are being implemented in the SPS agreement. There is a proposal on SPS measures from a group of 12 developing countries and LDCs.[9] According to this proposal, due to lack of technical and financial capacity, it is difficult for developing country Member to fulfil the sanitary and phyto-sanitary requirements of an importing developed country Member and thus market access opportunities for the product are restricted. In this regard, it is proposed to make the provision in Article 9.2 mandatory by modifying the text "shall consider providing" by "shall provide". Similarly, it is also suggested that if an exporting developing country Member identifies specific problems in complying with sanitary or phytosanitary measures of an importing developed country Member, the latter shall enter into consultations with a view to finding a mutually satisfactory solution upon request (Article 10.1).

The 12 country proposal also demands (in the light of Article 10.1) that while notifying a new SPS measure by a Member the systems and /or equivalent system to comply with such a measure; and the developing and LDC Members that could be affected in the process are to be indicated. India has demanded that as per the Doha Declaration the usage of word "normally", in context of longer time frame for compliance should be avoided and that it should mean at least six months. On the provisions under Article 10.3 the proposal suggests that the SPS Committee should grant time limited exceptions as and when any developing country approaches the SPS Committee. In the context of Article 10.4, where members are to encourage participation of developing countries, India has demanded that amendment should be made so as to read this as the 'duty' of developed countries.

Similarly, the Joint Communication from the African Group suggests that the term "substantial investments" in Article 9.2 of the Agreement on Sanitary and Phytosanitary Measures shall be construed as relative to resources of concerned government departments in developing and least-developed country Members and to their development needs. Any changes that would require additional resources to existing levels of current expenditure or their restructuring, or additional training or staffing, shall be construed to amount to "substantial investments".

Kenya has also submitted a similar proposal on behalf of the African Group in the WTO. The proposal has suggested the establishment of a Global Trust Fund (GTF) into which contributions shall be made by Members to assist developing and least-developed country Members in implementing the Agreement. Members that propose to introduce new standards shall, prior to adoption of the standards deposit amounts into the fund in accordance with assessments by the Committee based on resource implications for developing and least-developed country Members in complying with such standards. The proposal from Uganda also refers to the need of financial assistance for implementation of standards. It further demands that technology transfer and any technical and financial assistance under the Agreement to developing countries and LDCs would be free of all costs.

Trade Related Investment Measures (TRIMs)

In the TRIMs Agreement on flexibility of commitments, of action and use of policy instruments is provided under Article IV while Articles 5.1 and 5.2 provide transitional time period. In addition the Article 5.2 also provides special transition time period to the LDCs. According to this each Member shall eliminate all TRIMs which are notified under Articles 5.1 within two year of WTO coming into effect. The limit for developing countries would be five years while for least-developed countries this is seven years. If developing and least-developed countries demonstrate difficulties in implementing the provisions, the Council for Trade in Goods may extend the transition period (Article 5.3).

A proposal has been received from Uganda on behalf of the LDCs on the transitional period for the use of TRIMs as a means to meet their development objectives.[10] According to the proposal, S&DT measures specific to LDCs are contained in Article 5.2 relating to transitional period that for LDCs expired on 1 January 2002. This provision should be reviewed in the spirit of making it more effective in its operation, especially in the context of Paragraph 4 of Doha Ministerial Declaration and Task III for the Special Sessions of the CTD. It is not a mandatory provision but a right that LDCs may choose to exercise in addressing their development needs. According to the proposal, LDCs have always argued that TRIMs continue to be an important policy tool for strengthening production and export supply base necessary to take full advantage of the market access concessions and preferential schemes made available to them by their trading partners. Flexibility to apply local content requirements assumes particular importance in this regard. As long as they are LDCs, the transitional period for the use of TRIMs is ineffective as a means to meet their development objectives including industrial policy objectives.

Agreement on Subsidies and Countervailing Measures

There are almost 16 S&DT related provisions in the Agreement on Subsidies and Countervailing Measures. As part of Article 27.1 it is recognized that subsidies may play an important role in the economic development of developing countries while Article 27.15 provides for a review of a specific countervailing measure to examine whether it is consistent with other articles. The Article 27 Paragraph 1(a) suggests that the term developing country would not apply to the Members referred to in Annex VII. Article 27.9 suggests that actionable subsidies granted by a developing country Member other than those referred to in Article 6.1, may not be subject to action unless it results in nullification of tariff concessions and thus, impedes imports of a like product of another Member into the subsidizing developing country or injure to a domestic industry in the market of an importing Member. Article 27.10 suggests that any countervailing duty investigation of a product originating in a developing country Member shall be terminated as soon as the authorities concerned determine that: (a) the overall level of subsidies granted upon the product in question does not exceed 2 per cent of its value calculated on a per unit basis; or (b) the volume of the subsidized imports represents less than 4 per cent of the total imports of the like product in the importing Member, unless imports from developing country Members whose individual shares of total imports represent less than 4 per cent, collectively account for more than 9 per cent of the total imports of the like product in the importing Member. Article 27.14 suggests that the Committee shall undertake a review of a specific countervailing measure to examine whether it is consistent with its development needs, if requested by an interested developing country Member. Article 27.5 suggests that a developing country Member which has reached export competitiveness in any given product shall phase out its export subsidies for such product(s) over a period of two years. However, for a developing country Member referred to in Annex VII and which has reached export competitiveness in one or more products, export subsidies on such products shall be gradually phased out over a period of eight years.

The proposal from Uganda on behalf of LDCs has put across the point that there is an urgent need to remove the contradictions between time bound derogation in Paragraph 27.3 from the obligation in Paragraph 1(b) of Article 3 of the Agreement on Subsidies and Countervailing Measures, which prohibits subsidies contingent upon the use of domestic over imported goods. One way of removing this contradiction and thus providing the intended rights to LDCs in unrestricted recourse to the use of local content is to provide in both Agreements for the right as long as a country remains in the LDC status. The proposal from Cuba, India, Pakistan, Sri Lanka, etc. (TN/CTD/W/1) suggests that the usage of the word, 'may', in the Article 27.1 considerably dilutes the relevance of subsidies for economic development. As there is a need for unambiguous recognition of the role played by subsidies in developmental policies, the proposal suggests to delete the word, 'may'. The Joint Communication from the African Group suggests that under Article 27.4 Members should be granted extensions speedily and Members should refrain from invoking technicalities such as slight or reasonable delays to seek the extension within the prescribed time frames. The African Group also recommended that under Article 27.9 nullification and impairment in cases of actionable subsidies shall be construed to mean only the displacement of imports of a like product into the market of the developing country Member or injury to a domestic industry in the market of the importing Member.

Understanding on Rules and Procedures Governing the Settlement of Disputes

The Understanding on Rules and Procedures Governing the Settlement of Disputes contains 11 provisions pertaining to S&DT. Article 4.10 and Article 8.10 suggest that additional consideration would be given not only to the special needs of developing countries but also in terms of encouraging the participation of developing countries in settling the disputes. Article 12.10 recommends giving additional time for response from a developing country Member. The Chairman of the DSB shall decide, after consultation with the parties, whether to extend the relevant period and if so for how long. The Dispute Settlement Body would give special consideration to the possible impact on the economy of the developing country Members involved in the dispute (Article 21.8). Developing country Members are also entitled to obtain additional legal advice and assistance under S&D technical assistance provisions (Article 27.2). In the case of LDCs this support may come from the Director General, WTO or the Chairman of the DSB.

The joint communication from Cuba, India, Pakistan, Sri Lanka, etc. suggests that Article 12.10 should amend the words, 'whether' and 'if so for how long' by an expression, 'for not less than 15 days in cases of urgency as envisaged in Paragraph 8 of Article 4 and not less than 30 days in normal circumstances.' The proposal further demands more time at each stage after the initial submissions are made. The additional submission from India comes with the proposal to make provisions under Article 4.10 mandatory so that the idea of giving special attention to the problems and interests of developing countries becomes a mandatory provision. The proposal also suggests that if the defending party is a developing Member and the complainant is a developed Member then 15 months should be considered as a reasonable period of time (RPT) for compliance with DSB rulings. If the measure at issue is change of statutory provisions or change of long held practice/ policy [like Quantitative Restrictions/ Balance of Payment (QRs/BOP)], RPT should be two to three years and panels should indicate payment requirement of more RPT. Similarly, under Article 21.5 Procedures, the time for completion of 21.5 panel proceedings should be increased from 90 days to 120 days and the panel should give all due consideration as any normal panel would give to the particular situation of developing country Members.

Agreement on TRIPS

The TRIPS Agreement contains four provisions relating to S&DT which basically intend to provide transitional time period (Article 65.2 and 65.4); technical assistance (Article 67) and provisions relating to LDC Members (Article 66.1 and 66.2). Under the Article 65.2 a developing country Member is entitled to delay for a further period of four years the date of application as defined in Paragraph 1 of TRIPS. Under this Article the transition period for developing countries expired on 1 January, 2000. As part of Article 65.4 a developing country Member is obliged by this Agreement to extend product patent protection to areas of technology not so protected in its territory on the general date of application of this Agreement may delay the application of the provisions on product patents of such areas of technology for an additional period of five years (Section 5 of Part 2). Under the technical assistance provisions developing and least developed country Members would get assistance in the preparation of laws and regulations on the protection and enforcement of IPRs (Article 67). This assistance would also include establishment of domestic agencies and their offices including the training of personnel. In order to build a viable technological base for LDCs, the Council for TRIPS, shall, upon duly motivated request by an LDC, accord extension for implementing TRIPS.

In the Joint Communication of the African Group it is demanded that the developing country Members shall be entitled to extensions beyond the additional five year period under Article 65.4 relating to other areas of technology. It also demands that under Article 28 Members should have the freedom to define what constitutes exclusive marketing rights (EMR) and that EMR should not be equivalent to 'patent rights'. It also suggests that developed country Members should evolve laws and administrative instruments so as to encourage their institutions and enterprises to transfer technology to LDCs. The implementation of Articles 7, 8 and 66.2 should be regularly reported to the TRIPS council. The Joint Communication from LDCs presented by Uganda demands inclusion of part IV of GATT in the TRIPS Agreement.

Concluding Remarks and the Future Agenda

S&DT has been an integral part of the multilateral trading system right from the 1950s in recognition of the inherent inequality between the players. Despite the strong conceptual basis for S&DT stemming from the infant industry argument, the Uruguay Round Agreements tended to dilute them and reduced them into best endeavour clauses. Although the Doha Ministerial agreed to review the S&DT provisions to make them meet demand of developing countries, the progress has been unsatisfactory. All the proposed deadlines for reviews have been missed. The case for S&DT that may foster growth and development in developing countries by allowing policy flexibility to pursue development policy objectives today is stronger than in the 1960s. In the age of global economic interdependence, rapid development of developing countries eventually supports growth in developed world by creating demand for their goods and services. Hence, WTO needs to pay attention to implement the Doha Mandate on S&DT in letter and spirit. In what follows, some proposals for reform of overall S&DT as well as for some specific agreement are summarized for consideration by the WTO.

Framework Agreement on S&DT

In order to provide a legally binding framework to various S&DT provisions, there is need to negotiate a Framework Agreement as demanded by developing countries at Doha. Such an Agreement would provide for the notifications requirements and for inclusion of commitments in country schedules and dispute settlement. The Framework Agreement should clearly lay out an objectively defined economic criteria for S&DT provisions, as longer transition period is not adequate.

Granting Policy Flexibility to Developing Countries based on Objective Economic Criteria

S&DT provisions under different Agreements need to be further strengthened as longer transition period is not adequate as observed earlier. The S&DT provisions need to take cognizance of the varying levels of development of the member states. For instance, in the case of TRIPs, it has been found that most of the adverse effects on poor countries arise not because of the IPR regime but from the attempt to harmonize them across countries at different levels of development. In this regard flexibility to implement the provisions of the Agreement as per the level of development needs to be considered. A possible revision of TRIPs should in corporate a provision that grants to implement the TRIPs obligations until they reach a certain level of development defined in terms of some objectively defined criteria. One possibility is to adopt a threshold of US $ 1,000 per capita income as the Agreement on Subsidies and Countervailing Measures (SCM), as it would be easier to agree to, having been adopted in one of the WTO's Agreements. This would bring in an element of graduation in the treatment which would cease as they cross the developmental threshold. Another possibility could be to shorten the term of product patents applicable to low income countries.[11]

Similarly, under TRIMs Agreement, countries with per capita income of less than US $ 1000 may be allowed to exercise flexibility to employ trade-related investment measures, if they find them useful for their development policy objectives. [12]

Under Agreement on Agriculture, the countries with more than one half of population dependent on agriculture, could enjoy flexibility in implementing their minimum market access commitments. Similarly, small size holdings in developing countries may be given special consideration.

Under the Non-agricultural Market Access, policy flexibility could take the form of less-than-reciprocity. For instance, developing countries are required to cut tariffs in a proportion less than their developed country counterparts. Under the sector by sector/zero-for-zero modality, the tariff reduction could be zero-for-x where x is a variable rate applicable to developing countries depending upon their level of development as measured by per capita income.

Effective Technical and Financial Assistance

Empirical evidence available suggests that exports of developing countries have significantly declined due to difficulties in complying with sanitary and phyto-sanitary measures imposed by importing countries. It has been shown in Chapter 7 that the promised technical assistance as provided in the Agreement is not provided in adequate or timely manner. There are two proposals in this context. Firstly, implementation of the new standards is linked to provision of technical assistance. A complaint by a developing country on the lack of technical assistance should make the importing country liable to compensation of damages. Secondly, the adoption of standards higher than international norms should be linked to financial compensation to potentially affected developing countries in view of the fact that developed countries have been part of the process of formulating the international standards.

Transparency

It is important to promote transparency while S&DT provisions are being implemented. In order to enthuse developing countries about S&DT, a review mechanism to assess the performance of different donor agencies and the commitments made by them has been called for in the Doha Delaration. In this regard, greater convergence of various initiatives launched by international agencies to assist developing countries may also be initiated. This would help developing and least developed countries in honoring their commitments. This would also help in minimizing the compliance cost for developing countries.

Incorporating Effective Provisions for Transfer of Technology

Transfer and dissemination of technology is an explicit objective of TRIPs Agreement (Article 7). Although it provides for appropriate measures to prevent practices that adversely affect international transfer of technology, the Agreement leaves the provisions for transfer of technology quite vague. The access to technology is increasingly becoming difficult for developing countries due to stronger IPR regime, among other trends. There is need for defining conditions, norms and practices for facilitating transfer of technology to developing to countries.

Endnotes

1 Stevens, Christopher. 2002. 'The Future of Special and Differential Treatment (SDT) for Developing Countries in the WTO', Institute of Development Studies. *Working Paper No. 163*. England. September.

2 WT/GC/W/442 19 September 2001.

3 WTO. 2002g. WTO. 'The WTO Work Programme on Special and Differential Treatment: Some EU Ideas for the Way Ahead: European Communities.' November 20.

4 Annexe 2, Paragraph 3, Footnote 5.

5 WTO. 2002(d). 'Special and Differential Treatment Provisions.' TN/CTD/W/4. May 24.

6 Stevens, Christopher. 2002. 'Extending Special and Differential Treatment (SDT) in Agriculture for Developing Countries,' FAO Geneva Round Table on Special and Differential Treatment in the Context of the WTO Negotiations on Agriculture, Discussion Paper No.1, Geneva.

7 WTO. 2002(e). 'Special and Differential Treatment Provisions.' TN/CTD/W/6. India. 17 June and WTO. 2002 (f). 'Special and Differential Treatment Provisions.' TN/CTD/W/7. Thailand. 20 June.

8 WTO. 2002(c). 'Special and Differential Treatment Provisions.' TN/CTD/W/2. 14 May.

9 WTO. 2002(c). 'Special and Differential Treatment Provisions.' TN/CTD/W/2. 14 May.

10 WTO. 2002(d). 'Special and Differential Treatment Provisions.' TN/CTD/W/4. May 24.

11 Kumar, Nagesh. 2003. 'Intellectual Property Rights, Technology and Economic Development: Experiences of Asian Countries', *Economic and Political Weekly*. 18 January.

12 *RIS Discussion Paper # 14* on "WTO's Emerging Investment Regime and Developing Countries: The Way Forward for TRIMs Review and the Doha Ministerial Meeting" by Nagesh Kumar, RIS, New Delhi